THE BIG
INVESTMENT
LIE

MICHAEL EDESESS

THE BIG INVESTMENT LIE

What your
financial
advisor
doesn't
want you
to know

BERRETT-KOEHLER PUBLISHERS, INC.
San Francisco
a BK Life book

Berrett-Koehler Publishers, Inc.
235 Montgomery Street, Suite 650
San Francisco, CA 94104-2916
Tel: (415) 288-0260   Fax: (415) 362-2512   www.bkconnection.com

Ordering Information

Quantity sales. Special discounts are available on quantity purchases by corporations, associations, and others. For details, contact the "Special Sales Department" at the Berrett-Koehler address above.

Individual sales. Berrett-Koehler publications are available through most bookstores. They can also be ordered directly from Berrett-Koehler: Tel: (800) 929-2929; Fax: (802) 864-7626; www.bkconnection.com

Orders for college textbook/course adoption use. Please contact Berrett-Koehler: Tel: (800) 929-2929; Fax: (802) 864-7626.

Orders by U.S. trade bookstores and wholesalers. Please contact Publishers Group West, 1700 Fourth Street, Berkeley, CA 94710. Tel: (510) 528-1444; Fax (510) 528-3444.

Production Management: Michael Bass Associates

Berrett-Koehler and the BK logo are registered trademarks of Berrett-Koehler Publishers, Inc.

Printed in the United States of America

Berrett-Koehler books are printed on long-lasting acid-free paper. When it is available, we choose paper that has been manufactured by environmentally responsible processes. These may include using trees grown in sustainable forests, incorporating recycled paper, minimizing chlorine in bleaching, or recycling the energy produced at the paper mill.

Library of Congress Cataloging-in-Publication Data
    Edesess, Michael.
        The big investment lie : what your financial advisor doesn't want you to know /
    by Michael Edesess.—1st ed.
        p. cm.
    Includes bibliographical references.
    ISBN-13: 978-1-57675-407-8
        1. Investment advisors—Corrupt practices—United States. 2. Securities
    industry—Corrupt practices—United States. 3. Business ethics—United States.
    4. Deception—United States. I. Title.
    HG4928.5.E33 2007
    332.6—dc22
                                                                    2006020543

First Edition
11 10 09 08 07   10 9 8 7 6 5 4 3 2 1

To Graça, who made it easy
and to Hilary and Ariel

Contents

Part III: How You Are Sold   169

Conclusion: The Ten New Commandments for Smart Investing   253

Preface

I wrote this book because two pernicious trends I had been witnessing both in my business and private lives, year in and year out for many years, had recently become even worse. On the one hand, I saw individuals I knew—and institutions, too—throwing money away on expensive investment advisors and money managers. On the other hand, I experienced intimately those same advisors and money managers, polishing and repolishing, testing, and refining their sales pitches—and I knew they made no sense. All that mattered to these "investment professionals" was that their sales pitches sounded good.

In the last few years, these phenomena and my experience of them have only worsened. The expensive investment advisors and money managers have become even more expensive. And the massively unproductive transfer of wealth from ordinary lower-middle-income, middle-income, and upper-middle-income investors to the incredibly wealthy has not only continued unabated but accelerated until it has become a torrent.

This book is needed to counteract the finely tuned sales pitches and ad campaigns that keep what I call "the Big Investment Lie" in business. But this book alone is not enough. It must precipitate echo upon echo, news stories and media coverage, until it becomes widely known that most professional investment help, no matter how seemingly respectable, is in truth hazardous to your financial health. This fact should be as widely known as the now well-known fact that cigarette smoking is hazardous to your physical health.

The book is written for the general educated reader, with perhaps at least a little rudimentary knowledge of investments. Though the book assumes an elementary understanding of words like *stocks, bonds, assets, securities*, and *rate of return on investment*, it also provides a glossary where the definitions of those terms can be found. The book is written for readers with a general interest in investments or a need to know about investments to provide for their financial future or the future of funds that they oversee.

My book is intended both for small investors and for wealthy investors who qualify to invest in hedge funds. It is both for individual investors and for institutional investors—that is, those who oversee pension funds and endowments. And it is even for those who only have retirement funds through their corporate pension funds, who may not realize how much of those funds are squandered wastefully on expensive investment services.

Readers will receive from this book very important, practical information. First, they'll find out that professional investment help is a good deal worse than useless. Second, they'll find out that in spite of the apparent complexity imposed on investing by the investment profession, the most beneficial investment strategy is in fact quite simple.

Following the introduction, the book is organized into three parts and a conclusion. The first part shows how much professional investment advice and management costs (far more than you may imagine). The second part shows why this professional advice and management is virtually worthless and how Nobel Prize–winning theories show that an investment strategy skirting the professionals entirely is the best policy. The third part shows how professional advice and management are sold to you. In this part you will also see how hedge funds are sold to the wealthy and how conventional money management and hedge fund management are sold to institutional investors (with the costs paid by pensioners and stockholders of for-profit corporations, and by donors to nonprofits). Finally, the book concludes by showing that by adhering to simple investment principles and by plugging into their portfolios—in appropriate proportions— highly refined but ultralow-cost, readily available, sophisticated "chip"-like investment modules, investors can optimize the growth of their wealth.

I would like to thank my superb editor and publisher, Steve Piersanti of Berrett-Koehler (BK), for taking my project on and guiding me through numerous revisions. I would also like to thank BK's managing editor, Jeevan Sivasubramaniam, for shepherding the book through production to publication, and my marketing coordinator, Ian Bach, for overseeing the team that handles everything having to do with marketing strategy, as well as Kristen Frantz, BK's Vice President of Sales and Marketing. I would like to thank my agent, Craig Wiley, for finding so excellent a publisher and for offering astute comments and assistance when needed, and I would like to thank Clifford May for introducing me to Craig. And I would like to offer a hearty thank-you to the four outside reviewers retained by BK—Charlie Dorris, Ed Winslow, E. B., and Johann Klaasen—for reading carefully through the manuscript and offering crucially helpful comments—particularly to Charlie Dorris, who read two versions of the manuscript at different times.

I would like to thank Jim Sample and Bill Kleh for reading through early drafts and offering invaluable comments. And I would like to offer a special thanks to Mark Rubinstein, who read the manuscript carefully for technical accuracy and terminology. I incorporated as best I could their incisive comments and corrections. Any remaining errors or inaccuracies must remain the fault of the author alone.

Last, but far from least, are a few personal thank-yous. First, to my late cousin, Robert Edesess, who figures prominently in Chapter 2 but died in a tragic airplane accident a few months before the publication of this book. I am sorry he did not survive to see it in its published form. I would like to thank especially Maria de Graça Moreira and her wonderful family, Ana Rita and Gui, for providing the delightful company and warm environment that any author needs to keep going through thick and thin. And I would like to thank one of the world's best landlords, the engaging and entertaining Antonio Luis Pedro Baptista.

Introduction: Excuse Me, Is This the "Real" World?

This story goes back a long way, and so do I. In the spring of 1971, I was about to become a newly minted Ph.D. in abstract, or "pure," mathematics.

I was thinking about what kind of job to get. Almost all the other Ph.D.s in pure mathematics wanted to become professors. That, however, was not my plan. I wanted to apply mathematics, not to teach it. I had always been fascinated by science and technology, and I wanted to be the best at applying mathematics to those fields.

But the Vietnam War raised problems for that plan. In the war's earlier years, I had organized meetings opposing it. Now that the war was still going full tilt, every scientific or technological firm seemed engaged in the war effort. Nearly all of the big firms and laboratories played a role, researching or manufacturing components for weaponry or defoliants. Jobs that would have challenged and fascinated me were, for me, tainted because they only contributed to a war I didn't believe in.

Then a fellow student told me he heard that a brokerage firm in Chicago, where I was living, was doing "interesting things with mathematics."

I interviewed at the firm, A. G. Becker & Company, and was offered a job. I thought, I don't know anything about the stock market—I don't even know what it is—but I may as well learn about it. Besides, I should easily be able to get rich using my knowledge of mathematics, and why not? I'm smart; surely I can figure out how to beat the stock market.

Little was I to know how many people I would meet over the years with the same idea, all of whom would be wrong.

With my new Ph.D. in pure mathematics in hand from Northwestern University, I reported to work at Becker in July 1971. Immediately after starting, my bosses gave me books to read on stock market theories. I was the only mathematician with a Ph.D. in the firm, so I quickly became chief theoretician. I was assigned to work with a young assistant professor at the University of Chicago named Myron Scholes (later to become famous for the Black-Scholes option pricing model), who had been hired as a consultant. I was sent to conferences on quantitative finance, where I rubbed elbows and sat on panels with future Nobel Prize winners.

But within a few short months I realized something was askew. The academic findings were clear and undeniable, but the firm—and the whole industry—paid no real attention to them.

It was as if theoretical physicists knew the laws of thermodynamics, but engineers spent their time trying to construct perpetual motion machines—and were paid very handsomely for it.

The evidence showed that professional investors could not beat market averages. Professional investors couldn't even predict stock prices better than the nearest taxicab driver.

A study by a young professor named Michael Jensen published in the *Journal of Finance* in 1968 showed that mutual funds run by professional managers do not beat market averages. Its conclusion said:

> The evidence on mutual fund performance discussed above indicates not only that these . . . mutual funds were *on average* not able to predict security prices well enough to outperform a buy-the-market-and-hold policy, but also that there is very little evidence that any *individual* fund was able to do significantly better than that which we expected from mere random chance.[1]

Academic models showed that highly competitive markets would cause stock prices to change randomly and unpredictably. And many studies similar to Jensen's have been conducted since then, again and again, overwhelmingly supporting the conclusion.

A. G. Becker, at the time, had the largest database of tax-exempt investment funds in the world. It included pension funds, foundation funds, and endowment funds. There were funds overseen by corporations, state and municipal governments, government agencies, and unions. Some of these funds were enormous, with assets in today's terms of tens of billions of dollars. Becker's proprietary database was the largest database of professionally managed funds in existence.

I had access to this database, and I knew how to program computers. So I used the data to check the academic studies. Sure enough, they were right. The average stock portfolio in our database did not outperform a naive strategy of buying the whole market. Furthermore, the portfolios behaved unpredictably and randomly—there was no way to tell in advance which one would beat the market in any given year.

In spite of this evidence that trying to beat the market was futile, the whole business of the firm—and of the entire industry—was oriented toward trying to beat the market. Sales pitches to sell information (and information, bushels of it, is what Becker sold) always implied that if you have this information, then you'll be in a better position to beat the market.

The people who did the selling—who were the higher-paid and more impressively titled employees of the firm—did not give a fig for whether it was really possible to beat the market. What they did give a fig for was what would sell the product.

The product, in Becker's case, was a huge book full of statistics on fund performance that we sold to fund sponsors and fund managers. Believe it or not, this book sold for $20,000 to $30,000—in 1971. It could sell for this price because of the practice of "directed brokerage" or "soft dollars"—of which I will say more in Chapter 2.

Twenty thousand dollars for one book. This sum of money was, at the time, more than enough for four years of tuition at a top-notch college plus room and board. Such was my introduction to the world of incredibly high prices and high levels of compensation.

The huge payoffs brought about a Pavlovian process of sales pitch creation. People found out by trial and error what would work well for selling.

The scientific process creates a hypothesis and tests it against factual reality. The sales process creates a pitch and tests it against market reality to see what sells; factual reality—the truth—is not a necessary consideration.

One salesman I knew could carry on an extended monologue in highly technical-sounding language, punctuating it by repeatedly elbowing his interlocutor in the ribs and poking him in the tie with the wet end of his cigar. What he said made no sense at all, but he sold a lot of Becker books and became the sales manager. (The salespeople were called "consultants," but they were really only salespeople.)

I quickly realized that the whole industry was about what would sell, and not about what was true or factually based. This was an unaccustomed realization for a mathematician, whose entire course of learning and endeavor was oriented solely toward finding out what is true. Whether a mathematical proof would "sell" is never an issue.

In short, I was a fish out of water. I did not like the fact that the whole company—and, as far as I could tell, the whole industry—paid little regard to the truth. But I also thought that, perhaps, well, this was business. Academia—especially in cloistered fields like pure mathematics—is not thought of, even by academicians, as the real world. Business is the real world—and here I was. I resolved to try to make the best of it.

Making the best of it means

- going against the tide and sneaking the truth into the product while trying not to impair sales;

- accepting the language of the business as some sort of code that, though it sounds like a complete distortion of the truth, is really an Orwellian transliteration that everyone in the business understands and interprets correctly; or

- succumbing to cynicism, either despising the customers (Michael Lewis in his book *Liar's Poker* finally concludes, "The customers were our victims!") or believing they are so stupid that speaking to them in simplified lies is necessary to help them.

The alternative is to get out of the business. In my subsequent career, I alternated between getting out of the business and staying in it, but trying to go against the tide.

Getting out of the business usually meant accepting a much lower level of compensation. I tried working on renewable energy at a research institution in Colorado for a few years. But this alternative collapsed for me in the oil glut of the early 1980s. So I got back into the investment business.

I became a "lone eagle." *Lone eagle* is the Colorado term for an independent consultant who works alone and lives on a mountaintop, communicating with clients electronically and by FedEx. (As time wore on and we were still at it, we were called "bald eagles.") I consulted to institutional investors on the esoteric mathematics of dynamic asset allocation, risk hedging using options and futures, asset–liability modeling, and portfolio optimization.

I also authored a computer system to measure investment performance and select money managers. This system was used by a succession of investment firms, from E. F. Hutton to Shearson Lehman to American Express to Smith Barney, and by Dean Witter, Citicorp, and a number of other big firms. Once again, I found myself in possession of a large proprietary database of the performance of investment accounts. Once again, I tested the data to see whether professional managers could beat the market consistently and predictably; and once again, the answer was that they could not.

Each time I got back into the investment field, I tried to leave plenty of time for other activities that I deemed more important—primarily activities in the nonprofit world.

Finally, in the mid-1990s, I became a founding partner and chief economist of a new firm in the investment advisory field, Lockwood Financial Group. We tried to perform a useful function for the investor and stand by the truth, but our resolve tended to erode in the context of an industry that was already thriving on a lie. In the end, the firm was sold, in September 2002, for a large sum to the Bank of New York—the big New York bank founded by Alexander Hamilton.

Shortly after that, I experienced back-to-back, and at close range, several instances of incredible investment foolishness (which you will soon read about), exhibited by otherwise very smart people. I decided then that it was time to write this book. The message of the book is not new. It has been written many times before—though, it seems, not forcefully enough. If the book is imbued with a sense of outrage, it is because nothing else has worked. The lie perpetrated by the investment world to sell its services at exorbitantly high prices still works all too well.

The lie that it is worth paying a huge amount extra to professional investment service providers to try to beat the market prevails as much today as when I was at A. G. Becker thirty-five years ago. The field has progressed only in finding better and yet more profitable ways to skin clients.

When I occasionally go to a talk on investment theory and practice, I am amazed to find how little things have changed. The talks are still full of the same esoteric but simplistic mathematics. The constructs still begin by blithely assuming, against all the evidence, that many investment professionals have an innate ability to beat the market, that those who do have this innate ability can be identified early enough to benefit from their skills, and that it will be worth the cost.

This book will try to make crystal clear—through interesting and sometimes humorous experiences and anecdotes, simple explanations of theories, and evidence—what the truth is, what the Big Investment Lie is and how it is sold to us, and what we can do to avoid it. It begins by showing how easy it is to lie—even by accident—and to have that lie accepted, but it takes great marketing and salesmanship to pull it off on a sustained basis. It then shows what the Lie costs us, how it is conveyed using doctored statistics, what the real truth is, how the truth is distorted in the selling process, and how to avoid the Lie and do it right.

Other books have been written on these topics. But this is the first written by a mathematician. It is the first to draw not only on an insider's knowledge of the industry but also on in-depth mathematical expertise, exposing the Lie's rotting intellectual foundations. I show that for all the industry's claims of "sophisticated technology" and "sophisticated mathematics," its use of these claims to sell its services and justify its charges is absurd, nonsensical, and Swiftian.

For me, this book is a way—at long last—to find a useful application for my experience in the investment field.

PART I

HOW MUCH YOU PAY

1

The Beardstown Ladies versus the Professionals

. . . .

The Beardstown Ladies would have had it made for good if they hadn't been so naive and honest.

In the early 1980s, Mrs. Betty Sinnock, a grandmotherly woman of homespun wisdom, formed an investment club with fifteen other women—also senior citizens—in the town of Beardstown, Illinois, population 6,200. They called their club the Beardstown Business and Professional Women's Investment Club.

They got together regularly to study public companies and to select some to invest in. They joined the National Association of Investors Corporation (NAIC), an organization of investment clubs. They researched stocks, looking for companies with a solid history of growth. They saved and invested diligently, contributing $4,800 a year to their joint portfolio.

They stuck to companies they knew. When one of them came to a club meeting and announced she had seen a lot of cars parked at Wal-Mart, they bought Wal-Mart. One member brought some Hershey Hugs to a meeting. The members decided they tasted good. They wound up buying Hershey stock.

By 1992, they had accumulated a substantial portfolio, making them one of the larger investment clubs in the NAIC. The Beardstown Ladies' discipline and hard work had paid off. They were proud of their achievement, accomplished through their own efforts without professional advisors.

They were so unlike the conventional image of astute investors, and so appealing as a human interest story, that they attracted media attention. They appeared on the nationally televised program *CBS This Morning*, performing so well that CBS asked them back.

What happened next will go down in history. As one observer's account puts it, "For the Beardstown Ladies, it was the deviation from their comfort zone—in an attempt to quell the fast-paced, number-hungry media—that got them into trouble."

In senior partner Betty Sinnock's own words: "In 1991, a producer of *CBS This Morning* called and asked to feature our club for the second time. They wanted us to be on the show January 2, 1992 and they wanted to know what our annual return had been and how we had fared against the Dow."[1]

To respond to this request, the club bought the NAIC Accounting Software and received permission to use it at their bank, since Mrs. Sinnock didn't own a computer.

When Mrs. Sinnock finally got the data entered and read the results, the club had earned an average 23.4 percent per year for a ten-year period. The Standard and Poor's 500 (S&P 500) stock market index, a broader index than the Dow, had achieved only 14.9 percent per year.

The Beardstown Ladies had outperformed the stock market by a full 8.5 percent per year!

The mere human interest story of the Beardstown Ladies got a shot of adrenaline from that 23.4 percent ten-year return that Betty Sinnock had calculated with the NAIC accounting program. This was the stuff of big print on book jackets, a publisher's dream.

A book packager in New York asked to do a book based on the club. The book, *The Beardstown Ladies Common Sense Investment Guide*, became an instant best seller and soon was being published in seven different languages. Four more books followed, plus several audio and big-print editions and a video. The books touted in big bold letters the Beardstown Ladies' "23.4% per year return." The ladies were doing more traveling than they had ever dreamed possible. They were happy to share their knowledge to motivate others to save and learn about investing. They were constantly in the news, always in stories glowing with warmth and admiration.

In Betty Sinnock's words:

Television stations would fly us to New York or California for a four-minute segment. For us, coming from a small town, it was all the more exciting. Maybe a little frustrating and amazing, too.

In December 1994, Phil Donahue flew 13 ladies and our broker to New York to appear on his show to promote the first book. Six of the ladies had never been to New York City, and two of the ladies, in their 70s, had never flown before. It was a fantastic experience.

As we were being chauffeured around in limousines, I remember thinking, "we don't spend money like this." . . .

As part of the book's promotion, we were scheduled to be in a different city every day for 14 days. We were doing several interviews a day, for the print, radio and television media. It got pretty exhausting. . . . I was traveling nearly four days a week. . . .

It wasn't until the groups of people coming to hear us talk began to grow that we finally began to take in what was happening. At one point we were asked to do a program for the Smithsonian. Every time I talked to the people from the Smithsonian, the venue had changed because they needed more space to accommodate all of the people. Finally, we ended up in the auditorium of Washington University, where 1,500 people had made reservations to hear us speak.

For the first time, I felt that this must be how a celebrity feels.[2]

And it was all because of their 23.4 percent annual return.

When I heard about this on the news I assumed the number was wrong—but not because the Beardstown Ladies were inexperienced and untrained investment professionals. No, I assumed it was wrong because I knew how easily accidental or trumped-up statistics acquire lives of their own in the investment field. The gullible public and the mass media that cater to it, wishing fervently to believe in investment Holy Grails, regularly swallow these unlikely but facile figures whole, without checking.

On March 2, 1995, the *New York Times*, usually known for careful reporting and fact checking, nevertheless published a long and thoroughly uncritical piece on the Beardstown Ladies, in which their 23-plus percent performance was cited not just once but several times. The piece included a recipe for "Shirley's Stock Market Muffins (Guaranteed to Rise)."

A *Times* editor would reread this piece now with deep embarrassment. But from 1992 to 1998, the Beardstown Ladies had a spectacular run. Their books, audios, and videos sold in the millions. Their success spawned investment clubs around the country. They became investment advisors to the world.

In 1998, a journalist for *Chicago* magazine, Shane Tritsch, expecting to write the usual puff piece on the Beardstown Ladies, suddenly became suspicious. What aroused his suspicion was a fine-print disclaimer on the copyright page of the paperback version of the *Beardstown Ladies' Common Sense Investment Guide*. The disclaimer read, "This 'return' may be different from the return that might be calculated for a mutual fund or bank."

At the instigation of the Beardstown Ladies themselves, an independent audit of their investment returns was performed by the accounting firm Price Waterhouse. The study concluded that their investment return over the ten years had been not 23.4 percent but only 9.1 percent—underperforming the S&P 500 index by almost 6 percent instead of outperforming it.

The news should have come as no surprise to knowledgeable stock market and financial media observers. But it was of course devastating to the Beardstown Ladies' reputations as investment gurus. The error was apparently totally innocent. As Betty Sinnock described it:

> In 1992, the club offered to buy the NAIC Accounting Software if I could get permission to use it on a computer at the bank since I didn't own a computer. I entered the data as of 12/31/91 and I thought I was inputting the data so the first eight years would be included in our returns. Because of this, when the computer showed an annual return for our members in 1993 of 23.4 percent, I thought it was for the first 10 years and shared the information with the rest of the ladies and with the producer of our video, which had recently been completed. . . .
>
> We have since learned that the 23.4 percent was for a two-year period and not for the first 10 years as we had always thought.[3]

In giving this account of the error in a press release, Mrs. Sinnock added, "The Beardstown Ladies are just really, really sorry."

The error was duly reported in the media. *Time* magazine published an article under the tongue-in-cheek headline "Jail the Beardstown Ladies." The Beardstown Ladies' publisher dropped them. But the Ladies had clearly not connived, knowingly and maliciously, to propagate an erroneous number purely to enhance their own reputations and sell books. Their phenomenal success—though based largely on a falsehood—was not based on a deliberate, premeditated, and knowing falsehood but on an inadvertent one, a falsehood that the credulous public and the media lapped right up.

There was the expected, though muted, tut-tutting, implying that things had been set right again. Of course, mere amateurs like the Beardstown Ladies couldn't really beat the pants off the market and compete with professional investors on Wall Street. But this theme was surprisingly downplayed, not played very often, and not played much at all—in particular—by professional investment counselors themselves. It might seem like a case of professional courtesy, or just kindness and deference to some white-haired old ladies.

In fact, the muted quality and even nonexistence of "I told you so's" in the investment profession was also motivated by the perennial need of the investment advisory industry—the community of investment advisors, investment managers, investment consultants, investment commentators, and other investment "experts" of all stripes—to deflect attention from their own nakedness.

In March 1998, after the Beardstown unmasking, Tom Gardner, a founder of the offbeat Web-based investment commentary called "The Motley Fool," posted the appropriate comment on the Fool's Web site, fool.com. Noting that the Associated Press had run an article entitled "Beardstown Investors Called Frauds," Gardner wrote:

> Over the past five- and ten-year periods, between 85–95% of all mutual funds have done worse than market average, and we haven't yet come across a single article entitled "Mutual Fund Managers Called Frauds." This even as their advertisements cloud over the real underlying value of their managed funds (after the deduction of all costs and taxes) relative to that of an index fund. Do mutual-fund families plan to hire outside auditors to scrutinize and then publicize the after-tax

returns of their products over the past decade? (I've decided to start holding my breath now. Someone please tell me to stop.) [4]

Compared with the Beardstown Ladies (their inadvertent fraud having been exposed at their own behest, to the ruin of their enterprise) —whose fraudulent practice was naive, unintended, and strictly from Hicksville—the fraud of the investment advice and management industry is studied, refined, Wall Street minted and Madison Avenue packaged, and extraordinarily effective.

Unfortunately, the real message of the Beardstown Ladies—the example they represented of the virtues of self-reliance, disciplined saving, and thrift—was lost in the shuffle. For the prurient taste of the public and the media, these virtues had to be mixed with a hint of avarice. The Beardstown Ladies fell short, in the end, on the avarice quota. But they needn't have.

If they had been more artful, more worldly, more knowing, more cunning in the ways of the investment advice industry, they could have come out smelling like a crafty rose. They could have admitted and quickly apologized for their error, then swiftly moved on to emphasize the years in which they did beat the stock market. They could have explained away the years in which they lagged the stock market by saying their investment approach was "out of style" in those years or some such thing. Their publisher would not have dumped them, they would continue to be regarded as investment gurus, and they would have joined the ranks of the true investment professionals.[5]

The Big Investment Lie

The saga of the Beardstown Ladies may seem like an aberration and a curiosity in the annals of investment gurus. But it is not an aberration and a curiosity. On the contrary, it is typical. Behind the success of nearly every wealthy investment professional lie a winning way, an air of confidence, and an erroneous or highly selectively quoted statistic.

The success of nearly all prosperous investment professionals consists not in procuring higher rates of return on investment for their clients but in procuring astoundingly high fees *from* their clients—without the clients taking much notice.

In other fields, too, professional advice can be of doubtful value. An abundance of savage lawyer jokes makes it clear that many people think lawyers often do more harm than good—and overcharge their clients. Even in the medical field, doctors themselves will admit that their medical expertise can make a real difference only in a minority of cases.

But in no service field in which customers pay for professional advice and assistance is the failure to help so clearly measurable, and so clearly demonstrated, as in the investment field. Furthermore, *for this total and demonstrable failure, customers pay far, far more than they will ever pay for medical advice and treatment, or for the services of a lawyer, or for any other professional advice and assistance they will ever get.*

The investment advice and management industry encompasses a vast and complex array of advisors, managers, financial analysts, custodians, brokers, traders, performance evaluators, auditors, accountants, actuaries, conference managers, journalists and publishers, writers, ghostwriters, newsletter publishers, computer systems developers, and an endless array of consultants and consultants to consultants.

The investment advice and management industry is enormous, with total revenues well over $200 billion per year in the United States alone.[6] A percentage of investors' assets provides the entire financial support for this industry.

When an investor engages the services of an investment advisor or of a money manager, or both (usually both), the investor typically winds up with a combination of two investment strategies, one on top of the other.

The first is a sound, simple, low-cost strategy of investing in a diversified portfolio of stocks and bonds, a strategy that is almost certain to provide a strong positive return on investment in the long run.

The second strategy, which is skillfully and seamlessly overlaid on the first, is a gambling strategy, having expected zero return, and a cost paid to the croupiers rivaling the house take at any gambling casino in Las Vegas.

The vast majority of advisors and managers recommend not just the first strategy but also the second strategy packaged with it. Recommending both strategies as a package and collecting the large resulting fees is, quite frankly, like taking candy from a baby. Most investors—even those, surprisingly, who are very wealthy— seem totally unaware of what they are paying and equally unaware of the fact that they get nothing for it. On the contrary, they assume, against all the plainly available evidence, that they are getting something of great value.

In maintaining this situation, the community of investment professionals is helped greatly by what I will call "the Big Investment Lie." A Big Lie is a lie so bold, so often and so firmly stated that even in the face of contradictory evidence, people cannot believe anyone would be so assertive if it were not true. Once a Big Lie gains currency, it is repeated by many people, adding to its force.

The investing public has been fooled (and has fooled itself) for a long time by the Big Lie, a lie strongly supported by the investment advice and management professions. As the infamous former leader of Nazi Germany said,

> The size of the lie is a definite factor in causing it to be believed, for the vast masses of a nation are in the depths of their hearts more easily deceived than they are consciously and intentionally bad. The primitive simplicity of their minds renders them more easily prey to a big lie than a small one, for they themselves often tell little lies but would be ashamed to tell a big one.[7]

Indeed, the vast masses of a nation are not as primitively simple as the leader thought. Yet his insight into the nature of a Big Lie is still valid. It is harder to debunk a Big Lie than a little one, because the vast majority of people do not tell big lies themselves. Therefore, given the choice, on the one hand, of believing what a phalanx of ostensible authorities (at least as respectable in appearance as they are themselves) says to be true and, on the other hand, believing it is an outlandish whopper, most people will believe it to be true.

Therefore, it takes a major information campaign to debunk a Big Lie. It is a campaign that must be waged again and again—because the Big Lie keeps hopping verbal airships bound for bigger and more unearthly lies, while the Truth lags far behind, still putting on its boots.

If an investor interviews several investment advisors, she will find that they all say much the same thing. They will speak of a process of "asset allocation" and "selecting the best money managers or mutual funds." They may speak of "dollar-cost averaging" and, perhaps, "regression toward the mean," "efficient frontier," "mean-variance analysis," and "Nobel Prize–winning technology"—all with the predictable effect of snowing the client and helping to spread the Big Investment Lie.

Once you hear the same things from several different members of the same profession, all wearing nice clothes and occupying plush offices, you will assume a verifiable body of fact, theory, and evidence lies behind it—much as you would assume the same if you interviewed several doctors about a medical condition. And indeed there is a body of theory and evidence. But virtually all of that theory and evidence implies you should use the simple strategy, Strategy 1— never Strategy 2.

Strategy 2 is what advisors and managers add so that they can get paid handsomely. It is like the cable that a computer store sells you at a high price, to go along with the printer you thought you were buying for such a low price. It is like the maintenance insurance contract they try to sell you, too, because they can make a good profit on that, while they can't make much profit on the printer itself because price competition has driven the price of that commodity to rock bottom.

Similarly, in the field of investment advice and management, the advisors and managers add on features to the basic investment commodity that they can charge you for. But what a charge! When you buy a printer and then find you have to buy a cable too, it might cost you $15 extra. But the add-on for worthless investment advice and management will cost you tens of thousands, hundreds of thousands, even millions of dollars. The investment advice and management industry is trying to sell you a $10 million mainframe—almost all of it of no value to you—when all you need is a $499 laptop.

The Big Lie is perpetuated by a constant barrage of advertising. The typical ad is a two-page spread in a glossy magazine for a big brokerage firm or a big bank. The ad shows a distinguished-looking man in a conventional suit, graying at the temples (sometimes now it is a woman), who looks like he came from central casting (and he is, in fact, not an employee of the company but a professional model). The look implies "we know our business."

But that knowing look is a look of knowing . . . absolutely nothing, except how to sell a high-fee service.

This tactic is not that surprising or even shameful in a capitalist economy. The company is only doing what it is supposed to do: sell whatever its product is and try to maximize profits.

But the customer is *not* doing what the customer is supposed to do: try to minimize costs. Instead, the customers in the investment advice and management industry are so befuddled and so taken in by the Big Investment Lie, that they seem almost totally inattentive to costs. They will search for hours online to find the cheapest airfare to save $50, but they will not realize they are losing $50,000 on costly but worthless investment advice and management. In recent years, as the evidence has piled up and piled up that money management by professional investment managers adds nothing at all,[8] the exorbitant fees charged by money managers have not decreased but increased. And investors pay these fees, apparently unaware of the cost.[9]

Investors pay these fees because of what an investment professional I know, the chairman of a major investment firm, calls "optics." If you are an investment advisor or manager or any one of a veritable explosion of middlemen in the investment field, you state fees in such a way that they *look* small. This usually takes the form of stating fees as a "small" percentage of assets. Investors accept these "small" fees without quibble because they assume that the value of the advice, as a percentage of assets, will surely exceed the cost.

But this is exactly what the evidence, unequivocally, shows to be untrue. This is no secret. It has been published widely. It has been pointed out by the best writers of investment self-help books, people like Jane Bryant Quinn, Andrew Tobias, and many others. Public awareness of the fact accounts for the success of a mutual fund subindustry based on low-cost investing. Yet, still, far too many people pay exorbitant fees for investment advice and management. The message has gotten through, but it hasn't spread as widely as it should. The Big Investment Lie has seen to that.

Sauntering through the expensive, glossy outputs of the professional investment field, you may glimpse arcane, sophisticated-sounding articles, suggesting the discourses of an elite corps of exquisitely knowledgeable experts. Recent issues of *Institutional Investor* magazine, for example, and others like it carry stories about "portable alpha," "separating your alpha from your beta," and other impenetrable themes.

Yet in spite of the self-serving message trumpeted to both insiders and outsiders by these arcana—"we insiders are smart and extraordinarily capable"—the actual fact is that *professional investors do not do better than the random investment picks of a gaggle of monkeys.*

The Big Investment Lie is rather like the Big Lie perpetrated by tobacco companies in their advertising in the 1950s. As evidence that cigarette smoking was detrimental to health began to mount, cigarette companies' TV commercials featured men wearing white laboratory coats touting their brand of cigarettes. This "doctor" strategy finally fell apart under a barrage of negative medical evidence, after decades of resistance by tobacco companies and a torrent of advertising.

But the strategy of the Big Investment Lie is still working wonders. No equivalent of the federal Food and Drug Administration (FDA) rigorously checks the validity of the implied claims of investment advisory firms. If the tacitly implied claims of investment advice and management firms were subjected to a statistical test similar to the tests new pharmaceutical drugs have to pass, few or no investment advisory firms would ever be registered.

But because poor advice and investment management is not detrimental to your health, only to your finances, it is—perhaps properly—deemed a matter in which the buyer, not the government, must beware. The government will guard you against certain openly fraudulent practices in the investment advice and management industry; but it will not—as it does in the approval process for pharmaceutical drugs—protect you or even warn you against a remedy that costs far too much and doesn't work at all.

The investor is not an entirely innocent victim of the Big Investment Lie. The lure of getting rich quick, of finding the Holy Grail, can make the client a willing partner in assisted self-delusion. Perhaps, like Blanche DuBois in *A Streetcar Named Desire*, clients for investment advice and management would honestly say, "I don't want reality—I want magic!"

The investment industry by and large caters to this wish instead of discouraging it. Industry "professionals" are like physicians who invent medical-sounding reasons why their addicted patients should keep on smoking. Their advertising suggests that the investor is smart to hire professional assistance, but it is smarter by far to "just say no" to expensive and misleading help—and, as I shall show in later chapters, how much smarter, you cannot begin to imagine!

The typical investor—the buyer of hot mutual funds or the client of expensive advisors who imply they offer superior investments—is looking to get rich without working. He is looking for a vicarious road to riches, a road that enables him to suddenly wake up one day rich.

The odd thing is that this road exists. But its advantages are squandered away by investors who want their road to be better and richer than other people's. Diversified, low-cost, low-tax investment in stocks and bonds will make most thrifty people, who save their money and invest it, well off over time. But instead—because investors want not just a pot of gold but the rainbow, too—they make investment advisors and managers rich, while they themselves do only modestly well. In some cases, they do not do well at all.

Investors have a central role to play in breaking the back of the Big Investment Lie. They must give up the temptation of high-cost gambling and realize that it is much more likely to keep them poor than to make them rich. They must be supremely suspicious of investment advisors who imply they will beat the market or who do not fully reveal, in every minute and cumulative detail, what their services cost.

The job of genuinely professional investment advisors should be to disabuse investors of the get-rich-quick, beat-the-market mentality and tell them how simple it is, if they would only stop searching for the Holy Grail. And they should not charge them too much for this unadorned truth.

There are a few fine, upstanding people and companies in the investment advice and management field, who charge only reasonable fees and who honestly and learnedly advise you what will and will not add investment value. If you feel the need for a personal advisor, this book will help you find one. But it will also show you that you don't need one. The smartest investment strategy is so simple and so direct that you can easily do it yourself. This book will show you how.

It is not the purpose of this book to indict an entire industry and put it to shame. The investment industry is doing what businesses are, for better or worse, supposed to do in a capitalist economy: figure out what earns a profit and pursue it. It is inevitable that they will find ways to present their sales materials so that customers buy into it. As long as their activities do not clearly violate broad legal principles, they are entitled to persist. If the customers buy the sales pitch and the product, sellers can only presume they have given the customers what they want at the price they want to pay.

It is emphatically not the purpose of this book to call for new legislation or regulation, though requirements for the money management industry to publicize more balanced and accurate statistical information may be beneficial.

No, the proper check on a rogue industry is an informed consumer. The purpose of this book is to expose the Big Investment Lie and thus to enlighten consumers of investment services. The information in this book is already widely available, but it continues to be drowned in a sea of the Big Investment Lie. The steady drumbeat of the message, "You need professional investment advice and management," drowns out the relatively far weaker voices purveying the truth. Why? Because, of course, there's much more money to be made in selling expensive advice and management than there is in exposing the fact that it is far too high priced and adds nothing of value.

As I shall show, two types of professionals that could, if bent to the purpose, expose the truth in a louder voice have in large part been subtly co-opted by the reality, or even the whiff, of the money that can be made in the investment industry: financial journalists and financial academicians.

This book's aim is to start a communication snowball rolling that will enlist these voices as well as others, becoming big enough to combat the Big Investment Lie. Thus, perhaps, this book will reduce the investment advice and management industry to the compensation and size that are properly due it, and it may release a number of smart people from golden bondage to pursue more productive work.

2

The Extraordinarily High Cost of Investment Advice

....

Some years ago my cousin Bob, an oral surgeon in a mid-sized American city, told me someone was trying to sell him investment services. He wanted my thoughts on the matter.

A woman in his city, a local consultant with a large national investment brokerage firm, was calling him regularly to convince him to place his pension fund's assets in her company's wealth management program. Bob seemed to be responding to the marketing effort. He was considering entrusting the pension fund assets—about $1 million at the time—to the brokerage firm for advice and management. But he knew I might have a different view, and he wanted to know what I thought. Also, he knew I had a business involvement with her brokerage firm and thought I would be interested to know about the calls.

First, I told Bob never to tell anyone at the brokerage firm that I told him this. At the time, I had a fat contract with the firm. Its consulting division was making heavy and expensive use of a computer system in which I was a 50 percent partner. I had a good relationship with—and liked—the employees at the firm that I did business with, the people running the consulting division. Bob's suitor presumably worked for that division. Of course, I didn't want them to know I was working at cross-purposes. But I also didn't want to give my cousin a bum steer.

In response to Bob's inquiry, I quickly made a brash and ill-considered statement. I told Bob that if he hired the woman and her employer, his pension fund would have $1 million less when he retired than it would if he did not hire them.

Right after I told him this I felt a little sheepish, because I had made a quick statement about a matter of mathematical fact without really having done any calculations. I tossed the $1 million out without thinking, because I thought it would get Bob's attention. But then I went back and carefully did the calculations.

I was wrong. I had underestimated by a factor of three. He would have *$3 million less* if he hired the brokerage firm than if he did not hire them.

Here are the numbers. Bob's pension fund had about $1 million at the time. When it later paid out to retirees, in about twenty years' time, it would have to cover not only Bob but also his partner—another oral surgeon—a receptionist, and several assistants.

A reasonable assumption was that contributions to the pension fund would be about $100,000 a year for the next twenty years. In a long-term portfolio, a heavy weighting toward stock is desirable, and a return of 8 percent a year was—and is—a reasonable expectation.

A simple calculation, simple at least for those familiar with compound interest formulas—and readily available on popular handheld financial calculators—shows that at 8 percent return, Bob's pension fund would grow to about $9.6 million in twenty years.

Now let's deduct the fees the brokerage firm and its investment managers would charge. Total fees levied by the brokerage firm at the time were typically 2.5 percent a year. Most things about investment are unpredictable, but fees are highly predictable.

Deducting 2.5 percent from 8 percent leaves 5.5 percent. Performing the calculation again, we find that the same assets and contributions would grow at 5.5 percent in twenty years to about $6.6 million.

Without fees, $9.6 million; with fees, $6.6 million—a *predictable* difference of $3 million.

If you think this is a phantom figure—a mere hypothetical might-have-been, as in "If I had only invested $1,000 in Microsoft in 1986, I'd have $200,000 now"—remember that the brokerage firm would actually receive this amount. And it would come right out of Bob's account. Over twenty years, my cousin's payments to the brokerage firm would have accumulated to $3 million (see Exhibit 2.1). Almost a third of his assets, and almost half his investment gains, would have gone to pay the advisors.

Exhibit 2.1 Bob's Wealth Accumulation before and after Fees

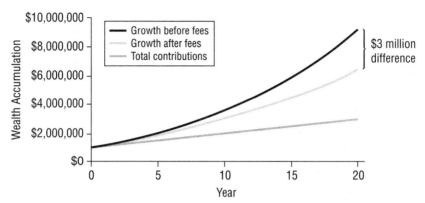

Fees of 2.5 percent may not sound like a lot, but $3 million *is* a lot. Yet that's what the 2.5 percent fees add up to. Now do you wonder how the brokerage firm and others like it can afford all those two-page spread-out ads in glossy magazines and those commercials on television that we are peppered with? And they still have plenty of money left for expensive offices in the most expensive parts of cities, expensive travel and expensive conferences, and very expensive awards for the best salespeople, and extraordinarily high compensation packages. It's done with your money, all the better to sell you their services with.

It's understandable that people would not realize that 2.5 percent of their assets is a lot of money. After all, the stock market's returns seem to fluctuate so widely that the difference between the return from one year to the next can be 10 or 20 or 30 percent or more. So what is 2.5 percent compared with that? But the 2.5 percent going to fees is a *sure* loss, while the other fluctuations average out in the long run and are unpredictable.

The selling point, of course, is the assumption on the part of the buyer that the investment advice and management will add more than it costs. That means it will have to add more than 2.5 percent per year, on average, than if Bob had just put it in the lowest-cost alternative, to be worth the cost.

What I shall show in the rest of this book is that investment advice and management does not add 2.5 percent per year. It does not add anywhere near that per year. In fact, what the evidence clearly shows is that the expert investment advice and management the brokerage firm's representative was selling my cousin Bob would add *nothing at all* to his investment results.

Investment managers are often divided into two main categories. Those who try to beat stock market averages are called *active* managers. Advisors typically recommend higher-cost, active managers. Those who do not try to pick stocks to beat market averages are called *passive* managers. They manage passive vehicles, the principal example of which is index funds.

I recommended to Bob that he invest his pension fund assets in a total market index fund, which at that time would charge him a fee of about 0.2 percent. (Fees for index funds and their sisters, exchange-traded funds or ETFs, are now 0.1 percent or less.) For that he didn't need to pay an advisor, didn't need to pay anything except the 0.2 percent per year. I don't know for sure what he did, but I hope he took my advice. I expected nothing and got paid nothing for saving him $3 million. Aside from the fact that he was family, it's hard to charge much for advice that's so simple. However, though I offered to pay my cousin for his oral surgery, my daughter did get her wisdom teeth extracted free of charge.

The Amazing History of Brokerage Fees

Excessive fees have always been a major issue in the investment field. It can be argued that the practice of overcharging used to be worse than it is now. Indeed, in many ways, it was. But far fewer people participated in the stock market a generation ago. And evidence that value added is minimal to none has continued to mount over that time.

About thirty or thirty-five years ago, most investment advice was delivered by stockbrokers. Their fees were the brokerage commissions they received on the purchase or sale of individual stocks, or commissions on sales-fee-loaded mutual funds. Commission rates for buying or selling stocks were much higher than they are now—ten times higher or more. Because fees for buying or selling stocks and mutual funds were the only ones brokers received, their fees were called "transaction oriented." To collect fees, brokers had to be transaction oriented themselves—that is, they had to urge clients to do a lot of buying and selling, to "churn" their portfolios.

Churning a portfolio racks up high commissions with resulting losses to the portfolio. It is "speculation" as opposed to "investing"—

investing involves sticking with a company for the long haul because its long-term prospects are good; speculation is fickle, trying to grab a big profit and run.

May Day

Until May 1, 1975, the New York Stock Exchange (NYSE), which is run by its member brokerage firms, thoroughly dominated stock trading. It allowed only member firms to trade its stocks. It required all brokers who traded on the exchange to charge fixed, high commission rates. The NYSE claimed that competition in commission rates would be destructive to the industry. And for many years the government regulatory body, the Securities and Exchange Commission (SEC), assented to these fixed rates.

Not being able to compete with each other on prices—that is, commission rates—brokerage firms competed by offering extra services, sometimes obtained from third party providers. The extra services usually carried a charge in the form of "directed brokerage" or "soft dollars." That is, to purchase a service, such as a research report, a customer of the brokerage firm was required to do a certain amount of trading. Buried in the exorbitant profit from the trading commissions was the cost of the service.

This is why the employer on my first job, A. G. Becker & Company, could charge such high fees for a single book full of statistics, graphs, and charts: $20,000 for a corporate pension fund and as high as $30,000 for a money management firm. Becker's clients had to pay the money to some brokerage firm for trading commissions anyway. Becker tried to beat out other brokerage firms for the business by bundling in extra services for the money.

This whole soft-dollar payment system became so messy and ridden with conflicts of interest that it was finally recommended that fixed commission rates be abolished. The NYSE fought this abolition tooth and nail, because its member firms were making so much money on the fixed rates and were using the system to maintain their exclusive club. But finally, on May 1, 1975, the SEC prevailed, and fixed commissions were abolished. "May Day," as the action was called because of the date it occurred (but also as an Orwellian reference to the Soviet Union, cooked up by the opposition forces), contributed heavily to changing the nature of the business from a transaction-oriented business to something else—something initially much better in many ways. But perhaps inevitably, reform gradually spawned its own new corruption.

Lower Brokerage Fees for Trading Stocks

When fixed commissions were abolished, discount brokerages like Charles Schwab were born, competing for brokerage business by drastically reducing commission rates. The cost of trading stocks became much, much lower.

"Full-service" brokers claimed their high fees were justified because their services included not only trading stocks but also recommending good stocks to their clients and telling them when to buy and sell them. The brokers claimed implicitly that they could add value to their clients' portfolios through their stock tips.

But it was long suspected, because of an abundance of anecdotal evidence and some statistical evidence, that the brokers' recommendations actually added little or nothing. So, many clients fled to the discount brokerages and began to make their own stock decisions.

The full-service brokerage business, of course, fought to hang on. A biography of Charles Schwab and the discounted brokerage firm he created, Charles Schwab & Co., by John Kador, gives an entertaining account of this struggle:

> [W]hen Schwab lowered trades to $29.95, *Fortune* Magazine reporter Katrina Booker overheard a Merrill Lynch broker's side of a telephone conversation with a customer. These are the Merrill Lynch broker's exact words, as reported by Booker. For fun, I took a guess at what the other side of the conversation must have been like. The exchange might have gone something like this:
>
> MERRILL LYNCH BROKER: *"I can't believe this. Suddenly you've got $29.95 trades, and you're empowered."*
>
> MERRILL LYNCH CUSTOMER: *"Look, I know what I want to buy. I don't need to pay for research. Why should I pay more than I have to?"*
>
> BROKER: *"Okay, fine. You want to trade on the Internet? Fine. Go right ahead. You have to do what's right for you. Just don't expect much service from me."*

CUSTOMER: *"We go way back. Why are you taking that tone?"*

BROKER: *"Why? Because I get goose eggs! I don't get paid, okay? So don't expect me to give you any more ideas."*

CUSTOMER: *"When was the last time you gave me an idea? I know what I want."*

BROKER: *"I have given you ideas. Okay. Maybe I haven't been as good about that as I could have. Starting today, that is going to change."*

CUSTOMER: *"Listen, you guys have got to wake up. Why should I pay you $250 when I can get the same trade for $29.95? It's a new game out there. Get with the program, or I'm history."*

BROKER: *"Look, I'm sorry. I didn't mean to piss you off. Hey, you want to go to the Mets game tomorrow? I've got tickets."*

Here we get a glimpse of the old-boy networking and schmoozing that cemented the high commissions in place for so many years. Booze, ball games, yacht outings, and dinners lubricated the relationship between brokers and their customers. Entertainment, more than investment research, often proved to be the traditional stockbroker's fiercest weapon. A pair of seats on the 50-yard line combined with an occasional stock tip could beat cheap trades any day. But brokers soon learned that investors are fickle: most will go where they can execute trades for less.

The fat commissions had fed an excessive lifestyle that was frequently lampooned by jokes and *New Yorker* cartoons. Chuck [Schwab] begins his first book, *How to Be Your Own Stockbroker*, by telling a broker yacht story.

> *I'm reminded of an eager-beaver stock salesman I knew in Florida who took a prospect to the harbor at Palm Beach. As they surveyed the various luxury craft floating before them, the salesman pointed out all the yachts owned by successful brokers.*
>
> *"But where are the customers' yachts?" the prospect innocently whispered.*[1]

The cash cow of the full-service broker was being killed. But a new and even better cash cow arose to replace it, albeit one that would serve a new, initially reformist, but ultimately exceedingly well-paid breed of investment service professionals.

The decline in dominance of the full-service broker, together with the fact that brokers were already under fire for causing their clients to churn their portfolios, led to a search for new ways for investment advisors to collect fees. This search helped create, and coincided with, a number of developments, many of which were good for the investor —at least up to a point.

A mutual fund industry grew to prominence that allowed small investors to invest in a widely diversified array of stocks, rather than just a few of them. This enabled small investors to reduce, through diversification, the risk of stock ownership.

Initially many full-service brokers offered these mutual funds to clients, taking large front-end "load" fees for themselves, on the order of 7 or 8 percent. But in due time "load funds," which were sold aggressively, acquired a bad name because of this front-end charge. The public became aware that no-load funds, which were not sold aggressively and therefore required no front-end sales charge, were a better deal.

So the gouging practices of the old full-service brokers were exposed and the public became aware and warned against them. Some, though, survived to cater to those who still believed they were being well served.

The New Percentage-of-Assets Fees

A new array of advisors and new forms of payment arose in response to the ethical crisis. It was intended to repair and move beyond the overcharging practices of the full-service brokerage industry. It was to provide new and better services to clients, with payment systems that made the interests of the advisor and the interests of the customer coincide.

In moving the payment system away from the one-shot brokerage commission charge and the one-shot mutual fund load charge, the burgeoning new array of service industries and professionals discovered something even better—the continuing, year-after-year percentage-of-assets charge.

In the brokerage business, the "wrap fee" was invented. The idea was to charge the client in a manner that had nothing whatever to do with how often or how much the client traded. It was also intended to "align the interests of broker and client" by giving them both an incentive to make the client's assets grow. The fee would be a fixed percentage of the client's assets and would include, or "wrap up," all broker services under one fixed fee—hence the "wrap" terminology. The typical fee quoted was 3 percent of investment assets, per year— and remember this is 3 percent of the investor's *total assets*, every year, whether it is an up year or a down year, not just of growth.

The interaction of these investment advisors with clients became a routine. First, the advisor gathers information about the client's assets, particularly investment assets. Then, the advisor does a "risk assessment" with the client, to determine how much investment risk the client is willing to take. This leads to an overall strategic asset allocation, a percentage allocation to stocks and bonds. Clients willing to take more risk get more stocks; those who are more conservative get more bonds. Then the advisor recommends a "style allocation," in which percentage allocations to categories of stocks, like "large growth stocks," are recommended. Finally, the advisor recommends specific mutual funds (or, these days, possibly separately managed accounts as opposed to investments that are commingled with others' assets, as are mutual funds).

The wrap fee charge is typically quoted as 3 percent but then discounted back to 2.5 percent or less, depending on the size of the account.

Of the wrap fee, about 1 percent goes to the advisor (much of it usually to the advisor's employer rather than to the advisor personally), about 1 to 1.5 percent to the recommended mutual funds, and the rest for various other purposes. Sometimes the fees are not wrapped but "unbundled," so that the client pays the advisor's fee, plus whatever happen to be the fees of the mutual funds, plus the other costs.

Almost all mutual funds have no front-end load now, because buyers became aware that it was better to buy no-load funds than load funds. But the mutual fund industry managed to get another, even better fee substituted for the load. By arguing that a start-up mutual fund needs to charge an extra fee to cover marketing to become known, the mutual fund industry got the SEC to approve what are called *12b-1 fees*; 12b-1 fees are an annual charge to customers, supposedly to cover the marketing of the fund. Much of this fee is often remitted back to the advisor who recommended the fund, causing a conflict of interest—advisors have an incentive to recommend the funds that remit back to them. (Some mutual funds do not remit back. Low-cost index fund providers, for example, will not remit anything back to a broker or other advisor who recommends their funds.)

By the original argument for 12b-1 fees—that they are needed for marketing to get a fund started—it would make sense that they be phased out as the fund becomes big. But they are not phased out. They are in part responsible for the fact that mutual fund fees are larger than they ever were. The typical mutual fund fee is about 1.5 percent of assets—and that doesn't even include the cost of commissions for trading within the mutual fund, which could add as much as 0.5 percent or more.

Financial Planners, 401(k)s, and the Advisory Service

In addition to the new wrap-fee brokerage business, a new breed of advisor arose independently: the financial planner. Financial planners assess the whole financial plan of a customer and assist with it and make recommendations. In practice, their recommendations usually consist mostly of investment recommendations, because that's where the fees are and that's what excites their clients. Hence, their routine becomes much the same as that of the wrap-fee broker. Financial planners can be almost anyone. They could be certified by one of the big financial planning industry organizations, or they could be certified public accountants (CPAs), or lawyers, or psychologists who add some financial planning knowledge to their repertoire, or even astrologers, or just someone who hangs out a shingle.

Both the financial planning and the wrap-fee industries grew rapidly in the 1980s and 1990s. They did their clients an important service by getting them to diversify their investments using mutual funds and by making them comfortable increasing their investments in stocks as a long-run investment. Their growth coincided with—and may even have done much to nourish—the stock market boom of the 1980s and 1990s. They rightly attempted in the late 1990s to beat back the rising lure of "day trading"—that is, frequent buying and selling of a small number of stocks—churning again, with lucrative profits to the brokers, even at the now much-lower fees.

The rise of the wrap-fee and financial planning industries also coincided with another development that encouraged investors to exercise choice in their investments—the *401(k)* plan. The term 401(k) refers to a section of the U.S. Internal Revenue Service tax code that went into effect on January 1, 1980. An employee benefits consultant named Ted Benna realized it could be used to design an employee benefit plan in which employer and employee contributions could be added tax free. The employee would have control over the plan's investment.

Corporations quickly realized that the 401(k) plan could save them money and the risk of investment, transferring that risk to the employee. The number of 401(k) plans increased rapidly, rivaling the conventional defined-benefit pension plans. As a result, many employees were faced with the decision about how to invest their 401(k)s. The demand for advice to help make that decision created more business for the investment advisory industry and introduced more of the U.S. public to investing in equity mutual funds (stocks are sometimes also called *equities*). The 401(k) investment decision was often included in the advisory process provided by a financial or investment advisor, whether the advisor was a financial planner or a wrap-fee broker.

Hence, the advisory service's value lay essentially in advising the customer to make a long-run commitment to a diversified stock portfolio. This is simple advice, easily followed. The rigmarole of risk assessment, asset allocation, style allocation, and selection of mutual funds or separately managed investments, and the frequent tedious repetition of the claim that "sophisticated" models and software are used to arrive at the recommendations, could be regarded as the window dressing necessary to get the customer to come in and get the simple advice he or she actually needs. From that viewpoint the whole process is valuable.

The question, though, is whether it is not only the window dressing to get the client to listen to good, simple advice but also the smokescreen set up to fool the client into believing the advice is much more complicated than it is—and therefore worth the enormous fees charged for it (albeit to the blissful disregard of the client).

"I've Never Been Able to Get More Than $3,000 from That Account"

A simple incident I witnessed shows what a boon the continuing, year-after-year percentage-of-assets charge is to the investment advisory and management profession.

In the last half of the 1990s and the early 2000s, I was a partner in a firm that catered to the investment advisory industry. We did not actually advise investors ourselves. Rather, we were the support system for the independent investment advisor.

Most investment advisors work for a big firm like Merrill Lynch, Smith Barney, or any of a number of other brokerage firms, banks, or other financial institutions. The big firm provides everything the advisor needs, including office space and equipment, sales training, computer systems, back-office paperwork and reporting, research reports, trading and custodial services, and so forth. But as the price for receiving this support, the advisor hands over to the firm at least half of her revenues from customers. Furthermore, the advisor does not own her "book of business"; that is, she can't sell it to someone else if she decides to move into some other business or retire or bequeath it to her heirs. (The advisor's book of business—her list of customers—can be of great value.)

Some advisors, though, can be independent of these large firms. They can set up their own business, get their own offices, keep most of the revenues from their customers, and sell their book of business if they want to. But they still usually need much of the support systems that employment by a big firm can provide.

What My Company Did

My company provided those support systems, charging a fee as a percentage of the assets invested by our clients' customers. We provided computer software systems to our clients—the independent investment advisors—to help them go through the usual risk assessment and asset allocation process, to help them automatically fill a recommended portfolio with recommended investments, and to automatically fill in all the required forms for them.

We provided various back-office services and sent out, on behalf of our clients (the advisors), regular reports to their investor-customers on the state of their assets and their rates of return on investment. We provided research reports and gave guest talks when requested. As the chief economist, I wrote occasional papers on economic and market issues and, when asked to (and when the client was a big enough client, that is, had a big enough book of business), gave talks to groups of our clients' investors and prospects. We also had a ghostwriter who would write articles that our clients were permitted to submit to their local newspapers or magazines under their own names.

At first we aimed for the "cream of the crop" of advisors, the broker-consultants who worked for the large "wirehouses" (the term is of historical derivation) like Merrill Lynch and Smith Barney. These people would generally have the largest books of business and would be most polished at selling and servicing clients. We hoped to have a relatively small but elite clientele. But it turned out to be more difficult than we expected to wheedle them away from their cushy situations. They were not used to furnishing their own offices. They asked silly questions to show that they didn't know how to do it, like "Where do you buy a Xerox machine?" Furthermore, and probably most importantly, they were locked into their big firms by stock ownership or stock options in their firms that didn't vest until years hence; in other words, they would lose the stock if they left.

Plan A was not working quite as we hoped, so we were forced to cast a wider net. Instead of limiting our clientele to a small number of the crème de la crème, we had to increase it to a large number of the not-so-creamy. Eventually our clients included not only a few brokers who left the wirehouses to go independent but also a number of financial planners of all stripes, CPAs, and others.

A Web of Business Alliances

One day toward the end of the boom market years of the late 1990s, I went to Minnesota to give a talk at a luncheon attended by the customers and prospects of a client of ours, a Minneapolis independent advisory firm. Besides speaking at the luncheon, I was also scheduled to join in a two-hour meeting with our advisor-clients and members of a local law firm. Our clients were trying to form a stronger relationship with the law firm.

This get-together helps illustrate the complexity of the relationships that can exist in the investment field. It's all about relationships and selling. The principal purpose of the relationship of the advisory firm with the law firm was to send each other business. It is a form of business prospecting. The more relationships you have with people in business, who know you are looking for more business, and who are also looking for more business, the more business you are likely to get.

Investment advisory firms have the advantage in this game that their clients are, in general, well-heeled. They are the sort of people who can afford expensive lawyers and whose businesses—the ones that brought them the money they have to invest—may need expensive lawyers. Furthermore, people who go to an advisor for investment advice frequently tap the advisor for other advice, like a recommendation of a good lawyer. The advisor is likely to recommend the lawyer who sends the advisor the most business. Similarly, clients of lawyers may also ask the lawyers for advice on other matters, like who is a good investment advisor. The lawyer is likely to send the client to the advisor who sends the lawyer the most business. And so it goes.

We Go After the CPAs

In the particular case of the Minneapolis investment advisors and the Minneapolis law firm, the law clients that the advisors—and we—were courting were the CPAs. CPAs hold sway over many of the decisions made by their clients about their finances. Why not advise them on their investments, too? If our client—the Minneapolis advisory firm—and we could recruit some CPAs to become independent investment advisors under our tutelage, and within our business network, then they could add to their revenues, and we could take a small (but substantial in dollar terms!) percentage.

In short, we wanted the law firm to help us recruit those of their clients who were CPAs to become investment advisors—because then they would use my firm's services and pay us fees.

This was not the first meeting of our advisor-client and the law firm. Rather, it was just an occasion for another meeting in the process of getting to know each other better, given that a representative of my firm—me—was in town.

They Were Wined and Dined

The advisors and the lawyers had, in fact, already met with CPA-clients of the law firm, had given them the pitch to add investment advisory services to their repertoires, and had then wined and dined them. (The more things change, the more they remain the same. Entertainment, more than investment research, is still often the advisor's fiercest weapon.)

Looking back on the process of pitching one of the CPAs on getting into the investment advice business, and then wining and dining him, one of our advisors told the following story.

When they met with the CPA during the day, they explained the whole investment advisory process—the risk assessment, the asset allocation, the selection of investment managers, yada yada. They used one of the CPA's clients as an example, a man with about $3 million in investment assets. They explained about fees—how the advisor's fee is 1 percent of the investor's assets, my firm's fees were whatever they were, the investment managers' fees were whatever they were, and so on.

Later on, they were having dinner with the CPA. They were no longer discussing the client with $3 million in assets. They were in the middle of the appetizer and having an exciting discussion about some sporting event or other, when the CPA suddenly stopped and said, "Wait a minute!"

The others at the table said, "What?"

The CPA said, "One percent of $3 million is $30,000!"

"That's correct," said the others.

Then the CPA said, "I've never been able to get more than $3,000 out of that account before."

Sale made. The CPA had seen the light—he had seen the power of the "small" annual percentage, charged every year. Charging for just doing tax returns, $3,000 was all he could ever get. But advise the client on how to invest his $3 million, and presto! Suddenly you've got $30,000 every year—and growing. What a business! What an opportunity! For the advisor, yes—but for the client?

And here I was—willy-nilly, like so many people in the industry, a part of the whole scam.

But little was I to realize that—as expensive as the investment advisors we were trying to recruit would be when they joined the party—they would be nothing compared with another group of investment "helpers" whose gravy train was about to arrive for real.

3

The Outer Limits:
Hedge Fund Fees

Now we come at last to the crowning achievement of the fee-charging business, the pièce de résistance, the masters of the fee-charging universe—hedge funds.

Hedge funds, like mutual funds, are pools of commingled investments shared among multiple investors. The difference between mutual funds and hedge funds is that hedge funds must restrict the type and number of investors that invest in them. Investors must be wealthy enough to bear significant loss (they must own at least a million dollars in investment assets or have income of at least $200,000 a year). As long as a hedge fund adheres to the restrictions on the type and number of investors, it escapes regulations applying to mutual funds. In particular, hedge funds can charge differently structured, higher fees, and they can use "leverage"—they can borrow to invest and use derivative investments mutual funds cannot use. They also don't need to make their numbers public or have them audited. The principle is that because the investors are wealthy and "sophisticated," they don't need the government regulatory structure to protect them.

A typical mutual fund, as we have seen, charges 1.5 percent of assets, plus brokerage commissions of perhaps a 0.5 percent. Given that an index fund product charging you 0.1 percent of assets—about one-twentieth as much as the typical mutual fund—is just as good or better, this is a pretty hefty fee.

But compared with hedge funds, mutual funds are real pikers.

Let's Do the Math

Hedge funds typically charge 1 to 2 percent of assets, plus a "performance incentive" fee of 20 percent of gains—though they can go as high as 4 percent plus 44 percent of gains. Sometimes there are additional administrative charges of about 0.5 percent.

For the sake of example, let's assume a hedge fund charges 1.5 percent fees plus a 20 percent performance incentive.

If the fund performs approximately like the long-term stock market—roughly 10 percent per year on average (and that, incidentally, would be good for a hedge fund)—then you would think the hedge fund manager gets 20 percent of that 10 percent, or 2 percent, as the performance incentive fee.

But, no, that's not quite the way it works. Returns fluctuate widely from year to year. Let's suppose the manager gets an annual 10 percent return over a two-year period but gets it by gaining 60 percent the first year and then losing 25 percent the second (that compounds to about 10 percent annually, on average).

Hence, the manager gets 12 percent for the first year—20 percent of 60 percent—and nothing for the second year, for an average of 6 percent a year. Not bad! That, plus the 1.5 percent base fee is a fee of 7.5 percent per year, on a return of 10 percent per year, leaving 2.5 percent for the investors—one-third as much as the manager gets.

Let's try this again with some real dollar numbers. You're a high roller like most hedge fund investors, so you've put a million dollars in this fund. In the first year your hopes are realized. The fund goes up 60 percent!

Now you've got $1.6 million—a whopping gain of $600,000. But you've got to pay the fees: 1.5 percent of assets plus 20 percent of gains. One and a half percent of $1.6 million is $24,000, and 20 percent of the $600,000 gain is $120,000. So you pay the hedge fund manager $144,000—that is, $24,000 plus $120,000. But you don't mind, because the manager's skill (or so you think—of course, it might have been just luck) has made you $456,000 after fees.

But in the next year the manager's skill fails her—or perhaps she just encounters bad luck—and the fund loses 25 percent of its assets. You had $1,456,000 after fees at the end of the first year, so at the end of the second year you have 25 percent less, leaving you with $1,092,000. But now you have to pay the 1.5 percent management fee, which on $1,092,000 is $16,380, leaving you with $1,075,620.

Over the two years, you've realized a gain of $75,620 on your $1 million while the manager received fees of $156,380, more than twice as much as you earned.

The Highest-Paid Business in the World

This anecdotal estimate is corroborated by the actual dollars paid hedge fund managers and their brokers. In 2004, those fees totaled $70 billion on an estimated $1 trillion in hedge fund assets—an average fee rate of 7 percent.[1] And that doesn't include an additional layer of "funds of funds" fees, to which I shall come shortly.

While not all hedge funds have large ups and downs, the ones that acquire the big names, essentially carrying the whole hedge fund business in the public mystique, do experience large ups and downs. They get famous for the ups and draw huge amounts of investment capital and then are usually not noticed so much for the downs. But the hedge fund managers make out very well on them.

Where are the investors' yachts? Indeed, where are the investors' *flotillas*? Hedge fund management is not just a license to steal; it is a license to steal literally billions. The hedge fund management business has created more billionaires than you can shake a stick at. In 2004, according to *Alpha* magazine, a magazine published by Institutional Investor, the average cash take-home pay for each of the top twenty-five hedge fund managers was $251 million.[2] Yes, you read that right. It doesn't take long to become a billionaire at that rate. And where does the money come from? It comes literally straight out of the investors' accounts.

Hedge Fund Celebrities

One of the controversial celebrities of the hedge fund business is George Soros, who, with Jim Rogers, started the Quantum Fund in the late 1960s. For a period of time it had outstanding returns, though later it busted so badly that it shut down. So how did Soros and the investors make out?

It's very difficult in most cases to know exactly how a hedge fund performed, because information is not public, numbers are only estimated by fund management itself, and numbers are not audited. I'll take up the question of hedge fund performance in another chapter. But we can get a rough idea, in the case of Soros's fund, of the relative return to investors and to management.

Appearing in the October 18, 2004, issue of *The New Yorker* was a mostly positive article about Soros's foray into politics in that year, written by the seasoned journalist Jane Mayer.[3] Anyone who can do simple arithmetic should find a revealing nugget of information embedded in Mayer's story.

Soros's wealth is attributable mainly to his management of the Quantum Fund, one of the earliest and most famous hedge funds. According to the article, Soros's wealth is estimated at $7.2 billion, on top of which he has given away more than $4 billion, for a total of more than $11 billion.

As to the source of Soros's wealth, according to Mayer: "The [Quantum] fund, which is registered in the Netherlands Antilles, turned an original investment of six million dollars, in 1969, into five and a half billion dollars by 1999."

Hence, Soros personally amassed over $11 billion while the fund amassed $5.5 billion. Of the fund's growth, we can rest assured that a large part of it, probably most, is due to the entry of new investors and their money, not to growth of the investors' assets itself.

The inevitable conclusion is that Soros himself earned at least twice as much as the investors, and probably a much greater multiple.

None of this is intended in any way to detract from Soros, who ranks among the great philanthropists of all time, especially for his work in formerly communist Eastern Europe. But the investors in his hedge fund may or may not feel proud to know that of their investment returns, two-thirds, at the very least, went to enrich the fund manager and as donations to socially responsible projects, while at most one-third went to themselves.

You would think that given the enormous amounts of money wealthy hedge fund investors pay out of their accounts to make billionaires of hedge fund managers, they would be extremely careful to research whether they are receiving equivalent value. Are they extremely careful? Not really. They might look, unscientifically, into the historical results of a fund they invest in—if results are even available. But do they evaluate in any serious way whether those results were due to skill or sheer luck, and whether there's any likelihood those results will continue? No, they don't.

One unique case of a hedge fund that won more fame in the public eye for its major down than for its ups was Long-Term

Capital Management (LTCM), of which I will say more later. After a period of several years of soaring returns—convincing many investors that those returns would continue forever—it encountered a decline so disastrous that it was effectively bankrupt, endangering several mammoth banks that had loaned it huge amounts of money. In the eyes of the U.S. Federal Reserve, its failure could have threatened the whole financial system if action were not taken. LTCM wound up being owned by the banks that loaned it money and recovered—essentially as a different company—but many of its investors did not.

No Bounds on the Ability to Charge Fees!

One problem that was noticed about performance incentive fees early on is that they create an incentive for highly fluctuating returns. As I showed, the performance incentive fee is much greater if the fund gets its return by experiencing huge ups and downs than by getting a steady annual return.

What performance incentive fees do for you is essentially give someone else the right to gamble with your money—and to collect a 20 percent fee when they win, while sticking you with all the losses when they lose (and collecting a 1 or 2 percent "administrative fee" into the bargain, whether they win or lose).

Yet getting a steady annual return—that is, avoiding the downs— is supposed to be one of the selling points of hedge funds (the very name itself—hedge funds—suggests that they hedge against downside risk).

To avoid creating this incentive to take on extra risk and volatility, the hedge fund industry introduced another feature in the fee structure: the high-water mark. With this feature in place, the manager can't get a performance fee in an up year if it wasn't sufficient to recover from a previous down—that is, if it didn't surpass the high-water mark created by the previous high.

For example, in the five years 1999–2003, the stock market as a whole (as represented by the S&P 500 index) gained 21 percent in 1999, lost 9 percent in 2000, lost 12 percent in 2001, lost 22 percent in 2002, and then regained 29 percent in 2003. If a hedge fund manager got those returns, she would have received her 20 percent performance incentive fee in 1999, but not in 2003, because 2003's 29+ percent was not enough to recover from the downs of

2000–2002. This is a sensible provision that helps rein in some of the worst potential excesses (as if the less-than-worst ones weren't bad enough).

Yet some of the newest breed of successful (they have the yachts) hedge fund managers are trying to sidestep that requirement. "No bounds on my ability to charge fees!" they say. An insider newsletter of the hedge fund industry, *Hedge Fund Intelligence*—not a place where the whistle will ever be blown on the entire industry, but a place where you might find a smidgen of self-criticism—published this report:

> Setting the fees . . . and the high-water mark used to be a relatively simple task. The fees were typically a management fee of 1%–1.5% and a performance fee of 20%. . . . And there was always a high-water mark above which a fund had to rise before performance fees were payable. Today, it is far more complex.
>
> A group of "hot" start-up managers have started to challenge the norm by setting aggressive fees . . . and scrapping the high-water mark in favor of a more flexible structure. . . .
>
> In some cases, there are good business reasons for these changes. But, more often than not, the trend is happening because some new managers have decided to charge whatever they think they can get away with. . . .
>
> In a recent case David Ganek, formerly with SAC, started the Level Global fund with an 18-month lock-up and a performance fee that moves up from the standard 20% to 30% when performance rises over 5%. He also scrapped the high-water mark in favor of a scheme that allows a manager to get a lower performance fee once the fund starts to recover from a drawdown. And he got away with it, raising significant sums of money on day one.
>
> His move to scrap the typical high-water mark was particularly innovative and borrowed from Steve Mandel at Lone Pine Capital. The way it works at Lone Pine is that the fund can charge half of the performance fee of any gain the fund makes from its low. This 10% performance fee continues until the fund has made up 150% of the drawdown from the previous high. Then the standard 20% fee kicks in again.[4]

OK, now do you understand hedge fund performance fees? The more complicated it is and the less investors understand the fee structure, the more you can charge.

Besides, if you find yourself submerged below a high-water mark and can't charge fees, hey, no problem! If your reputation as a bell ringer still lingers from some past year, then Allacazam! All you have to do is close your fund and open a new one. Then you can start charging fees again as if you had never fallen below the high-water mark.

The High Rollers Connive in Their Own Fleecing

So why do investors invest in these funds? And they are generally very wealthy investors, the kind who are supposed to be "sophisticated." Why do they do it?

Simple—it's the Big Investment Lie. They do it because they think they'll make more money by investing in these funds—or, at the very least, they think people will *think* they're making more money in these funds. People are vain—especially many wealthy people. Appearing to be a high roller can be more important than actually making money. But mostly it's just because investing in hedge funds is what their friends or associates told them to do—it's all part of the Big Investment Lie. It's all around them; they're enveloped by it. Suggestions that it is quite simply dead wrong do not wake them up but only confuse them. How could all those wealthy and respectable people be wrong?

Besides that, investors *like* the Big Investment Lie. They want to believe it. They collude in it themselves. They hire advisors who help them believe it. They want to get rich quick—or if they are already rich, they want to get *fabulously* rich—and they'll pay through the nose to someone who supports the belief that they can do it.

Funds of Funds

You may think we've now seen the absolute extreme, the outer limits, of fee charging. But oh, no! You haven't seen anything yet. As if hedge fund fees weren't high enough, an idea comes along to charge *yet another layer of fees*. Yes, some absolutely brilliant fee chargers created the "fund of hedge funds." Funds of funds often charge in excess of an additional 3 percent of assets and—would you believe—an additional performance fee . . . and even a front-end load! All this is on top of the already outlandishly excessive fees of the underlying hedge funds.

Funds of hedge funds, they claim, are for the purpose of diversifying away the risk of any one hedge fund. This is sheer nonsense because the use of hedge funds in the first place is supposed to be either to take a little extra risk with a small part of your fortune or to entrust a part of your fortune to a fundamentally conservative fund that demonstrably takes little risk by hedging against it.

Another purpose of funds of funds is to wrap hedge funds in a mutual fund–like instrument so that possibly smaller investors—those who aren't so wealthy—might invest in it, with lower minimum investments. But the legality of this idea has not been well tested yet. With the increased regulatory scrutiny hedge funds are getting, it is not likely that this avenue will go far.

That's all right, though, hedge fund and fund of fund managers are doing just fine living off the gullible rich.

Caveat Emptor: Let the Buyer Beware!

Much of what drives the investment advice and management industry is fees. This is not surprising. Business is first and foremost about collecting revenue. Without revenue businesses cannot survive, let alone thrive. Delivering a good product is important of course, but it can't be delivered unless fees are adequate to maintain the business. So thinking about how to collect, maintain, and increase fees comes first in business, even before thinking about how to improve the product, even how to make a good product.

But often—especially if the customer seems reasonably satisfied—thinking about how to get and increase fees completely replaces consideration of whether the product is any good or not. I've been in the thick of the business—and I know.

Strategy discussions about how to enhance revenue become the be-all and end-all. Discussions about how to ensure or improve the quality of the product or service don't take place at all, or they take place only in the context of how to retain revenue. This happens subtly, within a groupthink environment. It often doesn't occur to employees—except perhaps peripherally or in joking over drinks after work—that their product, to use the colloquial idiom of the after-work drinking environment, sucks. If the customer continues to pay, the product is de facto assumed to be what the customer, however ill informed, misinformed, misled, flat-out lied to, or simply stupid, actually wants.

Most employees continue to believe their own projected public image, that they are high-minded businesspeople performing a service that is—at the very least—worth the high level of compensation they are paid. If some employee pipes up and says something like, "Shouldn't we be trying to do things that actually benefit the customer?" others eye that employee with a look of bewilderment, as if they don't quite understand what he or she is saying.

Virtually the only check on this inexorable process is awareness on the part of the customer. In some professions, such as the medical and pharmaceutical fields, rigorous professional standards and government and industry regulatory bodies also provide something of a check. But in many fields, industry regulatory bodies are frequently handmaidens of the big players in the industry. Government regulatory bodies are often themselves "captured"—to use the economists' term—by the industry, because of the steady flow of employees back and forth between industry and government.

The agency that regulates the investment services industry in the United States, the SEC, does an excellent job within its mandate. It does not, however, have—nor perhaps should it have—as broad a mandate as do some other regulatory agencies. For example, the FDA has the authority to determine whether a new pharmaceutical drug performs better than a placebo before it will approve it for sale to the public.

The Corruption of Information

Governments and government regulatory bodies cannot wholly protect customers from themselves. They cannot protect them from being adamantly or willfully misinformed or from making bad choices.

In the end, the only true check is a sufficiency of information in the hands of the customer, enabling the customer to make a good decision. The customer must, therefore, find good sources of information, weigh them against each other, and make intelligent choices.

The companies themselves, trying to sell the customer investment services are, of course, one source of information. This source, however, as we have seen, is biased and suspect, because of the self-interest of the companies. The customer nonetheless has a tendency to weight this source too heavily because of what the customer believes to be the respected names of the companies. Because of the Big Investment Lie effect—the belief that it is surely impossible for so many authority figures to support an out-and-out bald lie—the customer tends to disbelieve information that flatly contradicts facts stated or implied by these highly respected brand-name firms.

The truly diligent customer will seek out unbiased sources like watchdog organizations, financial media, and academic studies. And many of these sources do provide accurate and unflinchingly truthful information. But many—probably the majority—put out information that is itself heavily tinged with the Big Investment Lie. Even the financial media and the academic financial community have been, by and large, subtly co-opted by the Big Investment Lie and the lure of money.

The co-option is the same as—if once removed from—the process whereby corporations begin to think only about what to tell customers in order to collect revenue and less about whether what they are saying is correct.

In the case of financial journalists and academicians, the incentive is not so much that they must earn revenue to maintain their businesses. The incentive is, rather, the possibility that the fabulously large levels of wealth accruing to so many people in the business could some day, somehow, come their way. To the extent that they stay in good graces with the investment services industry—parroting or at least not uncloaking too revealingly the Big Investment Lie— there is the chance they might join the party.

This happens frequently to academicians in the financial field. If an academician makes a name for him- or herself in academia and is not too much of a boat rocker, the academician could pull down a plum of a side job. Some are asked to become mutual fund trustees, with compensations well above half a million dollars a year—for doing very little. Some become money management or hedge fund consultants or even partners, with compensations potentially in the untold millions.

It is quite common for two professors to hold neighboring offices, one having lucked into a consultancy or partnership in an investment management firm that brings her millions, the other still subsisting on a meager academic salary, while keeping a constant lookout with envy, greed, and longing for his big chance. Is either one likely to become a whistle-blower and proclaim loudly that the whole industry thrives on a Big Lie? Not likely. Not when there are such big payoffs in the offing.

True, many important voices in the academic financial field do clearly speak the truth. Notable, among others, is distinguished Princeton professor Burton Malkiel, author of the best-selling book *A Random Walk Down Wall Street*. But many have been co-opted or remain silent—except among their peers—thus rendering their profession incapable of forming a strong counterforce to combat the Big Investment Lie.

The same is true of the financial journalism profession. Not only may financial journalists endanger their access to insiders and their ad revenues from the financial industry, but they might also endanger the possibility, however slim, that some day, in some way, they could themselves be cut in. Besides that, much of the financial journalism profession seems itself to be taken in by the Big Investment Lie. As Tom Gardner of "The Motley Fool" said when the Beardstown Ladies were exposed by the media as "frauds," "we haven't yet come across a single article entitled 'Mutual Fund Managers Called Frauds.'" Why not? Because the investment management industry's slick and polished methods keep the Big Investment Lie afloat, while the much more naive (and ethical) Beardstown Ladies could not even tread water once their own little inadvertent lie was revealed.

Although there are notable, laudable exceptions—*Forbes* magazine's consistent exposure of the absurdly high fees, sleaziness, and pointlessness of hedge funds is one outstanding example; *The Economist's* consistent skepticism about them is another—most financial coverage in the media gives the impression that everything, save for the occasional fraud case, is on the up-and-up. You would never know from the vast majority of media stories that the whole thing is shot through and through with a Big Lie.

4

Taxes Down the Drain

In January 1994, I spoke to a small gathering of the superrich at the behest of the Northern Trust Bank of Chicago. I was a speaker at their Family Financial Forum, which was held at an extremely opulent hotel in Dallas.

"Family Financial Forum" sounds like a nice little gathering, perhaps with tea and cakes, that you might have one evening at your local church or community center. But that's not what this Family Financial Forum was. The average wealth of the families represented at this forum was $400 million. This was not your typical community group.

The wealthy were represented either by family members themselves or by their staff, or both. Most superrich have family foundations managed by hired staff. A few of the people at the conference bore names that would be recognized for their wealth, but most would not be known to the general public.

Northern Trust spared no expense rolling out the red carpet for these, their most well-to-do clients. There were two "name" speakers. One was Dick Cheney. At that time he was known primarily for his understated televised briefings as secretary of defense during the Gulf War in Iraq. He was frequently mentioned as a possible presidential candidate. He seemed, in person as in his television briefings on the Gulf War, understated and modest.

The other name speaker—who may have cost Northern Trust even more as a speaker than Dick Cheney—was political commentator Norman Ornstein. Ornstein was in great demand for his biting political wit and insight.

Getting to the Meat

Those two speakers were the entertainment; the rest were the meat. The meatiest—and probably the longest speaking and most attentively heard—was a man from a big law firm who spoke on estate taxes. In his talk he displayed, and explained as best he could, the most complicated chart I've ever seen at a conference—save for conferences intended only for technical people. The chart was about how to create a tax avoidance strategy for a wealthy extended family. As I recall, a lot of it involved generation-skipping trusts. Apparently, if you can arrange to give a lot of money to your grandchildren but not to your children, you can avoid a lot of taxes.

It's not surprising that there was so much interest in avoiding taxes. Members of the U.S. private sector do not have friendly feelings toward taxes. They try to avoid them whenever they can. And this particular group included many people who were the least friendly toward taxes of all.

My Talk Bombs

Given this fact, it may seem odd that my talk might have been the least well-received one at the forum. I don't think it was a bad talk. I think, actually, it was rather good, if a little dull—but no more dull than estate taxes. I thought I made my small number of points clearly and well.

But the main thrust of the talk seemed to fly in the face of what people in attendance believed or wanted to believe. My talk was on "After-Tax Investment Returns." It doesn't sound very controversial, but it seemed to make some people indignant.

The main point of my talk was simple: "What you get is what you keep." That is, you have to take all costs into account before you decide whether an investment strategy is a good one or not. In this particular case, I was focusing on the tax cost. Some investment strategies cost you more in taxes than others. It pays to consider the comparative tax cost when you compare two investment strategies.

I gave a good example of two real-world mutual funds. One of them, Fund A—the Franklin Growth fund—had an annual return over the period 1963–1992 of 9.6 percent. Fund B—the Seligman Common Stock fund—had a much better return, 11.2 percent. Consequently, if you had invested $1,000 in each one of them, before taxes you'd have $24,400 with Fund B but only $15,800 with Fund A.

You'd think Fund B was a better investment than Fund A. But after taxes the story was much different. Fund B had high turnover—that is, stocks were frequently bought and sold. This meant the owner—if taxable—would have to pay short-term capital gains taxes at a high rate on the gains every year. Fund A, by contrast, had low turnover. The owner of Fund A had less in capital gains and would have to pay taxes only at the much lower long-term capital gains rate.

Because of this the owner of Fund A would have $10,800 after taxes, while the owner of Fund B would have only $8,400, even though—before taxes—the owner of Fund B had $4,600 more. That extra $4,600—plus $2,400 more—got eaten up by taxes.

I also pointed out that according to a study over the same time period by two Stanford professors, the average that taxable mutual fund investors lost to taxes was almost 3 percent annually. But you could reduce that greatly if you used—or if your investment manager used—a tax avoidance strategy.

To my surprise the audience reception felt icy. I thought my delivery was poor. Maybe my tie had a big stain on it from lunch. I wasn't sure what was wrong. One woman in the front row seemed particularly fidgety. Finally, she blurted out, "Well, isn't that the tail wagging the dog?"

She explained that paying attention to taxes would divert the manager's attention away from the most important thing, which was getting the best possible before-tax return.

I Keep My Mouth Shut

Could I have replied to her with the actual truth, which is that the manager's efforts to get the best possible return were probably a waste of time? Could I have pointed out that study after study shows that investment managers—even the ones who cater to the super-rich—don't beat a portfolio composed by a blind Ouija board operator? No, that would render her speechless with horror and would bring a complaint to a highly attentive Northern Trust executive vice president, perhaps to the president. That would be my last talk to the superrich at an extremely opulent hotel.

She was not the only person in the room who felt the way she did. To put the best spin on it, it was obvious from the general reaction that my message was ahead of its time. (In fact, that turned out to be the case. A perception of the importance of after-tax investing began gradually to dawn on some investors—though still not most—in subsequent years.)

This is my interpretation. Like most people in the room, the woman had a warm professional relationship with her investment manager, a person of good social standing and a fine manner. She extended feelings of trust and respect to that person for his supposed investing skills and his ability to keep confidences. She may possibly have gotten wind of rumors that professional investment management, on average, adds no benefit, but she could not believe that applied to her investment manager. She may have somehow detected in my talk the slightest suggestion that behind my emphasis on after-tax returns, there was a deemphasis of what may have been, in my view, the discredited quest for superior before-tax returns. She couldn't, and wouldn't, believe that.

The belief among many of the wealthy that they can have special access to superior money management becomes almost a part of their identity. Even to hint at questioning that premise is to eat away at their egos. Nothing else explains the stiff reaction I got.

The Dereliction of Duty of Money Managers

If you do not agree with the woman's premise—that an investment manager must not think about tax avoidance because it might interfere with the execution of his investment strategy—then you must conclude that the failure of investment managers to avoid taxes is nothing short of a dereliction of duty.

Tax avoidance doesn't matter, of course, if the investments are in a tax-deferred vehicle like a pension fund, endowment fund, 401(k), or IRA account. But if the investments are in a taxable account, then tax avoidance should be the first and foremost consideration of an investment manager. The ability of an investment manager to enhance a client's bottom line in this manner exceeds anything else he can do. (Fees are at least an equal consideration, of course, but that is the concern of the client and not the manager, whose concern is arguably to maximize his revenue without losing the client.)

But the vast majority of investment managers do not give taxes a thought. Evidence of this fact lies in the extraordinarily high turnover of most mutual funds.

The average turnover in equity mutual funds is now nearly 100 percent, according to the mutual fund–monitoring service, Morningstar, Inc. (it was much lower a few decades ago). That means most of the stocks in the fund are sold during a year, and others bought in their place.

A Free Loan from the Government

If a stock is held for less than a year and it gained during the year—as most stocks do in most years—then the gain is taxed at the income tax rate. For investors of above-average income, that rate is about 30 percent or more. Hence, if a stock gained 10 percent during a year, 3 percent out of that 10 percent goes to the government.

Therefore, a manager should have an awfully good reason to sell a stock before it is held for a year, because 30 percent of the gain will be lost if he does.

If the stock is held longer than a year and then sold, the gain will be taxed only at the long-term gains rate. The long-term rate is 15 percent for most investors—half as much as the short-term gains tax rate.

But there's even more reason not to sell a stock and realize a gain. The tax you pay on selling a stock is a tax you have to pay now. But if you keep the stock and sell it later, you can invest the tax money in the meantime.

The difference is huge. Deferring taxes has been called "getting a free loan from the government." If you can pay a tax later instead of now, it's like getting a zero interest loan. That's a very valuable thing to have.

Suppose, for example, you defer a $1,000 tax for twenty years that you would otherwise have to pay now. If you just invest it in certificates of deposit (CDs) at 4 percent, you'll have $2,191 in twenty years. Then after you pay the $1,000 tax, you'll still have $1,191, whereas you would have had nothing if you'd had to pay the tax now.

Furthermore, if you defer the taxes long enough, you could realize a really important benefit—you could die! Then the taxes won't have to be paid at all. This is not a joke. It can be a valuable thing for your heirs to inherit your investments before they are depleted by gains taxes.

The vast majority of mutual fund managers, not to mention hedge fund managers, pay absolutely no attention to these obvious facts. As a result, they lose for their clients, on average, about 1 to 2.5 percent of their money every year to the government, when with a little effort they could reduce that to as little as 0.5 percent.

That may not be an awful thing in a global sense. If wealthy investors don't pay extra taxes on their investments, someone else will have to make up the difference. But it should be an awful thing to admit to if you're the client's financial servant, charged with getting as much money into the client's pocket as possible. You're not doing that if you're letting 1 or 2 percent of it get away unnecessarily every year. Do you plead that you're making up for that loss with superior before-tax returns? Not a chance! That's a claim with not a scintilla of evidence to back it up.

Once again the Big Investment Lie is used to cover a multitude of sins—the lie that you can beat the market by a whole lot if you're smart and well paid. As soon as that lie is discovered to be illusory—like the emperor's imaginary clothes—the embarrassments of high taxes and high fees are revealed in all their nakedness.

Tax Avoidance Strategy in Investing

Capital gains taxes make up a very substantial part of United States tax revenues. One of the reasons the U.S. budget was hundreds of billions of dollars in surplus in the late 1990s, then hundreds of billions of dollars in deficit in the early 2000s, was because of capital gains taxes. When the stock market was soaring in the late 1990s, racking up increases in the 20 to 30 percent range, capital gains tax revenues poured in. Then when the market dropped in 2000, 2001, and 2002, these revenues dried up.

Obviously, somebody has to pay U.S. federal taxes to provide funds for the federal budget. But in the U.S. system—and all other systems, too—no individual, and no corporation, wants to pay taxes, and everybody tries not to. It's not considered shirking to try to minimize your taxes. It's considered good fiscal responsibility and good business sense.

Hence, advisors who help you minimize taxes are thought of as upstanding citizens and are well respected. The estate tax attorney who gave the complicated talk at the Family Financial Forum in Dallas was certainly a well-respected citizen and keenly sought after for his expertise.

Investment managers and advisors are also well respected and keenly sought after. The conference attendees' investment managers could, in some cases, have saved their clients as much in taxes as the estate tax attorney, if they had put their minds to it. But that was not thought to be their job. Neither they nor their clients thought it was their job. Their job was to beat the stock market. Never mind that they could save their clients far more in taxes than they could ever make for them trying to beat the stock market. The Big Investment Lie—that you can beat the market by a lot if you apply expertise and effort—means that expertise and effort are not applied where they really count.

The biggest problem, as usual, is that the best investment strategy is also the simplest. It is so simple that you wouldn't appear to need expert and hardworking managers and advisors to do it. Consequently, people who like to have expert, hardworking, and high-paid servants at their beck and call, and managers and advisors who like to have big inflows of revenue, don't consider that strategy.

The best tax avoidance policy in investment is a simple, well-diversified buy-and-hold strategy. If you hold stocks for a very long time, you won't have to pay tax on the gains, at least not for a very long time. And if you also want broad diversification, a passive index fund does the job quite nicely. Or you can try to use the strategy associated with investor names like Warren Buffett: choosing a portfolio of good companies and holding them forever. But if you aren't sure you can choose as well as Buffett (and who can be sure—not even Buffett himself), it's better to spread your investments across the whole market.

There are also more complicated tax avoidance strategies in investing. You can deliberately realize losses—that is, sell stocks at a loss—in order to offset gains. But these strategies have limited applicability. If you keep doing them for very long, you'll wind up with a portfolio concentrated in only a small number of stocks that have never declined. It's not a good investment strategy for the long run.

The best long-run strategy for tax avoidance is the simplest: buy and hold. You can do that by investing in a collection of stocks that you choose or in a passively managed, diversified, low-cost mutual fund. It doesn't just save you a little in taxes. It can save you in cash an amount equal to 2 percent of your portfolio every year. If your portfolio is a million or more, that will save you upward of $20,000 a year immediately and much more than that over time. If your portfolio is $100,000, it still saves you $2,000 every year. That's not peanuts.

That's a big tail, wagging a very small dog. The small—let's put it plainly, nonexistent—dog is the gain an investment manager can add by constantly buying and selling stocks like most mutual funds do, somehow winding up not even beating a passive market index.

The Bottom Line: Tallying Up the Costs

As I've already shown, many investors use high-cost investment services. Most of them don't even realize they're using high-cost services. These services typically cost 2 to 3 percent of an investor's assets annually.

To make things worse, higher-fee services tend to cost investors more in commissions than low-fee services and often in taxes as well, because higher-fee investment vehicles tend to have higher turnover.[1]

A Direct Comparison

Let's compare two investors, John and Mary. Each has $250,000 to invest. Neither one will touch the money for thirty years until after they are retired.

John considers that he knows little about investing. So he thinks he will be "smart" and hire a good advisor—or a "wealth manager," as the advisory firm he chooses calls it.

Mary decides to just invest 80 percent of the money in total market index funds purchased from Vanguard or Fidelity or one of a small number of other low-cost index fund providers. Mary decides to put 70 percent of this 80 percent in a domestic U.S. stock fund and 30 percent of it in an international fund. The other 20 percent of her money she will invest in a Vanguard intermediate bond fund.

John's comfort level with stocks is about the same as Mary's. So the wealth manager will advise him also to make a similar allocation of his portfolio to stocks and bonds—though the wealth manager will in all probability recommend different funds or investment vehicles, and a larger number of them.

Before fees and taxes, John and Mary will get about the same return over the thirty years—other than a small and unpredictable difference, plus or minus. Let's assume that return will average 8 percent annually.

Thus, their results before fees and taxes will be essentially the same. After fees and taxes, however, the difference between John's and Mary's results will be very large—*astonishingly* so.

Mary's total fees will be about fifteen "basis points"—or 0.15 percent per year. Her taxes will be a little over 0.5 percent a year.

But John's total fees will be more. They will range somewhere between 1.2 and 2.8 percent greater than Mary's. John's taxes will also be greater than Mary's. They will range between 0.1 and 1.7 percent greater than Mary's.[2]

The results will amaze you. I will summarize them in the following table at the bottom of the page.

The table speaks for itself. After fees, Mary will have somewhere between 40 and 121 percent more than John—with a midrange of 79 *percent more*—depending on how costly John's "wealth manager" and the investments he recommends are.

After both fees and taxes (if John and Mary are not able to put their money in tax-deferred accounts), Mary will have between 45 and 263 percent more than John—with a midrange of 137 *percent more*—by the time they need to access the funds. Mary will have at

What John's and Mary's $250,000 will be worth in 30 years with . . .

	After fees ($ THOUSANDS)			After fees and taxes ($ THOUSANDS)		
	JOHN'S	MARY'S	DIFFERENCE (% over John's)	JOHN'S	MARY'S	DIFFERENCE (% over John's)
HIGH-END FEES AND TAXES	$1,092	$2,413	$1,321,000 (121%)	$568	$2,064	$1,496,000 (263%)
MID-RANGE FEES AND TAXES	$1,351	$2,413	$1,062,000 (79%)	$872	$2,064	1,192,000 (137%)
LOW-END FEES AND TAXES	$1,720	$2,413	$693,000 (40%)	$1,428	$2,064	$636,000 (45%)

that time somewhere between $636,000 and $1,496,000 more than John. Of this amount, between $796,000 and $1,424,000 of John's money will have gone to pay his wealth manager, and between $292,000 and $523,000 will have gone to the federal government in taxes, while only $103,000 of Mary's money will have gone to pay fees and $349,000 to pay taxes.[3]

Now who do you think was smarter, John or Mary?

As silly as it sounds, the fees paid to the investment advice and management industry are largely based on the following circular logic: "We pay them a lot, so they become wealthy; they are wealthy, so we think they are expert and knowledgeable; we think they are expert and knowledgeable, so we pay them a lot."

5

Why Do We Give Golden Crumbs to Rich People?

W hat makes people fall for these high fees? It could be a certain well-documented chink in their good sense.

Classical economic theory makes a lot of assumptions about people's actions when their economic interests are at stake. It assumes, for example, that people act "rationally."

Some of these rationality assumptions seem a little out of keeping with common sense. At the very least, they are in a strange sort of jargon. For example, suppose someone decides to go to a three-hour baseball game for $20 instead of working overtime for $30 an hour. Economic theory assumes the psychic benefit of attending the baseball game must therefore be worth $110—$20 paid for the ticket plus $90 for the "opportunity cost" of not working. If the overtime option hadn't been available—assuming rationality— then the person would have been willing to pay $110 to attend the game.

Anyone can see that assumptions like these aren't going to predict economic behavior very well. People just don't act like that, for whatever reason. Nonetheless, the assumptions underlying this conclusion are the very backbone of economic theory.

Behavioral Economics

Recently a small coterie of economists and psychologists has staged a rebellion against the "rationality" assumption. Their heresy is called *behavioral economics*. Heresy though it may be, it has gone so far as to win a Nobel Prize for two of its proponents, experimental psychologist Daniel Kahneman and economist Vernon L. Smith. Behavioral economics consists largely of anecdotal and experimental evidence showing that people often don't behave in ways that economic theory labels "rational."

One of the people who collect and compile this anecdotal and experimental evidence is Richard Thaler, an economics professor at the University of Chicago. A lot of what Thaler does seems like just having fun at the expense of a few theoretical economist fuddy-duddies. For example, he likes to point out that one day when he was having several of his supposedly rational economist colleagues at his house, they couldn't stop eating a bowl of nuts he had put out. When he finally took the nuts away, they thanked him profusely.[1]

Some of Thaler's observations—and those of other behavioral economists—seem to point in a certain direction. One of his observations is that a person who drives across town to save $10 on a clock radio will not drive across town to save $10 on a much more expensive large-screen TV. Why not? It's the same $10 you save either way. But it's a big percentage saved off the clock radio price and only a small percentage off the large-screen TV price.

Another curious result Thaler obtained suggested that to buy the same item people will pay a rich seller more than they will pay a poor seller. He told subjects in a lab experiment to imagine they were stuck on a beach on a hot day and someone offers to get them a beer. How much would they be willing to pay? It turns out subjects are willing to pay more for the same brand of beer if they think it is being bought from an exclusive hotel than if it is bought from a neighborhood grocery.

One of the objections classical economists have to this new theory is that they think it is applicable only to trivia. Indeed, though behavioral economics and its sister field, behavioral finance, have generated a lot of buzz, it is not very clear how they should be applied. This makes it all the more curious that observations like Thaler's haven't been used to highlight one of consumers' most costly irrationalities.

People Don't Notice When They Pay Percentages to Rich People

As we noted from Thaler's observations and experiments, people seem to mind less paying a lot of money for something if (1) it is paid to someone who is already wealthy and (2) it costs a lot in dollars but little as a percentage. A person will drive across town to save $10 on a clock radio because it is 40 percent of the cost of the clock radio, but not to save $10 on a large-screen TV because it is less than 1 percent of the cost of the TV.

Is this behavior irrational? Yes, in an important sense it is. If you do everything this way, you'll go broke a lot quicker or get rich a lot slower than someone who realizes that saving $10 is saving $10, and it doesn't matter what you save it on.

So why don't behavioral economists spend more time and ink explaining to people the most costly result of these twin irrationalities—namely, paying high fees to investment professionals? People seem not to realize—or not to care—what they're paying because they're paying it to people who already are very well-off, and what they're paying, while enormous in dollars, is small as a percentage of their investment assets.

Co-opted

Behavioral economists could perform a service to the investing public by pointing out to them the very high cost of these particular irrationalities. But we've seen no such thing from the profession.

Why don't behavioral economists put their efforts into delivering this particular message? It could have something to do with the fact that—due to the recent popularity of behavioral finance and economics—many behaviorists are directors in their own professional investment management firms. To the extent that their firms draw substantial investments from clients and charge the usual percentage fees, they will earn far more than they ever could from their university salaries.

Why would a rational self-interested economist endanger this revenue stream by telling people how irrational it is to pay such high fees?

Perhaps Thaler and others like him just think their firms are going to make much more money for their investment clients by beating the market. But I'd be willing to hazard an educated guess that if you had a few beers with one of these academics–cum–investment managers—and it was off the record—he would admit he had no idea whether his firm would outperform the market in the future or not.

How to Get Rich

As a graduate student, I often needed extra money, so I picked up odd jobs using mathematics. For example, I did computer programming of mathematical solutions for the departments of physics, geography, astronomy, and engineering at my university. But I also fell into other jobs, some of them quite interesting.

The most interesting and unusual contract jobs were the ones I did for a man named Bud Bradley. Bud was very wealthy for reasons that were mysterious to me, until one day I finally figured it out. He had a small office on Dempster Street in Skokie, Illinois. Dempster was a street lined with the commercial generica that clutter a thoroughfare in the suburbs. Other than Bud's office, Dempster Street had mostly car dealerships, gas stations, and cheap restaurants.

Bud's small office was in a building one would never notice. It was completely unmarked. Bud had a single crucial and loyal employee, a Japanese woman named Tomi. Other than that he seemed to have no real work. But he had various business friends we occasionally met for drinks.

Most of my work for Bud was creating tables to be bound into little booklets. The tables showed loan repayment schedules at various levels of interest, along with credit life insurance payments. These booklets had to be different for different states, because insurance regulation is a state prerogative. At that time interest rates were capped by government. Allowable credit life insurance rates were also capped, but the caps were different in different states.

The calculations were a little complicated because you could charge interest on the credit life insurance payments, and you could also charge credit life insurance premiums on the interest payments. Consequently the calculations involved solving a small math problem each time I created a table.

Doing My Own Horoscope

This table making would soon have gotten boring—except for the fact that Bud was something of a character. He would also pick up oddball projects from time to time. One time he asked me whether I would be willing to program a computerized horoscope. It was to be a two-person project, me and an astrologer.

We met with the astrologer over dinner one evening. She was a woman with very big artificially blonde hair and a sparkling, over-friendly aura that seemed to go in everybody's direction but nobody's in particular. The idea was that she would write hundreds of paragraphs, each making a prediction about a person. After she finished the paragraphs, I read them and found them rather wimpy. The farthest out on a limb she went was to predict that the subject of the horoscope might get pyorrhea of the gums sometime in the subject's life.

My job was to write a program that, given the date and time of the subject's birth, would tell you the signs of the zodiac in which lay the moon, the sun, and the planets at that time. So I had to find out how to do that. I discovered quickly that there were so-called tables of the ephemerae that contained this information daily for centuries. But it was an enormous amount of information. How would we feed all that into a computer? And where would it be stored? (Computers didn't have much storage in those days.) Besides, there was a change from the Julian calendar to the Gregorian calendar in 1582 that confused things.

It occurred to me that those tables of the ephemerae had to have been created somehow. Somewhere there had to be formulas telling how to produce the numbers. So I went on a quest for those formulas. Remember, this was in the days before the Internet, the Web, and Google. Trying to find the answer to the question meant physically going around to different libraries and asking people until, if you were lucky, you got the answer.

I was lucky. I found the answer fairly quickly. The formulas that produced the tables of the ephemerae had been created in 1896 by Simon Newcombe, a man who was, surprisingly, otherwise well known as an economist.

I programmed these formulas. They would produce in a jiffy the precise azimuth and altitude of any of the planets as well as the moon and the sun on any given day at any given time. The program would then translate this into the signs of the zodiac these heavenly bodies were in. (As a bonus, I discovered I was a Virgo by three hours, not a Libra as I had always thought.) Depending on the combination of signs, the program would pluck out a series of ten or so paragraphs from the astrologer's list. That would be the person's horoscope.

The problem I ran into was printing this all out to make a hard copy. Believe it or not, this was not easy. The programming language I used, Fortran (this was the last half of the 1960s), was so inefficient at printing that it would take, as I recall, as much as an hour to print one horoscope. So we had to hire someone else who knew how to do it. To my deep chagrin, the fellow charged much more for his work than I had charged for mine.

This shows what kind of dabbling Bud occupied himself with, while the money just rolled in, from God knew what. It wasn't from things like horoscope programs. For that, the plan was to put little slips of paper in Kleenex boxes offering your computerized horoscope for $3. I suppose that could have made a lot of money if it really caught on, but unfortunately it never got off the ground.

The Dawning

One day Bud proposed another project. He said he knew of a warehouse where their accounting system was really terrible. They wrote everything on little pieces of paper. A lot of the pieces of paper fell from the backs of drawers behind desks and got lost. What they really needed was computerization.

I said I would be glad to take a look at the situation. Bud told me whom to call. I called the man, who told me how to drive to the place where the warehouse was and he would meet me.

As I drove to the warehouse, I started to get more and more worried. The year, I think, was 1968. I found myself driving deeper and deeper into the South Side of Chicago. It may not be something that is generally realized now, but for a small white guy to drive a cheap student's car that might break down at any moment into the all-black ghetto of South Side Chicago at that time was to kindle a rising panic. Besides, I wasn't at all sure where I was, or where I was going, or whether I was in the right place.

Just at the moment of greatest jitters, I saw a white man in a slightly rumpled business suit standing outside on the street, nervously watching for me. As soon as we made eye contact, he vociferously waved me into an underground parking chamber. From there, we went into the building.

We were in an enormous furniture warehouse where people—all black, without exception—were shopping for furniture. All of the furniture was marked on sale, and all of it was marked with terms for buying on the installment plan. Whenever someone bought on the installment plan, they were required by the sellers to buy credit life insurance. The credit life insurance would make the rest of the payments if the buyer died.

During the course of my calculations to produce the little books of interest and credit life insurance payments, I had noticed that the allowable premiums for credit life insurance were exorbitantly high. You'd have to have a death rate like that of the Black Plague years in the fourteenth century to justify credit life insurance rates like that. But nonetheless those rates were what the law allowed. Sure enough, those were the rates that were charged. Evidently people didn't really notice they were being charged outrageous rates for credit life insurance *because it was only a "small" percentage* of the cost of the item they were buying.

Now I realized how Bud got rich, why he had an unmarked office, and why he didn't seem to have to work much. He was the credit life connection. He raked off a little on each sale of furniture, kept a lot of it, and handed the remainder to an insurance company, who took care of the rest. The only thing he had to do was maintain the financial accounting, which is what Tomi did. I had just seen one of the sellers Bud worked with, probably only one of many. All told, Bud was selling credit life insurance on thousands upon thousands of transactions.

One time I was having drinks with Bud and some of his friends, and the subject turned to how to make money. The friends offered various ways they thought you might be able to make a lot of money. Then Bud leaned forward and gave the authoritative answer: "No," he said, "the way to make money is to *handle* money."

Golden Crumbs

Tom Wolfe's novel *The Bonfire of the Vanities* has a scene in which bond salesman and self-styled "master of the universe" Sherman McCoy is asked by his daughter what he does for a living. McCoy's wife volunteers an answer for him. It is a rather snide answer, suggesting she is more than a little put out by his inflated ego. She says that what Sherman does is to shave golden crumbs off a golden cake as the cake is passed around.

This characterization has a lot of truth to it. Because of the irrationalities we pointed out earlier—and that Thaler identified—people do not seem to take much notice when a large amount of money is shaved off a much larger amount. If you can get involved in some business that passes big pieces of money around, a business that *handles* money—even if it's only aggregates of smaller amounts of money—and shave a small percentage off, you can amass truly astounding sums rather quickly.

An example of this made the news a few years ago when the high-est-paid corporate executive in 1996 was announced. The amount was $102.4 million, paid to Lawrence M. Coss, chairman of Green Tree Financial Corporation. What business was his company in? Green Tree Financial was the biggest company engaged in financing the purchase of mobile homes. It made its money from interest pay-ments on mobile home mortgages.

People who live in mobile homes are by and large the poorer people in the United States, so Coss made his $100 million from a small percentage of the aggregated money paid by poor people for their homes.

Is there any justification for the amounts of money the golden crumb shavers, the money *handlers*, make? Do they perform a serv-ice commensurate with what they are paid? Or do they make so much money for no better reason than that people are irrational and don't know or care that they are paying huge amounts of money, as long as they perceive it as only a small percentage?

The mobile home mortgage provider was getting rich off the backs of poor people. Reprehensible? Perhaps. But Coss could defend himself as follows. Poor people are bad risks. It's very hard for them to find someone who will lend to them so that they can have a home. Someone who does lend to them is willing to take big risks. They have to charge high interest rates to compensate. If they're lucky and the economy is good one year, with rising employment rates, all their borrowers might pay up at the high interest rates and none of them default. In that year, the president of the lending company might be paid $100 million from the profits. But the next year the economy might turn down, the default rates could go way up, and the com-pany could go broke on its lending.

The good thing, at least, about this defense of the mobile home mortgage-lending bonanza is that the explanation is also the whole truth. It's true that most banks won't lend to people poor enough to be able to afford only a mobile home. Only someone willing to shoulder a lot of risk will do it. But they'll need to be compensated for that risk.

Can anything similar be said about the huge profits in the invest-ment advice and management business? The principal defense of the business is that people want professional advice and management and feel more comfortable when they get it. But the business would be gradually reduced to a much smaller, much less lucrative business if it made a practice of telling the whole truth and advising clients accordingly. Therefore, it must—as an entire industry—engage in a Big Lie to keep its business lucrative. It must underplay its fees and overstate benefits in any way it legally can.

This is not providing an advisory service to a client; it is providing a delusion. Maybe the defense of the Big Investment Lie is merely that the client desperately, urgently, wants to be lied to.

I've shown you how much investors pay for the services of investment professionals. Now it's time to examine what they actually get for their payments.

PART II

HOW LITTLE YOU GET

6

Why Investment Professionals Can't Predict Markets

In previous chapters, I've shown what professional invest-ment advice and management costs. Now I'll show why it doesn't benefit you—that is, why it doesn't increase your wealth.

In this chapter, I'll explain the very sound reasons why professional investment managers should not be expected to beat the market. Then, in the next chapter, I'll describe the extensive evidence that shows that, indeed, they cannot.

Active and Passive Management

Suppose you were asked which investment manager you would like, one who tries to beat the stock market aver-age or one who is content just to equal it. What would you say?

"Well, it depends on the cost" is the best answer. Is it worth spending more than a minimal amount to try to beat the market?

As I explained earlier, managers of equity investment assets are divided into two main categories. Those who try to beat stock market averages are called *active managers*. Their practice is called *active management*. Paid investment advisors typically recommend higher-cost, active managers.

Those who do not try to pick stocks to beat the mar-ket averages are called *passive managers*. Their practice is called *passive management*.

Passive Management

Passive management strategies don't try to determine which stocks are better than other stocks. Instead, they usually invest in nearly all the stocks in the stock market or all the stocks in some subcategory—for example, the S&P 500 index. This investment methodology is called *indexing*. The idea is to hold a portfolio that is allocated exactly the way the whole market or submarket is allocated. Thus, investment performance will neither beat nor fall short of (except for a small fee) the market index.

It is not really necessary for a passive strategy to adhere strictly to a market index—though, in theory, that can afford the best possible diversification. All that is necessary for a strategy to be passive is that it not attempt to pick stocks or to time when to get into or out of the market or any market segment.

In some cases, like that of mutual fund management firm Dimensional Fund Advisors (DFA), trading is passive also. On the assumption—to put it plainly—that other people trade for dumb reasons or give up too much profit when they trade, DFA simply takes the other side when another trader is aggressively buying or selling. Hence, DFA's index funds may not adhere precisely to the index allocation at all times, but they add a little in performance by taking advantage of others' eagerness to trade.

Fees for passive investment management are low—about twenty basis points (twenty-hundredths of a percent, or 0.2 percent) or less for individual investors in major market index funds, and as low as five basis points (five-hundredths of a percent, or a 0.05 percent) or less for large investors and institutional investors. For investments of $100,000 or more, the lowest fees for broad U.S. domestic index funds are now ten basis points or less. Institutional investors get still lower basis point fees because their passively managed portfolios can be gigantic, in the hundreds of millions or billions of dollars. This size results in a cost reduction due to economies of scale.

In addition to index portfolios allocated the same as the market or a submarket, there have arisen—as a marketing reaction to the popularity of index funds—a variety of so-named index funds, quasi-index funds, and fake index funds that lose many, most, or all of the benefits of true index funds. These can usually be spotted by their higher fees.

Active Management

In contrast to passive investment management, active management tries to distinguish stocks that will perform better—that is, will have higher future rates of return—than other stocks in the market. Fees for active investment managers are much higher than for passive management because people who pick stocks are paid extremely high salaries, because they often buy outside investment research, and because they have higher profit margins.

Fees for actively managed mutual funds—the domain of the individual investor—range from a low of about 0.3 percent to a high of well over 3 percent per year, with averages in the 1 to 1.5 percent range. Individual investors can also invest with separate account managers who charge only about 0.5 percent for a minimum investment of $100,000. But they can invest with these managers only through an advisor—which means they'll also have to pay the advisor.

For institutional investment funds, the cost for active management is lower than for individual investors because the funds are usually larger than individuals' assets. But the cost for active management is still much higher than for passive management.

How Active Managers Pick Stocks

For active managers, most of the effort goes into picking individual stocks. Sometimes they try to evaluate the stock market as a whole—when to get into it and out of it—and how much to allocate to individual market sectors, like energy or technology.

The routine for picking stocks at a typical active investment management firm goes something like this. The database of all stocks (such as all U.S. domestic companies) is screened to reduce it to an eligible set of about two hundred stocks. The screening is done with the help of database filters on characteristics like earnings growth, trading volume, price/earnings (P/E) ratio, and debt/equity ratio. Companies with too high a P/E ratio, too high a debt/equity ratio, or too low earnings growth or trading volume might be screened out— or an entirely different screen might be applied, depending on the manager's investment philosophy. In addition, research from independent research reports, industry contacts, and general reading comes into play.

Fundamental analysis of the companies in the remaining list—exhaustive analysis of their financial statements and filings—is then performed to generate earnings forecasts. The forecast is usually of the earnings in the next year and the earnings growth rate thereafter. The *present value formula*, a mathematical formula that discounts back to the present day the value of future earnings, is then used to deduce the "true" price—the price at which the stock of the company "ought" to be trading. This "true" price is compared with the actual price in the market. If the true price is higher, then the stock is a bargain at current market prices and should be bought. If the true price is lower, then the stock is currently overpriced and should be sold or not bought.

Such is the procedure at active money management firms—along with similarly determining whether the market as a whole or sectors of the market are overvalued or undervalued. For this activity an extra 1 percent or so of assets (less for larger clients) is charged by the manager.

Then, on top of the fee charged by the manager, an investment advisor—if the investor has one—attempts to select among the stock-picking money managers to determine which are best at stock picking. For this additional service, the advisor charges up to another 1 percent.

The trouble is, these activities—and the attempts to discern who is best at them and who is not—are of no value whatsoever to the investor. Let us examine why.

The Myth of Centralized Information

What do the former Soviet Union and active investment managers have in common? Both believe prices can be determined independently of the market.

The error of this belief is now well established due to the demise of the Soviet Union. Not trusting the market, Soviet central planners set up huge bureaucracies to determine what the price of every item, large and small, in an industrial economy should be. Every nut, bolt, tractor, assembly line belt, potato, bag of fertilizer, oil well drill, swatch of fabric, button, item of clothing, bed, chair, lamp, cow, soup can, loaf of bread, bottle of vodka, and on and on and on, had to have a price determined for it by the central planning bureaucracies.

What a challenge! How well do you think you would meet this challenge? As you might expect, they didn't do it very well.

The results of their exercises ran up against the fundamental economic laws of supply, demand, and prices. Prices present people with incentives to produce or consume. If prices are too high, too much will be produced and too little consumed. Massive surpluses will build up and waste will occur. If prices are too low, not enough will be produced. Waiting lines will form to buy what little exists of the product.

It will be a complete mess. In the former Soviet Union, these exact things happened, and it was a complete mess.

In China, they tried to do the same thing, but they were a little smarter about it—at least, some of the central planning bureaucracy employees were a little smarter. Assigned the task of determining a price for a good, they would sneak out of the office and go observe the black market. They would see what price was being charged for the good on the illegal market and then sneak back to the office. There, they would magically come up with a price for the product that actually worked. They may have had difficulty explaining to their bosses how they came up with the price, but they got away with it, especially when the results were good.

History proved finally that the central planning method of deducing prices inside bureaucracies in the Kremlin doesn't work. The Soviet Union was rife with colossal economic inefficiencies—severe shortages of some items, overproduction of others, and an economy that was at last revealed not to be working at all.

At the same time, statistical evidence proves that active investment managers' methods of deducing prices in their offices in Manhattan don't work. Before examining the abundant statistical evidence, let us explore the reasons why active managers' methods don't work. This exploration brings us to the work of the man who was probably the greatest political economist of the twentieth century, Friedrich August von Hayek.

An Economic Life Spanning the Twentieth Century

Friedrich von Hayek's lifetime spanned nearly the entire twentieth century. The landmarks and ups and downs of his life were closely connected to the great events of the era—the rise of National Socialism in Germany and socialism in England and northern Europe, and, most spectacularly, the rise and fall of the Soviet Union.

Hayek was born in Vienna, Austria, on May 8, 1899, into an upper-class family. He served as an artillery officer in World War I. In the 1920s, he was educated in and became a prominent exponent of the Austrian school of free market economic thought led by Ludwig von Mises. He was hired by the London School of Economics in 1931 as London's counterweight to Cambridge's John Maynard Keynes, the other economist frequently mentioned as one of the greatest of the century. Though their creators were friends on a personal level, Hayek's and Keynes's economic belief systems were nonetheless at odds, and they were sparring partners professionally. Hayek later, in 1950, joined the faculty at the University of Chicago—though not in the economics department but as part of the Committee on Social Thought, because the work Hayek was doing was not regarded as economics but as social and political philosophy, even by seemingly like-minded economists like Milton Friedman. In 1962, feeling more comfortable with European ways, Hayek moved to a university near the Black Forest in Freiburg, Germany.

For all his long professional life, from the late 1920s to the early 1990s, Hayek was an ardent opponent of socialism and "collectivism" of all stripes—fascist, communist, or socialist. For most of his professional life, he was badly out of step with the times. In the 1930s and 1940s, capitalism was seen to have failed miserably. It had given the world the Great Depression, leading to fascism. The prevailing belief was that government must exert strong control to rein in the excesses released by capitalism.

Hayek ventured into many areas of economics and social thought, and he changed his mind about some things, but he never varied from his belief that socialist and collectivist tendencies were dangerous and led to totalitarianism. In 1944, he published his famous and influential popular work, *The Road to Serfdom*, which warned that England and other countries were traveling down a political path that could lead to excesses like those of Nazi Germany and Soviet Russia. Though the book made him an outcast within the welfare-state-oriented economics profession of the time—he later recalled that "it went so far as to completely discredit me professionally"—the book was popular, especially among anti–New Dealers in the United States, selling more than six hundred thousand copies and propelling him on an extended lecture tour. Nevertheless, in the 1950s and 1960s, the Soviet economy appeared to be doing well, and the partially socialist economies of Western Europe, with their large nationalized industrial sectors, were prospering. Hayek's thesis seemed disconnected from reality. His professional standing, and he himself, fell into a depressed state.

By something of a fluke of Nobel Prize politics, Hayek was elected to share the prize in 1974 with welfare state economist Gunnar Myrdal. According to John Cassidy of *The New Yorker*, Myrdal later said he wouldn't have accepted the award if he had known he would have to share it with Hayek—so blemished was Hayek's reputation among the dominant left-wing economists of the day.[1]

The Nobel Prize revived Hayek's spirits and his professional career, but subsequent events were to raise it to the level of unparalleled greatness. Margaret Thatcher of England adopted Hayek's works in the mid-1970s as the philosophy of Britain's Conservative Party and of what later became the Thatcher Revolution. Ronald Reagan followed suit in the United States in the 1980s.

Then in 1989, the Soviet Union fell under the weight of its own unsustainable economy. Cassidy writes that according to Hayek's son, the then-ninety-year-old Hayek would watch television coverage from Berlin, Prague, and Bucharest, beam benignly, and say, "I told you so."

Hayek's Theory of Prices

Hayek's central argument was developed in the late 1930s and early 1940s, when it was presented mainly in two journal articles, "Economics and Knowledge" in 1937 and "The Use of Knowledge in Society" in 1945. He repeated it and refined it in many forms numerous times thereafter. His main thesis is that the knowledge required to run an economy is, by nature, necessarily dispersed among many people with differing local knowledge—that is, knowledge that is specific to place and time, and not available to any one person or centralized body. Therefore, the problem of an economy is how to organize the transfer from person to person of the most needed elements of this information.

Fortunately, the required system of transfer in an economy with open competition organizes itself spontaneously, without central control. It is the pricing system. No one person or group of people alone has sufficient information to determine what all prices should be. Prices are set naturally through many local interactions between people having only local knowledge, knowledge that is specific to time and place, knowledge that cannot be obtained or concentrated in any central location. In the current jargon, price is an "emergent property" —a property that cannot be assigned to a system but that arises from it spontaneously.

Hayek had strong objections to the prevailing wind of economics (it still prevails today to a large extent) that assumed perfect knowledge by individuals of all information. Given this perfect knowledge, mathematical formulas could be used to determine the most efficient allocation of resources. Hayek called this error *scientism*—the imitation in the social sciences of the methods of the physical sciences, or "the erroneous transfer to social phenomena of the habits of thought we have developed in dealing with the phenomena of nature." Hayek believed it assumed away precisely the problem that is the central problem of economics: how to share most usefully information that is, of necessity, dispersed, and therefore not available in its entirety, or even in large part, to any one person.

Because of this belief of Hayek's—this certainty—Hayek knew that the central pricing and planning policies of the communist Soviet Union could not work. It took many years for the house of cards to collapse, but collapse it did. In retrospect, we now know it was inevitable. But it did not seem inevitable for a long time, except to Hayek. We have learned a lot from the experience and should now know how to apply what we have learned.

The Scientism of Active Money Management

Curiously, a profession that now practices its own brand of scientism, the profession of active money management, includes many people who would consider Hayek a great social and economic philosopher, one who was right all along. I believe this is because they do not fully understand his theories or do not understand their implications. Meanwhile, day in and day out, they practice their scientism, forecasting future earnings and discounting them back to the present using mathematical formulas to obtain a so-called true price, as if they alone had access to all the local and dispersed information in the world.

The real information is precisely what the Beardstown Ladies had, though they had only minuscule pieces of it—pieces of dispersed information intimately familiar to them because of their situation in place and time. One of the ladies, on her way to a meeting of their club, noticed a Wal-Mart parking lot overflowing with cars. That was a piece of information, which influenced their buying decisions. Another of the ladies brought Hershey Hugs to a meeting. They all liked them, and that influenced their buying decisions. Did everyone know these things at the time? No. These pieces of information, however small, are the true information of the market, the information that forms prices—not earnings forecasts and discount rates made by centrally located planners and calculators in Wall Street offices. This is why the Beardstown Ladies were admired—because they represented the genuine information of the heartland, modest bits of dispersed information, information that won't allow them to second-guess in any major way prices set by the market and thus render them fabulously rich, but information that might allow them to make buying decisions a tiny, tiny bit better than they might have if they did not have the information.

Wall Street stock pickers, by contrast, have the hubris to believe they can pole-vault over all those little people, with their vast but widely dispersed collection of local knowledge, shared only through the miraculous mechanism of the pricing system. Swayed by scientism, they believe that by dint of the sheer fact that they use mathematical formulas like physical scientists, they can deduce truths inaccessible to the multitude.

Scientism is an astoundingly resilient fallacy. Anyone who has used the present value formula—and many of the other formulas comprising the "sophisticated" mathematics of the investment profession—knows perfectly well that any pretense of using the formulas to get precise results is a sham.

The present value formula, for example, is exquisitely sensitive to data inputs. Very small changes in the assumptions—the forecasted earnings growth rate or the discount rate—make a huge difference in the resulting "true" price. The user of the formula can, in effect, get any result he wants, just by jimmying the inputs. One forecasted growth rate will make the "true" price much higher than the market price, while a forecasted growth rate only 0.5 percent lower will make the "true" price much lower than the market price.

The result of this sensitivity is that analysts actually make a subjective decision and then cook the numbers so the formula backs them up. It's a funny way to do things. But it doesn't seem to persuade the stock pickers that what they're doing bears no relation to real science or mathematics.

Endless Variations

One of the reasons investors seek out investment advice is because of the bewildering array of investment options. An ordinary investor could invest directly in any combination of more than six thousand publicly listed U.S. domestic stocks and tens of thousands of bonds of U.S. companies as well as federal and state governments and municipalities.

Or the investor could—instead, or in addition to—invest in any one, or a combination, of thousands of mutual funds that combine stocks and bonds for you.

Or one could invest in the stocks or bonds of foreign companies or the bonds of non-U.S. governments or mutual funds that combine them. One could invest in diversified real estate through real estate investment trusts (REITs) or mortgage-backed securities like GNMAs. One could invest in TIPS—Treasury bonds issued by the U.S. government that are inflation protected; that is, they offer a small fixed return above the inflation rate. Or one could invest in commodities like soybeans, pork bellies, coconuts, or oil, or in precious metals, or in commodity pools that combine them.

And that doesn't begin to cover derivatives, which I'll talk about later.

All of the investments mentioned have two things in common. Their common factors make them near-equivalents—virtually indistinguishable, from the point of view of the investor, except for their different names.

The first common factor is that all of them have prices that are set by the market and by the market alone—and a very active market at that. Therefore, they are all competitively priced.

The second common factor is that each investment product has one and only one output: a stream of cash flows at varying intervals.

These differently named investment alternatives are not like the dazzling array of consumer goods you can get in a Wal-Mart or a downtown big city department store. There, you can get products that play tunes or make toast, products you can play tennis with, products that water your garden, products you can ride, products that take photographs, products that protect you from the rain, products that protect you from the sun—in short, you can get products that all do completely different things for you, in your choice of colors.

Investment products, by contrast, do only one thing: they produce streams of cash flows at varying intervals. That's all. No choice of colors, no choice of sizes or shapes or musical accompaniments. All you get is a choice of when the cash flows will occur and whether they're fixed or uncertain. Other than that, there's nothing to distinguish these investment products, except their names.

And even the difference in timing of cash flows is not that much of a difference. These days, there are so many ways to make cash flows "fungible"—that is, to turn a cash flow at one time into a cash flow at a different time—that it doesn't matter much when they occur. For example, if you bought a bond that matures in six years, but it turns out you don't need the money until a year after that, no problem—you just invest the proceeds in a bank CD or a money market mutual fund for a year. On the other hand, if it turns out you need the money in five years, one year before the bond matures, no problem—you can sell the bond on the market, or, if you prefer, you could get a bank loan for a year using the bond as collateral. In either case, you might lose a little because you couldn't time things perfectly, but not much. Or if you've invested in a stock that pays dividends and the dividend isn't enough to cover some financial need, no problem—you can sell a few shares of the stock to make up the difference.

Furthermore, because the investments are priced continually by market bidding, they are near-equivalents in terms of price-to-value ratio. Well-known consumer commodity items—personal computers, for example—for which there are many brand alternatives and competition is fierce, are priced by the market to compete very closely with each other. Similarly, investment vehicles are priced by the market to compete very closely with each other. When you shop for a PC, you will be faced with a broad range of alternatives. But when you come down to it, they are nearly all clones of each other. You're not likely to find an unusual bargain—you'll get what you pay for. If you pay more for one PC than for another, for the same set of features, you'll probably find it is more reliable—that is, less risky. The same is true for investment vehicles. They're all alike except for risk.

This reduces the fundamental differences among all those investments to only one difference: how risky they are. Other than differences in their risk and differences in how one investment's risk correlates with another's, there is no material difference.

Thus, a complicated choice among a bewildering array of alternatives can be reduced to rank simplicity. I'll show you how simple it is a little later, after introducing the Nobel Prize–winning theories.

Don't let anyone—especially not for a high fee—tell you how complicated it is.

Theories Explaining the Unpredictability of Market Performance

The most prominent economic theory explaining why active money managers can't outperform market averages is called *efficient market theory*. Unfortunately, efficient market theory, as usually stated, is—in my opinion—itself redolent of scientism.

Efficient market theory is often stated something like this: "The market price is the best estimate of the true price." This statement assumes there exists such a thing as the "true" price—as if price were a hard, enduring physical reality, instead of an expression of the wants and desires at a particular moment of thousands or millions of people with widely diverging, scientifically unaccountable, and even indeterminable, fundamental tastes. Efficient market theory is built on the highly unlikely supposition that, because of the assumed complete transparency of information in the modern era, people have perfect information and, as a group, interpret it "rationally" to set the correct price.

Hayek Explains It Better

This is all very un-Hayekian. This unfortunate standard formulation of efficient market theory has prompted the current senseless debate over whether investors are "rational." Both sides of the debate seem to take it for granted that each investor has perfect knowledge of the information needed to determine market prices. But one side argues that investors interpret it "rationally," while the other side argues that they do not.

There isn't really any reason we need to wonder whether investors —or consumers—are rational or not, whatever that means. Prices are determined by the interacting wants and tastes of consumers and investors—and there is no accounting for taste.

At the end of the twentieth century, the demand for Amazon.com stock had become so great, its price had been driven higher even than noted financial academician Burton Malkiel, author of the best-selling and highly informative *A Random Walk Down Wall Street* and an efficient market believer, thought rational. Malkiel published an article in the *Wall Street Journal* pointing out that on the basis of the discounted present value of future earnings, there was no way on Earth that Amazon.com could be worth so much.

Yet apparently it was, to its investors. Why is a painting of soup cans on a shelf worth $50 million if it is painted by the right artist? Not because of the present value of its future earnings, of course, but because it is believed someone in the future will pay $100 million for it, which is probably the same reason why people bought Amazon.com stock at a high price. It's a tricky game, of course—one must guess what others will pay for it later and time it right. But is it "irrational"?

No, the Hayekian formulation is much better, and it leads to essentially the same end result. It assumes merely that people have their own wants and tastes and that, combined with their massive volume of widely dispersed information based on each person's direct experience specific to place and time, at a vast number of different places and times, these lead naturally to a system of prices conveying the essence of the information needed to trade with others as well as anything possibly could.

In the same way, though, in which efficient market theory does— probably better—Hayekian price theory leads directly to the remarkably rich mathematical theory of the development of prices over time usually referred to as the *random walk model*. We will soon explore the random walk model and its amazingly broad range of implications.

But first, let's take a brief look at the statistical evidence that professional investment managers can't outperform the market.

7

The Abject Failure of Professional Advisors and Managers

If Hayek's arguments have not convinced you that money managers cannot deduce true prices that are better than the prices set by the dispersed knowledge of the multitudes, the empirical record of active investment management's dismal failure should convince you.

I will now review that record. I'll do it first in a simple way, then more extensively with a review of the research studies.

The Unpredictability of Market-Beating Performance

The statistical record of performance of professional investment managers and advisors is voluminous and thoroughly well documented. It has been analyzed dozens of times in academic studies and in private studies by companies in the investment field having their own proprietary databases.

I myself performed studies using the largest then-existing investment performance database for institutional fund managers in the early 1970s, while working at my first job at a brokerage firm.

I performed more studies in the late 1980s and early 1990s when I had access to a large quantity of data on the performance of managed investment accounts, which was input by brokerage firms who subscribed to a computerized investment performance measurement system in which I was a partner.

In both cases, I was working with proprietary databases. The results of the studies couldn't be published. But a large number of studies have been performed using publicly available data. The conclusions of those studies have been the same as the conclusions I reached when I performed my studies with private databases.

The Simple Facts about Investment Performance

The results can be stated in a complicated manner or in a simple manner. So let's first describe them in a simple manner.

STEP 1: *Obviously, the average performance of all investors will be equal to the market average, right?*

Market averages are measured by market indexes like the Wilshire 5000, which includes nearly all the stocks issued in the domestic United States. Sometimes the S&P 500 is used as a proxy for the U.S. stock market. This is a pretty good approximation. Though the S&P 500 includes only five hundred large stocks, it covers over 70 percent of the U.S. stock market's value. The Dow Jones index, because it includes only thirty stocks, and the NASDAQ, because it represents only a sector of the market (mostly technology), are less representative.

Therefore, if you bundled together all the investments of all investors in the U.S. stock market and measured the performance of the aggregate, it would be substantially the same (before all costs and taxes) as the performance of, say, the Wilshire 5000 or the S&P 500.

STEP 2: *Investors in the U.S. stock market are of two types: professionals who are paid to invest their clients' money and everybody else.*

The dividing line is pretty sharp. Professionals who are paid to invest other people's money must register as investment advisors. They run mutual funds and money management firms, and—outside certain niche markets like hedge funds, which still make up a small percentage of the market—their performance record is publicly available.

STEP 3: *If professional investors know how to get better investment performance, then their performance as a group ought to be better than everybody else's, right?*

Professional investors and everybody else together make up the total market, so if professional investors outperform everybody else, then they must outperform the market.

But . . . .

STEP 4: *Professional investors as a class do not outperform the market.*

Virtually all reputable statistical studies, time after time after time, show that on average, the performance of professional investors as a class is no better—in fact, usually a little worse—than the market average. In short, the statistical evidence shows that professional investors, as a class, add nothing for their fees.

STEP 5: *Now, wait a minute. You keep saying "as a class." Everybody knows that some professional money managers—the good ones—outperform the market.*

But . . . .

STEP 6: *Some investors will always outperform the market—probably about half of them.*

If nobody outperformed the market averages, then nobody could underperform them, either. Everybody's performance would be the same as the market average. This could be true only if everybody held the same portfolio of stocks, because the performance of stocks varies widely. So, in any time period, some investors will beat the market average, and some will fall short.

STEP 7: *But don't some professional investors consistently beat the market averages?*

The answer is no.

STEP 8: *Nearly all reputable statistical studies show there is no significant consistency or predictability in the performance of professional investors.*

It's easy to explain this using the results of studies I did while employed years ago at the brokerage firm A. G. Becker & Co.

We had a huge database of performance statistics for professionally managed employee benefit funds, foundation funds, and endowment funds. Our computer programs calculated the rates of return for all the funds for all time periods, placed them in rank order, and found the medians and quartiles. If a fund was in the first quartile, that meant it was among the 25 percent of funds that performed best; if in the second quartile, it was among the 50 percent of funds that did better than median but not among the first-quartile performers; and so on.

If good performance were consistent, then funds that were above median in one time period would have better than a 50 percent chance of being above median in the next time period. If they were first-quartile one period, they would have better than a 25 percent chance of being first-quartile the next period.

But that's not what the data showed. Only half the above-median performers in one time period performed above median in the next time period, and only a quarter of the first-quartile performers in one time period performed in the first quartile in the next time period. It was as if performance were completely random.

The same results have been obtained again and again and again. This leads to . . . .

STEP 9: *Market-beating performance is unpredictable.*
In short, you can select and hire professional managers until you are blue in the face, but you will not be able to select one with better than a 50 percent chance of beating the market (before all fees and taxes, not to mention after!).

At this point, the still-incredulous will blurt out, "But what about Peter Lynch and Warren Buffett!" I will deal with this point at more length in Chapter 13. But for now, suffice it to say that you would have had to be either clairvoyant or merely extremely lucky to have found and picked either of these men as your professional investment manager in time to be on board with him during the period when his performance was terrific. Outstanding performance seen in hindsight is a very different thing from (and much less useful than) outstanding *and predictable* performance.

Is it worth the extremely high cost to pay a professional money manager and perhaps a professional advisor to find her, when the probability that the manager will enable you to outperform a market index (before all fees and taxes!) is no better than

50-50 and no better than you could do yourself at negligible cost? The answer should be no.

The Best Shall Be Worst

A striking example of the point that past performance does not predict future performance is a story in the July 11, 2003, issue of *The Economist*. *The Economist's* story relates the astonishing fact that the top ten mutual funds for the three years from the end of 1996 to the end of 1999 were all among the *worst*-performing 7 percent of mutual funds in the next three years.

If you had invested at the beginning of 2000 in the top ten performers for the previous three years, you would have experienced a brutal come-uppance. In the next three years, you would have lost 70 percent of your investment. Many investors actually did this—a large proportion of them on the advice of professional investment counselors.

It is not really typical that the best performers in the past actually become the *worst* in the future. Statistically, it is more typical that half the best past performers become better than average and half become worse than average. But the overall lesson is simple, if counterintuitive: past investment performance *is definitely not* a predictor of future investment performance.

I'm not saying that professional money managers are not smart or knowledgeable people. They are usually well educated. They try to keep themselves well informed about the economy, market sectors, technologies, and current public affairs. This doesn't mean that they can predict the market or the price of stocks.

The Academic Research Record

Having outlined in a simple manner the statistical facts of the failure of expert investment management, I'll now describe briefly the voluminous record of research behind them.

This research goes back more than a hundred years. It has included spasms of fervent debate and the frequent finding of "anomalies." But in the end, the results have been remarkably consistent. The results are encapsulated in the following three statements:

- Professional investment managers on average do not outperform market averages; in fact, they tend to underperform them by the amount of their fees.

- No patterns or trends in securities prices or investment returns can be reliably depended on to continue, other than the expectation of positive long-term returns, underlying a pattern of random fluctuations. The expected returns are greater for diversified baskets of securities with higher risk than for those of lower risk, but the risk of possible loss is higher.

- Any patterns and trends that may, for a time, appear to have persisted in the past either do not continue or are not strong enough for an investor to exploit them advantageously after paying the normal costs (fees, commissions, and expenses).

If the professional investor has any advantage at all, it is an advantage that only she can exploit—namely, that she can invest and trade for her own account at lower expense than can the nonprofessional investor. This advantage is not, of course, of any use to the nonprofessional investor who hires the professional (unless the professional is willing to either suspend fees entirely or charge fees that are a tenth or a hundredth of those generally prevailing).

The Earliest Work on Randomness in the Securities Markets: Louis Bachelier

In 1900, five years before Einstein, the French mathematician Louis Bachelier outlined in detail in his doctoral dissertation[1] the mathematics of Brownian motion, or "random walk."[2] In later life, Bachelier pursued an undistinguished career in small academic institutions in France. Although his work was known in the mathematical field of probability, he might never have been known to the finance profession had it not been for the rediscovery of his work in 1954 by economist and Nobel Prize winner Paul Samuelson.

Bachelier described mathematically the phenomena of randomly varying prices, validating his mathematical characterizations using prices of securities on the Paris Bourse. It may surprise the reader to learn that securities in 1900 were no less complicated than they are now. Some derivative securities on the Bourse had peculiar names like "contangoes" and "call-o'-more's." There were also futures, options, spreads, and straddles like we have now.

Probability of exercise of options at twenty-five

	Calculated Probability	Observed Frequency
EXPIRING IN 45 DAYS	0.41	0.40
EXPIRING IN 30 DAYS	0.47	0.46
EXPIRING IN 20 DAYS	0.53	0.53
EXPIRING IN 10 DAYS	0.65	0.65

Before launching into his mathematical model and the empirical evidence for it, Bachelier made this insightful prefatory remark about fluctuations in prices:

> The determination of these fluctuations depends on an infinite number of factors; it is, therefore, impossible to aspire to mathematical prediction of it. Contradictory opinions concerning these changes diverge so much that at the same instant buyers believe in a price increase and sellers in a price decrease.[3]

Bachelier then proceeded to set forth the precursors of the modern mathematical formulas for Brownian motion or random walk. To check that his formulas corresponded to reality, he calculated the predicted probabilities that the prices of these financial instruments would be in certain price ranges, using his Brownian motion model. Then he compared these predictions with the frequency with which the instruments actually were in those ranges. In almost all cases, the correspondence was very close. He did this for many cases. (One example is shown in the table at the top of the page.)

It is less important to understand the meaning of the options terminology in this table (I will cover that in Chapter 18 as well as in the glossary) than to note that the mathematical hypothesis of randomness developed by Bachelier did a very good job of explaining the results found in the data.

The Cowles Commission

The crash of 1929 and the subsequent Depression kindled an interest in exploring whether such stock market disasters could be predicted. The millionaire Alfred Cowles, who had sustained severe losses in the crash, gave an endowment to establish a commission in his name, the Cowles Commission. The Cowles Commission continued to perform research in economics and securities markets for many years afterward.

One of the first research projects of the Cowles Commission was to study whether it was possible to predict the movement of stocks and stock markets.[4] The preliminary version of the 1933 report, titled "Can Stock Market Forecasters Forecast?" was summarized in a famous three-word abstract: "It is doubtful."

The Cowles report reviewed the stock recommendations and market forecasts of sixteen financial services, twenty fire insurance companies, twenty-four financial publications, and those of William Peter Hamilton, the editor of the *Wall Street Journal*. In each case, the recommendations performed worse than the average common stock, by an amount ranging from 1.2 to 4 percent per annum. For example, the report's summary states:

> Sixteen financial services, in making some 7500 recommendations of individual common stocks for investment during the period from January 1, 1928, to July 1, 1932, compiled an average record that was worse than that of the average common stock by 1.43 per cent annually. Statistical tests of the best individual records failed to demonstrate that they exhibited skill, and indicated that they more probably were results of chance.[5]

In other words, the stock forecasters not only performed randomly, but their performance was actually even a little worse than random.

The Random Character of Stock Market Prices

Over the next thirty years, studies of securities prices were carried out by researchers in a variety of fields. Typical was a study in 1953 by statistician Maurice Kendall, a professor at the London School of Economics. Kendall thought that stock and commodity markets would provide a good source of data to study predictable patterns. To his surprise, he could find no such patterns.

Several other studies were performed with similar results, by Holbrook Working, who studied agricultural commodity prices; M. F. M. Osborne, an astrophysicist working at the U.S. Naval Research Laboratory; and statistician Harry V. Roberts. All of their findings, together with Kendall's study, Bachelier's thesis, and a number of other papers, were reprinted in 1964 in a book titled *The Random Character of Stock Market Prices*, edited by MIT professor Paul Cootner.[6]

Typical of the careful analyses in this volume is Kendall's guarded conclusion:

> In series of prices which are observed at fairly close intervals the random changes from one term to the next are so large as to swamp any systematic effect which may be present. The data behave almost like wandering series. . . . Until some way has been found of circumventing this difficulty, trend fitting, and perhaps the fitting of any model, is a highly hazardous undertaking.[7]

In short, Kendall found that the "noise" overcame the "signal" (if there was any) to such a degree that determining any underlying pattern was either impractical or impossible.

Studies of Mutual Funds

As the performance of large numbers of professionally managed mutual funds became accessible in publicly available databases, several studies were performed in the 1960s on the performance of mutual funds.[8] In no case did the studies find evidence of better-than-random performance of mutual funds. In fact, their performance was consistently worse than market averages when expenses were deducted. William F. Sharpe studied thirty-four mutual funds over two successive ten-year periods, 1944–1953 and 1954–1963. Typical of the results of the studies is Sharpe's statement that "the odds are greater than 100 to 1 against the possibility that the average mutual fund did as well as the Dow Jones portfolio from 1954 to 1963."

Soon after, the study performed by Michael Jensen referred to in the introduction was published in the 1968 *Journal of Finance*. Jensen's study of mutual funds showed that (1) the average mutual fund managed by investment professionals could not beat market averages, and (2) the pattern of mutual funds' underperforming or outperforming market averages appeared to be a random pattern, with no predictability.

Jensen's unique and enduring contribution was that he measured the risk-adjusted performance of the mutual fund portfolios with a measure he called α, or alpha. This measure stuck, and it is now enshrined in the jargon of portfolio management and measurement, along with beta. I will revisit these measures in Chapter 12.

If the mutual funds' performance on a risk-adjusted basis was no better than the market's, then their alpha would be zero. Jensen found that "The average value of α calculated net of expenses was –.011 which indicates that on average the funds earned about 1.1% less per year . . . than they should have earned given their level of . . . risk."[9]

Mutual funds have been studied intensively because their data are so readily available. Mutual funds are required to report their results by the SEC. A problem does exist with mutual fund data, however, called *survivorship bias*.[10] Mutual funds that have not performed well tend to be expunged; they are either closed or merged with other funds that have performed better. Therefore, their data tend to disappear from the database, leaving only the better-performing funds. To correct for this problem, researchers of mutual fund performance have had to go to lengths to dredge up data for funds that went out of existence in the past and to include them in the database.

When survivorship bias is corrected for, studies of mutual fund data invariably reach the same finding: the average mutual fund, adjusted for risk, does not outperform the market average; in fact it usually underperforms it by an amount approximately equal to the fees and expenses of the fund. For example, Sharpe says that "results actually obtained by the holder of mutual fund shares (after the costs associated with the operation of the fund have been deducted) fall somewhat short of those from the Dow-Jones portfolio. This is consistent with our previous conclusion that, all other things being equal, the smaller a fund's expense ratio, the better the results obtained by its stockholders." And in a careful study in 1997 of 1,892 diversified equity funds from January 1962 to December 1993, Mark Carhart, then a professor at the University of Southern California, stated in his conclusion:

> I also find that expense ratios, portfolio turnover, and load fees are significantly and negatively related to performance. Expense ratios appear to reduce performance a little more than one-for-one. Turnover reduces performance about 95 basis points [that is, nearly one percent] for every buy and sell transaction. . . . Surprisingly, load funds substantially underperform no-load funds . . . the average load fund underperforms the average no-load fund by approximately 80 basis points per year.[11]

The inevitable conclusion is that the investor gets not just nothing, but worse than nothing for the fees spent on mutual fund expenses, loads, and trading costs.

The Rise of "Anomalies"

By the late 1960s, due to extensive evidence as well as the cogency of the efficient market theory, it became generally accepted in academia that the stock market was a random walk and that professional investors could not beat the market. This academic view did not, however—as I showed in the introduction—deter the business community of professional investors from claiming that they could beat the market and that they should be paid very well for it.

Subsequently, some academicians began to focus on "anomalies" in stock market data that seemed to call into question whether the market was really "efficient." For example, it was found that if in the past you had invested in the market on the first day of January each year and sold several days after that, you would have done very well indeed. This was called the "January effect." Similarly, if you had bought each Monday morning and sold soon after you also would have done very well. This was, not surprisingly, called the "Monday effect."

Many other so-called anomalies were also discovered in the data by a variety of researchers. The following evaluation of these anomalies by G. William Schwert, a professor at the University of Rochester who is also affiliated with the National Bureau of Economic Research, summarizes the best judgment that can be made about them:

> After they are documented and analyzed in the academic literature, anomalies often seem to disappear, reverse, or attenuate. This raises the question of whether profit opportunities existed in the past, but have since been arbitraged away, or whether the anomalies were simply statistical aberrations that attracted the attention of academics and practitioners.[12]

What Schwert is saying is that so many statistical studies are being done—both by academicians with a need to publish and by industry professionals with a need to find something that might work—that they are bound to fall on random statistical patterns, with no predictive capacity. But even those that might have been more than aberrations, once they are discovered and publicized, will go away as soon as they are divulged.

Doesn't this suggest, though, that professional investors who know about these aberrations before they are publicized will be able to beat the market? Doesn't it mean that you need to find an investment manager who is very much in the know and doesn't tell others what he knows but just acts on it?

If that were true—if most, many, or even a significant and persistent minority of professional investment managers were regularly aware of anomalies in the market and capable of acting on them—then the findings of the studies would have been different. Instead of showing that professional investors don't beat the market on average and that market-beating performance is unpredictable, they would show that some professional investors consistently beat the market, with statistical predictability, and that on average they do better than the market.

But unfortunately the studies don't show that. If there really are professional investment managers who can consistently and predictably beat the market, you won't be able to find them.

Behavioral Finance

Efficient market theorists set themselves up right from the very beginning for a rebuttal from a theory with a name like "behavioral finance." They did this by making "rationality" a cornerstone of their argument for the unpredictability of prices.

It would seem more likely that "irrationality" would be an explanation for the randomness and unpredictability of prices. Indeed, it is a good explanation. But efficient market theorists—in their explanation why market prices should be "correct" (i.e., as close to the "true" price as possible)—invoked the assumption that investors are "rational" and therefore that they price things right (as if there were a "right" price, other than what the market thinks it should be).

Sure enough, a field arose calling itself "behavioral finance" that argued the obvious—that investors are not necessarily "rational" after all but depart from rationality from time to time in important and sometimes foreseeable ways.

These supposedly predictable irrationalities are called on by those in the field of behavioral finance who believe they can be used to predict price movements. They are used to explain some of the anomalies that have been observed in the statistical data.

But no less than the other anomalies, the ones "explained" by irrationalities observed by advocates of behavioral finance either are confusing and contradictory, or tend to disappear as soon as they are found. As a result, they cannot reliably be taken advantage of to help an investor beat the market.

Eugene Fama, a professor at the University of Chicago, performed a thorough study of the "anomalies" that behavioral economists claimed could be predicted due to the predictable irrationalities of investors.[13] These anomalies fall into two categories: (1) overreactions of irrational investors to stock market or economic events and (2) underreactions of irrational investors to stock market or economic events.

The problem, Fama found, is that in the behavioral economists' studies, investors would seem to overreact around half the time and underreact around half the time. Furthermore, measurements of whether investors have underreacted or overreacted are sensitive to the time period studied after their supposed under- or overreaction. Studies of short time periods seem to show that investors underreact to events (so that the subsequent correction in prices, after the event, goes in the same direction as the first), while studies of long time periods seem to show that investors overreact (so that the later price correction goes in the direction opposite to the first). In the end, Fama concludes:

> Apparent overreaction of stock prices to information is about as common as underreaction. And post-event continuation of pre-event abnormal returns is about as frequent as post-event reversal. Most important, the long-term return anomalies are fragile. They tend to disappear with reasonable changes in the way they are measured.[14]

In short, just as Schwert noted, pricing anomalies claimed to exist by behavioral economists appear to be nothing more than that—anomalies. They may be due to statistical accidents of the way they were measured or to actual existing conditions that were unique only to the time period over which they were measured; but in either case, they cannot be expected to continue in the future, and therefore they cannot form the basis for a stock market–beating strategy.

Other Institutional Investors

Although the data for mutual funds are the most widely available, some studies have been performed using data for other professional investors as well, especially the money management firms that invest the assets of pension funds, endowment funds, foundation funds, and trust assets of high-net-worth individuals (many of these money management firms also run mutual funds). Though the studies are fewer—because data are less easily available—they tend to come to the same conclusions as do the mutual fund studies. For example, in a comprehensive study for the Brookings Institution of the professional investment management industry entitled "The Structure and Performance of the Money Management Industry," the five authors of the study conclude that "pension fund managers have consistently underperformed the market."[15]

Much of the data for private pension and endowment funds are proprietary—that is, not available to the general public. In most cases, studies using these data are performed by people with special access to them—such as I had in the two situations where I was able to compile a large quantity of data. In general, the owners or providers of the data are industry insiders. It would do the industries that employ or retain them no good to sponsor and divulge studies, released to the general public, showing that their efforts to advise investors and manage their assets for high fees are fruitless.

But that is what my studies showed, studies that I could not publish. Fortunately, studies based on the publicly available data for those institutional investors who manage mutual funds say the same thing.

Hedge Funds

It is even more difficult to study the performance characteristics of hedge funds, because thousands of them start up and many hundreds go out of business every year, so it's hard to keep track—and they publicize their data only if they want to. Hence, the data are rife not only with survivorship bias but with self-selection bias and other forms of bias, too. Also, hedge funds have proliferated like rabbits in the last several years (responding to the absurdly high fee scales, for those who manage to stay in business), so not very many of them have long-term performance records.

Nevertheless, two studies[16] have been performed providing strong evidence that the same statistical characteristics that apply to mutual funds also apply to hedge funds: on average, they don't beat market indexes, and their performance is inconsistent and unpredictable.

A study by Burton Malkiel of Princeton and Atanu Saha of the Analysis Group describes the typical way a hedge fund gets started and how this contributes to biases in the data:

> Unlike mutual funds, which must report their periodic audited returns to regulators and investors, hedge funds provide information to the database publishers only if they desire to do so. Managers often establish a hedge fund with seed capital and begin reporting their results at some later date and only if the initial results are favorable. Moreover, the most favorable of the early results are then "filled back" into the database together with reports of contemporaneous results.[17]

Because of the resulting biases, the statistics on hedge fund performance cited in business and financial publications are highly inaccurate—so much so that they should be ignored completely. Malkiel and Saha attempt to correct for the various biases by leaving out the cherry-picked backfilled data and by adding back historical data for defunct funds that have dropped out of the database, usually due to poor performance. Even though they were still unable to correct for some significant upward biases in the reported data—notably that hedge funds usually stop reporting when their performance gets bad shortly before they go out of business—Malkiel and Saha were able to make a better estimate of hedge fund performance than is found in other published data.

Malkiel and Saha found that from 1995 to 2003, hedge fund returns underperformed the stock market index by more than 3.5 percent—an average annual return for hedge funds of 8.82 percent compared with an annual return on the S&P 500 index of 12.38 percent. True, the reported variability of returns for the hedge funds was lower than that of the S&P 500 (hedge funds claim they get better performance with lower "risk," but it is their managers themselves who report their risk measures, in the form of standard deviation or volatility, and not outside examiners). However, as revealed in the fact that a statistic called the *kurtosis* is much higher for hedge funds, the probability of either an unusually good or, more troubling, unusually bad result is much higher than if you invest in a broad stock market portfolio. (Higher kurtosis in a probability distribution means "fatter tails"—that is, higher probabilities of extreme events.)

Malkiel and Saha also investigate whether there is "persistence" in hedge fund returns—that is, whether the good ones persist in being good, whether their past returns are predictive of their future returns. Their result is encapsulated in the following passage:

> We tested this hypothesis by analyzing whether winners tend to repeat their success in the subsequent year. We called a hedge fund manager who realized a return larger than the median hedge fund return for that year a "winner." A "loser" was a fund that realized a below-median return. For the previous year's winners, we then asked whether these funds were winners (winners-to-winners) or losers (winners-to-losers) in the next year. . . . We found [that] the probability of observing repeat winners during the period was basically 50-50.[18]

In sum, hedge funds realize worse returns on average, and higher risk of very poor returns, than a broad stock market portfolio. Furthermore, those hedge funds that do better than average in any particular year or series of years cannot be counted on to have better than a 50-50 chance of doing better than average in subsequent years.

Considering the exceedingly high fees of hedge funds—averaging at least 7 percent a year, according to one estimate (see Chapter 3)—you would need better than a 90 percent chance that they would outperform the average—not a 50 percent chance—just to come out even.

These results are far from the popular image of hedge funds as a perk for the rich, enabling them to get better returns than those that can be obtained by ordinary mortals.

The Jury Is Always Out

Because of the enormous amount of data and the ease of mining it for statistical studies, more anomalies can always be found in the data than can be disproved with careful research. Furthermore, the existence of small anomalies from time to time is a natural condition of a market. Buyers and sellers will be constantly on the lookout for a good price, and they will be ready to take advantage of it when they see it.

The problem is that there is no evidence that it is worth paying an expensive professional to help you find a good price. Any gain you might reap from uncovering a favorable pricing situation, in a competitive and efficient market, will be wiped out by the fees you pay the professional—unless the professional works for much, much lower fees than those in the investment services industry tend to do.

8

The Market Can Turn on a Dime

. . . .

Now I shall explore with you, in an easy-to-understand way, the fascinating—and frequently weird—mathematics and chaotic patternlessness of securities markets that occurs when markets are highly competitive and liquid (i.e., easy to trade in).

In the late 1960s, having exhausted my taste for political action as a small part of the early vanguard of student protest against the war in Vietnam, I turned my attention back to my studies. I was a graduate student in pure (theoretical) mathematics at Northwestern University. I had elected to concentrate in probability theory. I had never taken a course in economics or finance or anything faintly resembling those fields. I had no idea what a stock or a bond was. I assumed they were probably different names for the same thing, but I didn't care anyway. Like virtually all mathematics students and professors at the time—and most students in many fields of study—I was disdainful of business applications.

To begin my studies in the subfield my thesis advisor had designated for me, he gave me a crudely mimeographed set of notes "published" by the Tata Research Institute, a research institution in India funded by the highly successful Tata family business. The notes were written by an obscure Japanese mathematician named Kiyosi Itô. Mathematical symbols like the Greek letter capital sigma for summation and the integral sign were hand drawn, undoubtedly by Itô himself.

Reading the notes was difficult. Reading higher mathematics always is. It is chock-full of integral signs, summation signs, logical symbols, Greek letters, Hebrew letters, very few actual words, and—the layman is always astonished to hear—virtually no numbers at all, other than the occasional zero or one, and two numbers written as symbols, the letter e (for the base of natural logarithms, 2.71828...), and, of course, π (for 3.14159265...). Sometimes the writing is so dense it can take a day or more to read a page. The notes dealt with stochastic processes—variables whose values evolve uncertainly over time and can only be described using probabilities. The mathematical objects had names like the "Wiener process," "Brownian motion," and the "stable Paretian distribution."

Market Price Movements Fit These Models

When, soon after receiving my Ph.D., I took a job at Chicago brokerage firm A. G. Becker & Co., I learned fairly quickly what stocks and bonds were (though I remember some slow learning in the case of bonds—it took me a little while to understand why bond prices go down when interest rates go up). But I learned very quickly the theory of stock (and bond) price movements because it fit perfectly the mathematical model I knew most intimately.

Whether arrived at from a Hayekian or a "perfect information" perspective, the prevailing (at least among academicians) view was the same. It was—and is—best expressed in the statement "Prices reflect all available information."

If price at a given time—say, 10 A.M. on October 3—reflects all available information at that time, then any subsequent change in price can only be due to new information that was unknown and unknowable at that time. The change in price must arise from new, previously unforeseen and unforeseeable information, arriving unpredictably since 10 A.M. Hence, prices themselves must change unpredictably and randomly.

This conclusion was probably first noted in recent times by M. F. M. Osborne, in an article titled "Brownian Motion in the Stock Market," and by Holbrook Working, in an article titled "Note on the Correlation of First Differences of Averages in a Random Chain."[1] The French mathematician Louis Bachelier also said the same thing much earlier, in his doctoral dissertation in 1900.

Hence, future price changes are completely unpredictable from any past or present information. This simple fact leads to a whole mathematical model of enormous richness describing price movements—though, of course, the mathematical model does nothing to help predict prices with any certainty. Nonetheless, the model can help to predict *probabilities* of various price movements.

The Random Walk Model

The model is usually referred to as the *random walk model of stock market prices* or the Brownian motion model—what I worked on in my Ph.D. dissertation.[2]

This is not a model that can be *proved* to be true. It is merely a model that *can't be disproved* given all the available data. Of course, the same holds even for physical models of science. Almost nothing can be proved with finality; it can only be said that a scientific model fits the data more or less well.

The random walk model fits the price data very well. Such a large volume of price data is available that it has been possible to test the random walk model over and over again. It has held up in the tests like a champ. As with models of physics, it is supported not only by the data but by an underlying theoretical model—in this case, by the efficient market model or the Hayekian theory of prices.

If the random walk model fails *one* test on a small set of data from time to time or even a few tests over time, this is not sufficient to disprove it. The overall results are statistical. It is inevitable that statistical flukes will occur occasionally if enough tests are run. The evidence for the random walk model is in the sum total of all tests analyzed in a statistical manner, not in any one piece or few pieces of anecdotal evidence.

There Are No Trends

But the model has implications people find remarkably hard to accept. These implications are extremely counterintuitive.

For example, the model implies there are no such things as "trends" in securities prices. A trend is a pattern in the recent past data that one can expect to continue. In stock market prices, according to the random walk model, there is no such thing. No pattern can be expected to continue (other than that securities prices, over the long term, will rise—on average—in a random, unpredictable, meandering pattern).

This squares with the findings about the consistency of money management performance we mentioned in an earlier chapter. The "trend" of excellent (or poor) past performance has no statistical tendency to continue into the future. Because of these findings, all mutual fund advertising is now required by the mutual fund industry governmental overseer, the SEC, to state that past performance is not necessarily indicative of future performance. The whole truth is a little stronger. Past performance, according to all available evidence, not only *is not necessarily* but *is not at all* indicative of future performance.

Let's Change Our Verb Tenses When Speaking of Investment Markets

This finding poses a problem for our very manner of speech. It is often said that "the market is going up" or "the market is going down," "McDonald's stock is going up" or "Microsoft stock is *going* down." The very use of the word going seems to imply a continuity of movement—a tendency to trend, an implication that the market or the stock *has just recently been going up (or down) and is continuing to go up (or down).*

We must change our vocabulary. You can only say "the market has just gone up" or "the stock has just gone down," never "the market is going up" or "the stock is going down." You could even say (for whatever reason) that you believe "the market is *going to* go up" or "the stock is *going to* go down," but you can't say it's "going up" or "going down."

Making the mistake of using the phraseology "going up" or "going down" sometimes leads to senseless advice. Advisors, financial journalists, newsletters, and advice columnists often say something like, "When the market is going down, it is better to hold a more conservative mix of stocks and bonds" (i.e., less of one's portfolio allocated to stocks). Of course, it is better to hold less in stocks just *before* the market goes down, if that's what you mean by "when the market is going down."

But how are you supposed to know *before* the market goes down that it is *going to* go down? Not from what it just did, that much is clear. Not from what it "is doing." Let's take a quick look at what the mathematical theory says the market "is doing."

The Market *Always Turns on a Dime*

Please allow me to launch into a little mathematical discourse, very briefly. Sorry—I get a kick out of it (it's the old college instructor in me). But besides, if you'll bear with me a little while I think it will help to clarify price movements.

There are many paths the price of a stock or a market index could hypothetically follow. For example, on a single trading day, between the market open at 9:30 A.M. New York time and its close at 4:00 P.M., the price could follow any one of a very large number of paths. But because of the fact that there are no trends—future price changes are completely independent of past price changes—only one kind of price path is possible.

The kind of price path that is possible is stated mathematically in the sentence "The paths of Brownian motion are *continuous* but nowhere differentiable." The word continuous refers to a line you could draw without taking your pencil off the paper—a line with no breaks in it. The idea that prices move continuously (while not strictly true, because prices actually move in little jumps) merely means you could connect the prices with a continuous line.

A curved line is "differentiable" if it is smooth everywhere—you can tell roughly where it's going next by where it came from. To say that "the paths of Brownian motion are continuous but nowhere differentiable" is to say the paths that prices take are *never* smooth (see Exhibit 8.1). Not only can't you assume there are price trends, but the statement says there *never are* price trends. The paths of prices *are all corners*.

A layman's translation of the mathematically complicated-sounding statement "The paths of Brownian motion are continuous but nowhere differentiable" is "*The stock market can turn on a dime and always does.*" Prices are constantly twisting and turning without trend or predictable pattern. Their recent movement gives you nothing to go on.

A new word, *fractal*, invented by the mathematician Benoit Mandelbrot to describe lines that are highly irregular has taken root in popular imagination, probably because of the beautiful abstract images generated by Mandelbrot's computer programs using fractals.

Exhibit 8.1   Example of a Line That is Continuous but Nowhere Differentiable

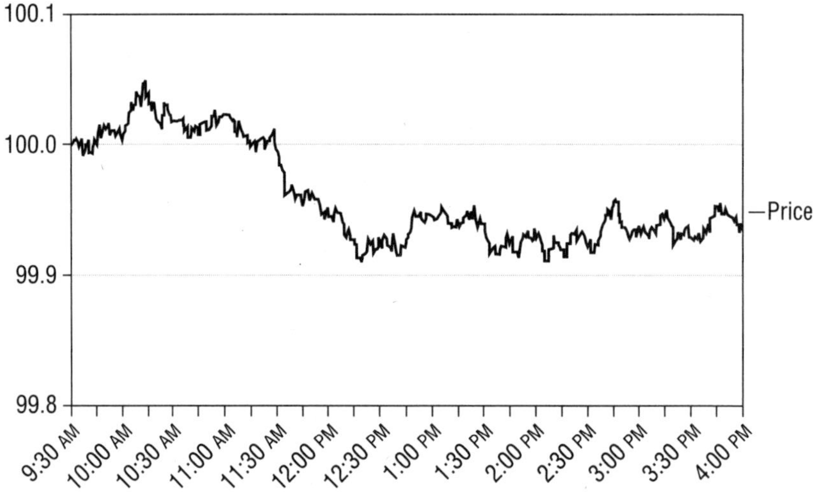

Irregular patterns like coastlines or stock prices are fractals. They are all twists and turns, no straight lines to be found, even for short distances. They also have the characteristic that their pattern as seen through a magnifying glass is similar to their pattern as seen through a telescope.

Would you expect to be able to follow a coastline as it reveals itself beneath you—say, by holding a piece of opaque paper over a map and moving it gradually to uncover mile by mile of it—and predict which direction the next mile of coastline will head based on the direction the last mile went? No, you wouldn't. If you did, you would be wrong as often as you were right. Similarly, you can't predict which way a price path is going to head in the next minute or hour or day or week or year, based on the direction it went in the last minute or hour or day or week or year.

You can see what a problem this poses. Managers and overseers and evaluators in every field are accustomed to scrutinizing past performance, on the expectation that it will be the best predictor of future performance. In the case of investment management, past performance is not predictive of future performance.

Yet investors continue doggedly to comb through past performance records of investment managers as if they were the only thing that counted. If they have hired an advisor or consultant to help them select and evaluate money managers, then the advisor is paid in part—especially if the investor is an institutional investor (I'll have more to say on this later)—to slice and dice past performance in a bewildering variety of ways, none of which has the slightest tendency to predict future performance.

Meanwhile, investors ignore completely or relegate to an after-thought the only thing that is predictable and that really does matter (along with taxes)—and that in fact matters in a very big way—which is, of course, the manager's (and the advisor's) fees. A large part of the Big Investment Lie is that all this minute examination of historical performance data can enable the investor to do better in the future, which it can't—and it helps justify advisors' large fees.

At Long Last Itô Comes into His Own

A measure of how thoroughly the Brownian motion or random walk model of securities prices has been accepted is the fame that has come to that once-obscure Japanese mathematician Kiyosi Itô. In inducting Itô into foreign membership in 1998, the U.S. National Academy of Sciences said, "If one disqualifies the Pythagorean Theorem from contention, it is hard to think of a mathematical result which is better known and more widely applied in the world today than 'Itô's Lemma.'"

Itô began developing his theory of stochastic differential equations in 1942. Thus, the recognition was long in coming—fifty-six years. Itô's recognition probably never would have arrived even in 1998 had it not been for another honor conferred in the previous year, 1997.

In 1997, two American professors of finance, Robert Merton and Myron Scholes, were awarded the Nobel Prize in economics for their development of the theory of pricing of stock options. The best-known manifestation of this theory is the Black-Scholes option pricing formula, developed by Scholes with Fischer Black (who would also have been awarded the Nobel Prize if he had survived) in the early 1970s.

The seminal Black-Scholes paper—at first rejected by academic journals before finally being published in 1973—did not actually mention Itô's name or reference his theory directly. But it invoked a mathematical solution that, some devotees of financial mathematics realized (especially Merton), was embedded in the mathematics of Itô.

Now, virtually no textbook on mathematical finance (and there are many) fails to have a chapter on the "Itô calculus." Itô's mathematics concerns stochastic processes that are—in the phrase frequently used by professors teaching mathematics—"forgetful" processes. That is, you might as well forget the history of the process up to now, because it won't tell you anything about what it will do next.

Both the widespread use of Itô's formulas (among, e.g., those who estimate the prices of derivative securities like options) and the ubiquitous use of Monte Carlo and binomial simulation programs (the computerized versions of random walk) mean that the Brownian motion model of securities price movements has now been thoroughly accepted in the investment industry, hook, line, and sinker. Virtually all simulations and calculations of securities and stock market prices performed in the industry assume the random walk or Brownian motion model.

Many Processes Are Approximately Random, but None Is Perfectly Random

Beating the market is nothing but a coin toss—but it is a very different kind of coin toss.

The outcome of an ordinary coin toss is determined by physics. The coin is spun into the air and—depending on air currents, how it was tossed, the distribution of weight in the coin, and how far it is to the floor—it will land heads or tails. In principle, it should be possible to predict the outcome. All the factors determining the outcome are physical forces—and the effects of physical forces are predictable.

But there are far too many minute physical forces acting on the coin during its journey to calculate the outcome. No matter now expert you are in the laws of physics and the conditions under which the coin is tossed, your estimate of the outcome must be "50 percent chance of heads, 50 percent chance of tails."

Unlike a coin toss, the future movement of the price of a stock or a portfolio of stocks is determined not by physics but by economics and human nature—forces far less predictable than physical forces, even on the best days. But like coin tosses, price movements are subject to so many minute economic and human forces that the only possible expert forecast of the outcome is "50 percent chance of better than average, 50 percent chance of worse."

No matter how much you know about it, no matter how much of an expert you are on the stock market or anything else, your chances in any given time period of beating the market are 50 percent. And if you count fees against you, your chances of beating the market after fees are much less than 50 percent. If you count taxes against you, too (if your investments are taxable), then your chances of beating the market average fall substantially again.

The Inevitable Small Departures from Randomness

Why is this so hard for people to accept? They accept with little question that a coin toss has a 50 percent chance of coming up heads and a 50 percent chance of coming up tails.

Yet this firm belief, knowledge, and understanding—which most of us have—that gambling games and coin tosses are matters of sheer luck and not of skill are not, in fact, exactly correct.

The mathematician Ed Thorp specialized—often just for sport—in finding the occasional nonrandom event in hypothetically random processes. He wrote the books *Beat the Dealer* (on the game of blackjack, or 21) and *Beat the Market* (on a fleeting market-beating opportunity he exploited in a small way; then he wrote the book when the opportunity vanished). He also found a way to beat the game of roulette.

Roulette? Isn't that a game of fixed probabilities that you can win only by sheer luck, not by skill?

Yes, usually. But that's a theoretical roulette wheel you're talking about—a roulette wheel that is perfectly balanced. In the real world no roulette wheel—or anything else—is perfectly balanced. Thorp found out that about 25 percent of roulette wheels were out of balance enough that, if you observed them at great length, you could figure out how the probabilities departed from the theoretical ones. And in some small percentage of those cases, you could actually win the game often enough to come out ahead after the house took its share.

But Is It Worth the Cost?

Could you win often enough and big enough to pay yourself a good salary to compensate for all the time you had to put into finding and beating the odd roulette wheel? And could you do it for long enough to make it worth it, before the house performed maintenance on the roulette wheel and spoiled your game?

The answer to both questions is probably no. No industry of roulette wheel beaters arose in the wake of Thorp's roulette wheel research. (An industry did arise to follow his blackjack strategy in *Beat the Dealer*.) But the questions make a point, a very important one. In the real world, nothing corresponds exactly to its theoretical or statistical model. That goes for coin tosses and roulette wheels as much as it goes for the game of trying to beat the stock market. The question for coin tosses and roulette is not whether it is occasionally possible, because of some unusual situation or aberration, to beat the game. The question is whether it's worth the time, effort, and trouble to do so—in short, whether the cost is worth the gain.

This applies to the game of beating the stock market as much as to the game of beating roulette. Perhaps in some earlier time the probabilities were higher that a knowledgeable person could do significantly better than one who was less knowledgeable. Perhaps even in the present time, someone could find "unbalanced roulette wheels" among the stocks, enough to pay a modest salary.

But the statistical evidence is overwhelmingly, inexorably, undeniably (except by those with a fast tongue, a good line, and a great deal to lose) crystal clear that there are nowhere near enough unbalanced roulette wheels among the stocks to pay the boundless salaries hauled in by many mutual fund providers, investment advisors, consultants, and—most outlandishly of all—hedge fund managers.

This is the sum total of the statistical evidence. But to repeat what I said earlier in the chapter: If a statistical model fails one test on a small set of data from time to time or even a few tests over time, this is not sufficient to disprove it. It is inevitable that statistical flukes will occur occasionally if enough tests are run. The evidence is in the sum total of all tests, analyzed in a statistical manner.

Allow me to show you now what happens when this warning is ignored.

9

The Claims of Money Managers: "Smoking Our Brand Prevents Cancer"

Welcome to Fumaria, a vast but little-known country in central Asia.

Fumaria is a land of very heavy smokers. Ninety-nine percent of Fumaria's eighty million people over the age of twelve smoke an average of four packs of cigarettes a day. As a result, the cigarette and tobacco industries are enormous and highly competitive. The country has more than a hundred major cigarette companies, each offering an average of a hundred brands.

The Fumarian cigarette industry and its advertising are moderately well regulated. Since 1999, when the Fumarian minister of health attended a conference in Washington, DC, organized by a trial lawyers' association, all cigarette packs have had printed on them in large letters in Woldu, the official national language, "Smoking Kills." But this warning seems to have had little effect on the level of smoking in Fumaria.

How to Prevent Cancer, Fumarian Style

Cigarette companies and their brands compete fiercely in advertising campaigns. Most of the ads focus on claims of reduced cancer risk.

Although the vast majority of the population smokes, the cancer rate in the nonsmoking population has been determined from the eight hundred thousand nonsmokers. The companies' advertising implies they are able to beat this benchmark. Cigarette companies compete in claims that their flagship brands can reduce cancer rates *below the nonsmoking* level. The implication is that smoking their brand prevents cancer.

The companies back their claims with results of carefully monitored studies of the smokers of various brands. The Fumarian Ministry of Health, believing in the merits of transparency, requires that this information be fully disclosed.

Each cigarette company advertises in full-page advertisements in Fumarian newspapers and magazines, on billboards, and on television. The centerpiece of each ad is a table of numbers showing the cancer rate over some recent historical time period among smokers of its brand, compared with the cancer rate among nonsmokers. The cancer rate for the advertised brand is invariably lower than the nonsmoker rate.

Periodically some brand name beats the benchmark by a large amount. Smokers switch to that brand in droves. In subsequent years, the cigarette company usually does not advertise the cancer rate statistics for that brand, because it is not necessary. Many smokers stay with the brand for years because they remember from the original advertising that its cancer statistics are excellent. Instead of cancer rate statistics, advertisements for the brand feature a ruggedly handsome ox driver.

With so many brands, some are phased out frequently, especially after their statistics have been poor. Some are merged into other brands, creating new brand names.

The Booming Big Bertha Industry

A new variety of tobacco product has arisen recently, not calling itself a cigarette at all but a "Big Bertha." Because Big Berthas are so expensive—a single Big Bertha costs fifty-two thousand camels, the equivalent of $10—the tobacco regulatory authority does not require filing of the usual disclosures, on the assumption that Big Bertha smokers are the wealthiest among the population and can fend for themselves.

Because of the enormous profits to be made selling $10 Big Berthas, thousands of Big Bertha manufacturers have arisen in recent years. Statistics reported by Big Bertha Research, Inc., a company generously supported by the Big Bertha industry to maintain a database of Big Bertha information, show that smoking Big Berthas reduces the cancer rate by even more than smoking cigarettes.

Some enterprising companies offer Big Bertha selection packs that combine Big Berthas from several manufacturers whose Big Berthas have exhibited the lowest cancer rates. These packs sell for the equivalent of $15 for each Big Bertha. One even offers a "Big Bertha Index" package that combines the Big Berthas with the lowest cancer rates in the database.

A small group of tenured professors at Lucky Strike University in Chesterfield, the capital of Fumaria, have argued that smoking any cigarette or Big Bertha subjects you to a much greater cancer risk than if you did not smoke. Their studies are published in academic journals and occasionally reported by the press. They are not, however, advertised in newspapers or magazines, or on billboards or television. Therefore, their conclusions are not widely known.

The Fumarian Data-Mining Miracle

What is going on in Fumaria? How can they possibly show that smoking some cigarette brands actually prevents cancer? Are they cooking the data, falsifying the statistics? No, they are not faking the figures—it is not necessary.

What is happening is simpler than faking the figures. Cancer incidence is random. It does not occur with certainty to anyone who uses tobacco. The now well-known fact (though not well known a short few decades ago) that smoking causes cancer is a statistical phenomenon. It is not the result of an ironclad, 100 percent certain causal chain.

Because cancer is a statistical phenomenon, results can vary. One person may smoke four packs of cigarettes a day for a lifetime and not get cancer. Another may get lung cancer without ever having smoked.

The same can happen to groups of people. If you looked hard enough, you could find ten people who all smoked four packs of cigarettes a day for thirty years and never had cancer. And likewise, you could find ten lifelong nonsmokers who all got lung cancer. If you look harder, you may find one hundred of each or even one thousand.

What the cigarette companies in Fumaria were doing, de facto—that is, without necessarily having planned it that way deliberately—was looking very hard for groups of people who smoked and didn't get cancer, at least not as much as nonsmokers got. By creating many thousands of brands, they were certain to find that smokers of some of these brands got cancer less often than smokers of other brands. They were even able to find that smokers of some of the brands got cancer less often than nonsmokers. It's a statistical fluke, resulting from a practice called *data mining*. If you run enough tests of a random phenomenon, you will eventually get—at random—the result that you want.

By creating thousands of test groups—one for each brand—the cigarette companies were guaranteeing that there would be a wide variety of results, a wide spectrum of cancer rates. Then by cherry-picking the best rates and touting the cigarette brands that achieved those rates, they were lying with statistics. But they were lying in a way that didn't require them to actually have to tell an outright lie.

By phasing out or merging brands that had bad cancer statistics, the companies were getting them out of the database, so that statistical database studies across all their brands would not count them. That would make the cancer rate statistics in aggregate look better than they actually were.

The Big Bertha Phenomenon

What about the Big Berthas? Why were their cancer rates so much better?

The answer to that is simple also. Big Bertha companies were not required to report to the database. Only the ones that wanted to report did so.

Which Big Bertha companies do you think will report to the database and have their numbers scrutinized by anyone who can gain access? Why, the ones with the better numbers, of course. And because thousands of Big Bertha companies were created in order to chase the profits that could be made from them, plenty of opportunities were created for some Big Berthas, by random chance, to achieve much better-than-average cancer rates. The ones that do so report their results to the database. The ones that don't achieve good numbers don't report. In most cases, they simply close their doors.

The end result is that even if you scrutinize the entire Big Bertha database, you'll find that the average cancer rates are relatively low. Only the Big Bertha companies whose customers had low cancer rates reported to the database.

Will Smoking Help You Prevent Cancer in the Future?

Do any of the claims of the cigarette companies and the Big Bertha companies have any predictive value? Their claims, as we have seen, were derived from real data for real customers (barring the occasional faking or shading of figures). When a cigarette company advertised that smokers of one of its brands had lower cancer rates than nonsmokers over a specific time period, it was really true. But did it imply that your cancer risk in the future would be reduced if you smoked that brand?

Of course not. The results presented by the cigarette companies have no predictive value. The fact that customers for a particular brand had one rate of cancer or another is nothing but a statistical artifact, signifying nothing but the randomness of the data—and certainly signifying nothing about what would happen if you smoked that brand in the future.

The relative rate of cancer in smokers of a particular cigarette during a particular period of time is not a characteristic of the cigarette but an accident of the smokers over that time—a random statistical event. In the next time period, a different random statistical event will occur, and the cancer rate will be different.

The Vast Tobacco-Consulting Complex

In spite of what I have just said, the cigarette and tobacco industries in Fumaria are big and sprawling. Not only do they include tobacco growers, cigarette manufacturers, and their advertisers. A huge service industry has arisen to feed off the widespread assumption that cigarette smoking—and to an even greater extent, smoking of Big Berthas—is good for your health, if you smoke the right brands. Much of the effort revolves around exhaustive research and analysis to find the right brands.

In Fumaria, health advisors—often translated from the Woldu as "doctors"—prescribe cigarette smoking to prevent cancer, just as doctors in the West prescribe cholesterol-lowering drugs to prevent heart attack. Doctors recommend specific cigarette brands, usually those with low cancer rates.

Doctors frequently procure a long-term supply of their recommended brand for their patients. The brand's manufacturer then pays the doctor a percentage of the sales in gratitude for his recommendation. These remittances from the cigarette manufacturers represent a substantial portion of doctors' incomes.

Corporations in Fumaria engage health maintenance organizations to cover their employees. Fumarian HMOs offer a limited selection of cigarette brands as part of their health plans. Numerous consulting firms serve both corporations and HMOs. These consulting companies perform research studies on cigarette brands, at high cost to their HMO clients. The costs are passed on to HMO members, becoming part of the high cost of health care. In these research studies, the consultants analyze cigarette and industry data in depth, attempting to isolate factors that explain cancer rates obtained with the various cigarette brands.

Consulting firms are often hired by HMOs to help select cigarette brands for the HMOs' health packages. The consulting organization performs studies to help select the brands. The consulting organization attempts to attribute a cigarette brand's cancer rate to various factors, trying to explain its superior or inferior performance over time, and why it may have performed well at one time and not at another.

For example, statistical analyses may show that 12 percent of the performance is due to tobacco produced by agribusinesses in the Fumarian northwest, 26 percent to agribusinesses in the southeast, 44 percent to agribusinesses located south of the central mountains, and the rest to firms in the northeast region near the Gray River.

The consultants combine these results with separate studies of the turnover of executives in tobacco companies in those parts of the country. From these data, the consultants are often able to draw conclusions about whether good or poor cancer rate statistics may have been caused by the management retention rate in tobacco agribusiness companies.

Because these consulting organizations are believed to take great care in their analyses and have large numbers of experts in the tobacco and cigarette fields, as well as in statistics and mathematics, they are compensated very well, and their recommendations are usually followed.

We're Not in Fumaria Anymore

What we're talking about here, obviously, is mutual funds and hedge funds, not cigarettes and Big Berthas. We had to make a change of venue to elude the Big Investment Lie that holds people in its grip. Truths that would otherwise be self-evident seem to escape us if they imply that important-looking people in expensive suits in plush offices making really big money and generating scads of statistics actually rack up investment results that are totally random and worse than you could do yourself—worse, so to speak, than if you didn't smoke their brand at all.

Until a little more than fifty years ago, the tobacco and cigarette manufacture and sales industry in the United States was as respected as the investment services industry is now—probably more so. Cigarette companies were the lead advertisers on the best television programs. Although some studies were beginning to show that cigarette smoking caused cancer, industry-funded studies proved the opposite. It took a long time and years of antismoker activism and major government intervention to cut the industry and its reputation down to size—and to finally controvert the misrepresented statistics.

That process has barely begun to scratch the surface of the lies in the investment field.

A Perfect Analogy

Everything about the cigarette and Big Bertha industries in Fumaria has a direct analog in the investment management and services industries. Well over a hundred companies sell mutual funds. Some offer a choice of as many as one hundred funds, comprising over ten thousand funds in total.

The spread of performance across these funds is very wide. Every company that offers a large number of funds can always find one or more for which it can advertise outstanding, market-beating performance, at least over some time period. But in the aggregate, they perform worse than a market average—just as, in aggregate, smokers of the Fumarian brands got more cancer than nonsmokers.

Advertisements for mutual funds feature tables in large, bold typeface showing the performance of a particular fund in comparison to a market benchmark like the S&P 500 index. Every advertisement is required by the SEC to display the statement "Past performance is not necessarily indicative of future performance." But hardly anyone seems to pay much attention to it.

Statistics of the mutual fund industry have now been studied for decades. Government and industry oversight restrain most of the worst excesses of statistical chicanery. As a result, lying with statistics in the mutual fund industry is largely confined to the basic Fumarian lie—advertising statistical flukes as if they were trends that could be expected to continue.

Thus, mutual funds, because of their level of transparency and industry and government oversight, are not very amenable to blatant statistical manipulation—other than the Fumaria-like fraud I've described. The same, however, is not true of hedge funds, the "Big Berthas" of the industry.

Hedge Funds and the Big Bertha Lie

Currently there are more than eight thousand hedge funds, many of which assume very high levels of risk. That is enough to find any performance you can imagine, good, bad, very good, very bad, and indifferent. Hedge funds have few regulatory constraints. Their performance data are not required to be audited, so the way is open to them to fudge their data. They are not entirely free to do this, of course. Outright fraud can land them in a lawsuit (a common event for hedge funds, as readers of the financial press will know). But there are surprisingly many degrees of freedom in data reporting that allow for statistical manipulation, even without outright fraud.

The implication often made from hedge fund database statistics—that hedge funds perform better than other funds or than the market as a whole, with less risk—is completely wrong. It is as wrong as the claim that Big Berthas reduce your risk of getting cancer. That claim was made in Fumaria because the Big Bertha smokers who were reported in the Big Bertha database actually had lower cancer rates. But the database held only that portion of the data—among the thousands of Big Berthas—that was *voluntarily* reported.

Similarly, data in the hedge fund databases consist only of what is voluntarily reported. Just as the Big Bertha manufacturers were likely to report their data only if they showed low cancer rates, hedge funds are likely to report their data only if they show good performance. Combining these data to imply that all hedge funds perform well on average is to commit a grave statistical error.

Trying to Get Behind the Doctored Statistics

More careful studies have recently attempted to avoid using only the cherry-picked data that the hedge funds decided to report. They still couldn't avoid the problem that failing hedge funds—those with poor performance—tend to stop reporting when their performance gets bad. But at least the studies eliminate some of the statistical bias.

When these data are used, it turns out hedge funds have done worse on average than the S&P 500 market index. Furthermore, hedge funds' range of performance has been extremely wide, from phenomenally good to horrendously bad—but unpredictably so.[1]

Hence, an investor undertakes more risk by selecting a hedge fund than by randomly selecting a mutual fund. You could get one whose results will be very, very good; but you could also get one whose results will be very, very bad—and it may be impossible to predict which it will be.

The phenomenon of the Big Bertha selection packs—the ones with Big Berthas costing $15 each—is found in the parallel fund-of-hedge-funds phenomenon. Funds of hedge funds group several hedge funds together—usually the ones with good cherry-picked past performance records—and resell them as a higher-cost package to gullible investors.

I have found that many people are astonished, incredulous, and downright indignant to be told that hedge funds are a worse investment than a market index fund or virtually any common run-of-the-mill mutual fund with low fees. They are indignant because so many seemingly respectable people they know—not to mention the hedge fund managers themselves, who are respected only because they have grown incredibly rich—believe that hedge funds are superior investments. This is an archetypal instance of the Big Investment Lie in action. People believe it because so many "respectable" people say it is so.

The Investment Industry's Entourage
Sprawls Like Fumarian Tobacco

The analogy with the sprawling Fumarian cigarette industry continues to be apt in the investment advisory and consulting businesses. Investment advisors recommend their favorite mutual funds, usually citing past performance records and recommending funds that charge enough to kick back a portion of their fees to the advisor. Mutual funds' historical performance records cannot, of course, be shown to be anything but random results—anymore than can the rates of cancer for smokers of Fumarian cigarettes.

This sounds appalling when placed in the Fumarian context of a doctor recommending to her patient a particular brand of cigarette to smoke, then getting a kickback from the cigarette's manufacturer. But the analogy with an investment advisor's recommendation is flawless.

The Fumarian "health advisor" recommends smoking a certain brand of cigarette when not smoking would be better for the patient's health.

The real-life investment advisor recommends a mutual fund or manager who charges substantial fees when a very low-fee alternative would be better for the client's finances.

Both the Fumarian health advisor and the real-life financial advisor get kickbacks from the manufacturer of the brand they recommend, calling into question their objectivity in making that recommendation.

More intricate still in its cynicism is the lucrative institutional investment consulting business. Having spent many years in that field, I am familiar with its ins and outs. I will say more about it in a later chapter, but a brief reference to the Fumarian analogy is relevant here.

The ludicrous-sounding study performed by the consultant to the Fumarian HMO—involving precise attribution of which agribusiness the tobacco in a cigarette came from and whether the changes in management in tobacco growers' firms occurred too often—is mother's milk to the institutional investment consultant.

Where the Fumarian consultant helps the HMO select cigarette brands, the real-life institutional investment consultant typically helps a pension fund select money management firms. The compensation both for the consultant and for the money management firms ultimately chosen is very large. Therefore, a great deal of caution and analysis (or at least the appearance of it) is needed in the process of making that recommendation—just as the Fumarian consultants, to satisfy their HMO client, needed to perform careful analysis to determine what cigarette brands to recommend to the HMO for its employee health plan.

The end result is a strange combination of technohubris ("It must be right because we used a lot of mathematics and ran a lot of statistical tests") and conventional good-old-boy wisdom, like the assumption that your product will be better if you have stable management, even when you know already that the product is awful no matter what kind of management you have.

Fumaria is a strange place indeed. But it's where we live our lives as investors—unless we know better.

An old psychiatrist joke says that neurotics are people who build castles in the air, while psychotics are people who live in them. Now, let's visit the people who spend most of their working lives in a virtual Fumaria.

10

Idle, Greedy Hands and Too Much Data Do the Devil's Work

Given the abundant evidence that trying to beat the stock market is a waste of time and effort, I have often wondered how smart people can do so much of it. Those who are professionals in the business do it, of course, because they are paid very handsomely to at least pretend to try. Thousands upon thousands of people are engaged one way or another in the effort.

When I was a child, I would look out on the roadway and see all the cars going to and fro. I would wonder where each and every one of them was going. Now I wonder what each and every one of those would-be market beaters is doing, day after day after day. Of course, I have been involved in the investment business in one way or another for most of my career, so I have some idea what they are doing.

But I have never been so close to a group of people in a corporate environment who were determinedly trying to beat the stock market as I was a short time before starting to write this book, in the fall of 2004. The experience was, in fact, what provoked me to write it.

I'll describe the situation, changing the names, locations, and a few other irrelevant details about the company. The essence of the story—the personalities involved, how the company tried to beat the stock market, and how I was reluctantly drawn into the effort—is accurate.

The Saga of Seagull Unlimited

The company was called Seagull Unlimited. It was set up in a pleasant location in the Florida Keys by its founder, Bruce, a bear of a man, a larger-than-life, hard-partying social climber. Bruce had been involved in a number of professions, some of them of the daredevil kind, like skydiving. But he had also run serious projects for major corporations. He had two chief skills. The first was salesmanship, in the form of glowing and grandiose but often well-phrased descriptions of projects that Seagull Unlimited was engaged in or was planning. The second skill was the ability to attract smart and interesting people to his company. He also aspired to be—and was, to a degree—an intellectual, having read widely and accumulated a library of technological, scientific, and philosophical books that anyone with a love of science and technology would envy.

I was drawn to the company by its diverse and intellectually stimulating aspirations and by its projects and plans, which included applications of advanced computer technology, science projects, and language analysis. The company also believed—not entirely without reason—that they could use some of their technologies for stock market prediction. They thought that I, being a mathematician, could help them do this, though I thought that was doubtful.

As I discovered when I learned more about the company, they were experiencing a serious cash flow problem. But I joined them nonetheless for several months as a consultant, payment deferred contingent on future revenue. I hoped that Seagull's overblown but fascinating, and in principle attainable, dreams could be fulfilled. I liked the people, I liked the agenda, I liked the place, and I had hopes the venture could be turned into a success.

Once I got there and spent a few weeks learning more, I discovered that the company's business was far more about predicting the stock market than I had thought. The exciting technology and science projects were real, but they weren't profitable. Venture capital funding of several million dollars had been raised to launch the company. I was told that the founders—Bruce and a couple of associates who were involved with him from the start—had tried to raise venture capital funding for the technology and science projects. But prospective venture investors would invest only if the company worked on developing a model to beat the stock market, presumably because that's where the big bucks are, the golden crumbs.

The company had hired an expert group of computer programmers. Almost all of them, I discovered, were engaged in developing the market prediction program. The program—like so many market prediction programs—had a beautifully colored but very busy output screen showing the value of a stock market index over time and an array of predictors, indicators, and signals saying when to buy or sell.

The Prediction System's Two Clients

Not only had there been a quantity of venture capital invested, but there were also two major clients testing the market prediction software. These clients paid an astounding amount every month, on the order of $100,000, to use (actually, to beta-test—i.e., to help get the bugs out of) the software. They were paying so much because they thought it could make them tons of money once fully developed and because they would have exclusive rights to resell it.

The two clients were Scott and Nigel. Scott was a man with illustrious achievements in another field, who was nevertheless in a bad period in his life. He was in the middle of an ugly family situation and living alone in Montreal. He spent his whole day, while the New York stock market was open, trading futures contracts on the stock market using the online software provided him by Seagull Unlimited.

Seagull Unlimited's founder Bruce would spend most of the day sitting at his desk on the phone with Scott, explaining to him how to interpret what he saw on the screen of Seagull's stock market prediction program and how to use it to trade contracts on the stock market.

Scott was an intractable client. He would often refuse to do what the program told him to do, to trade when it told him to trade. He would always have a reason why he did not follow its dictates. The relationship with Scott was clearly a difficult one for Bruce and a thorn in his side. Nevertheless, Scott was a major source of funds and important contacts for Seagull Unlimited, and he had to be placated.

The second client, Nigel, seemed to use the program to trade less often, but he did what he thought it was telling him to do. When I talked to him on the phone before I met him, he offered—in his mild-mannered way—a thundering endorsement of the market-predicting program. He said it was amazing, that it worked better than he would have believed possible.

Later, when I met Nigel, he confided that whenever he used the program, he lost money. I thought—because he seemed to have a rather self-effacing demeanor—that what he was saying was that he must be doing something wrong. The clash with his earlier endorsement was otherwise inexplicable. What I think was happening was that Nigel was a friend of Bruce's, a part of Bruce's social-climbing orbit and somewhat in awe of him. He was therefore a believer and a supporter. To the extent that an invention of Bruce's seemed not to work, Nigel blamed his own inability to understand it or apply it correctly.

Bruce's prediction method was based on trying to exploit, very rapidly by fast computer, a flow of information that was not available as quickly to the vast majority of investors. Because of this, I thought it had a chance—but only a small chance—of actually working.

Evaluating Seagull's Predictions

Nobody at the company knew how to evaluate the results of a stock market trading strategy. They asked me to undertake that task. I agreed, having done the same sort of thing many times before.

Evaluating the performance of an investment strategy employs a standard and simple method. It involves calculating the return that would be realized on an investment of a dollar between each pair of trades, then stringing those returns together over time. One must also subtract brokerage fees and any other expenses.

Once the return on the strategy has been calculated, one must determine a benchmark to compare it with. It is simplest to compare it with putting your money under the mattress or in a low-interest-bearing bank account. Then all you have to do is determine whether the strategy made money.

But that is not usually what people want to know. They want to know whether it beat a market index. It is not enough, however, just to compare it with the market. It must be compared with the market on a risk-adjusted basis. (I'll go into this in more detail in Chapter 12.) If the strategy was to borrow money so as to be leveraged ten times over—that is, to increase risk by a factor of ten—then its results must be compared with investing in the market index but with 90 percent of the invested money borrowed.

I discovered it was not easy to determine exactly what Bruce's strategy was. True, the computer program's screen turned a light on or off to say when to buy or sell. So there definitely was a strategy. But it kept changing. Bruce would come down at random times to the area where the programmers worked and, in his booming voice, ask for a change in the way the strategy was programmed.

The programmers were experts at what they did. What they did included such skills as extracting data from databases, programming numerical computations so they ran quickly, and displaying graphs and tables on a computer screen so that the screen looked very impressive, refreshed itself quickly when information changed, and responded well to user inputs. It was not the programmers' job to second-guess Bruce's requests or even to keep a record of them. And Bruce was an imposing personality, appearing to be very certain about anything he came up with.

As a result, it was difficult to find out exactly what the stock market–trading strategy actually was at anytime. But finally I got a precise description of it that both Bruce and the programmers seemed to agree to—though I had the feeling Bruce didn't really want to be pinned down.

Unfortunately, the verdict of the evaluation was that the strategy worked terribly. Running the strategy over the previous six months—thus simulating a hypothetical investor who invested for that period using the strategy (this process is called *backtesting*)—produced a loss of 80 percent. It was a bad period in the stock market. The risk-adjusted benchmark happened to lose 20 percent over that same time period. But a loss of 80 percent, even compared with a benchmark loss of 20 percent, was not good.

I was not that surprised. True, the prediction method had seemed to have some potential. The raw data it analyzed almost instantly to make its forecasts were not available to the whole market as quickly as it was to Seagull's computers. But the method of analysis was simplistic. It was hard to determine, moreover, what refinements to that method might enhance its predictive capacities. It is one thing to have data more quickly than the public at large has it. It is another thing entirely to analyze that data to produce a better prediction than the market.

Furthermore, the strategy was eaten alive by brokerage commissions, even though the brokerage rate the company could get was very low. The strategy involved trading very frequently. Brokerage commissions can be a substantial percentage of capital when leverage is high.

Bruce Sees the Patterns

Bruce seemed unfazed. He continued to sermonize in his grandiloquent way, giving the impression that Seagull's system was beating the market by as much as 100 percent per year. I would periodically remind him, sometimes forcefully, that it was doing no such thing. If it was to beat the market by even a little bit, then serious refinements to the methodology would be needed.

Bruce did not like my way of looking at it. He thought I needed convincing. He would occasionally call people, including me, to look at the screen of the Seagull program to see how well it was doing predicting the market. He said he *knew* the patterns were there. He said he had years and years of experience recognizing patterns.

But whether or not the pattern on the screen showed that the indicators were accurately predicting the market was no more than a matter of personal interpretation and predisposition. It was not, to say the least, a scientifically proven conclusion.

Bruce was exerting pressure to find statistics proving that the method predicted the market. He referred to my "skepticism" as if it were some form of heresy and a bad attitude. He said, referring to me, he would never again have someone working for him he couldn't pay because he couldn't control them. The implication seemed to be that if he could control someone, he could get them to prove the system was beating the market.

I'm sure that if he could have paid someone to do that, he could have gotten an employee who would indeed produce such a proof. One can comb through statistics over and over, again and again, and find some way to align them so that they seem to prove some—any—foreordained conclusion.

I Try to Sell the System

I hoped, though, that the company could survive to fulfill its more exciting ambitions. So I began to do my best to find a way to produce revenue with the "market prediction" system.

In the investment business, there is a market for "research," meaning any information that may prove valuable to an investment manager in pursuing an investment strategy. I tried to plumb this market for business. It was receptive. Like a good salesman, I tried a newly popular buzz phrase in my pitch—"behavioral finance." It worked. I also tried to find ways that might improve the prediction strategy.

In addition, I contacted hedge fund firms. Using contacts I had built up in the investment field, I called the president of a European-based hedge fund complex and also the venture funding arm of a U.S. hedge fund company.

Everybody who is touting a new investment strategy performs backtests to show that the strategy would have worked in the past. We weren't ready to show this yet. The results of our backtests were, in fact, beyond dismal. But given time and effort, and trial after trial after trial, I knew there was a good chance we could find something that backtested well. I hoped it would have at least some predictive validity. But even if it didn't, I knew we could find something that at least appeared to work. Then, I thought, we could use the money from the lucrative investment management business to do something useful.

My contact in the hedge fund venture-funding department said something interesting. He said, "We don't believe the backtests." Then, in an incidental, matter-of-fact tone, he added, as an obvious footnote, "Of course, you've got to have them."

What he meant was that anyone can trump up a good backtest. All you've got to do is try hundreds or even thousands of variations of your strategy until you get one that backtests well. It's all done by fast computer, so it's easy. Therefore, a successful backtest is meaningless. Yet you have to have one for marketing purposes.

The hedge fund complex agreed to perform live tests of our trading strategy if we sent them the buy-sell signals. The venture funding arm indicated they would invest seed capital of $20 to $40 million if we enlisted the hedge fund complex to manage the fund.

The ducks seemed to be in a row. All we needed was an actual strategy that worked. For that, I was willing to mine the data. I suggested we rapidly try one thing after another after another until we found something that seemed to have at least a little predictive value. I still thought there was a chance. Then we would submit it to the hedge fund complex for testing.

There's always a 50-50 random chance a strategy will work anyway in practice—that is, that it will beat the market (before fees)—whether it has any real validity or not. And when it uses a lot of leverage, if it works, it will work very well. If we were lucky, maybe it would work in the live test. Then the European hedge fund complex would agree to manage the fund, the U.S. firm would seed it with $20 or $40 million, and we would be in on the hedge fund gravy train. Then we could use the money to do genuinely productive work on science and technology.

But it was too late. Time had run out, both on my relationship with Bruce and on the company itself. The company was about to run out of money. It would have to let the paid staff go. And Bruce, in a fit of pique over what he perceived as insubordination, asked me to leave immediately.

The Story of Ralph

There's more to the story. A plot strand of nearly equal importance was developing itself in parallel.

Another man named Ralph was the second in command of the company. He spent only half his time at the company in the Florida Keys, however. The rest of his time he was a partner in a completely different business in New York. Ralph really wanted ultimately, though, to move to the Keys and spend all his time working at Seagull Unlimited.

The relationship between Ralph and Bruce was a classic geek–jock symbiosis. But both Ralph and Bruce had aged well past their prime geek and jock years and had acquired, respectively, some jockish and geekish qualities in the process.

Ralph had been a devoted computer geek in his teen years but had gone on to other things, at which he had been successful. He nonetheless kept abreast of the state of the art of computer technology. He still regarded himself as—and was—a master geek. Ralph was officially the boss of the programming department. Unfortunately for the company's organizational clarity, he played little or no role in the company and had little contact with the programmers or anyone else when he was away in New York.

When Ralph was in the Keys, he would work very hard. He did little else, except relax occasionally with late nights of talk involving much wine, beer, and vodka. He and I had numerous fascinating, far-ranging, wee-hours conversations.

Ralph's days were spent partly in meetings with the programmers, with Bruce and others, but the meetings were admirably brief. Almost all of his time was spent banging away at stock market data. He would do this for hours on end, using Excel spreadsheets and other tools. He was trying to find patterns—cycles and curlicues in minute-by-minute and second-by-second stock market index data. Unfortunately, the data he used were very limited. He used data only for the past few days. He would find a pattern and then run a hypothetical trading strategy based on it to see whether it would, hypothetically, make money.

He did this for hours and hours and hours, with his head down, barely aware of the world around him. When a strategy appeared hypothetically to make money, he would announce how much it made per trade to me and others. Subsequently, he would often find that he had made a mistake in his calculations and the gains weren't that much. He did not hide this when it happened. It is not at all unusual for someone doing computer calculations to find an error—a bug—so there is no embarrassment in finding one.

The problem, of course, was that there was no reason for any of the patterns Ralph found to continue. If you pound through the data enough, you'll find a pattern somewhere. It's like the game we used to play as kids on a long, boring drive somewhere. We would look at license plates and find patterns. "Hey, look, there's a license plate with four threes in it!" "There's a full house!" "A straight!" The feeling was that if you looked hard enough, you'd suddenly transport yourself to the land where everything follows a pattern, and you could even tell what the next license plate would be. We have some built-in reason to want to believe this, to want to be able to predict the future. This, I think, is what motivated Ralph—the psychological need to be able to predict the future and the rush you get from tiny bits of feedback that suggest that you can.

Ralph's methodology was completely different from Bruce's. But he exhibited the same hope for it, if a lot less salesmanship. The difference was that Ralph believed he could find it if he tried hard enough. Bruce seemed to believe he already had it.

Bruce and Ralph hadn't, they said, aspired originally to beat the stock market. Far from thinking primarily about the stock market, they thought they had a concept of computing that was a step ahead, and they wanted to pursue it. It could be applied to many things, so, well, if the investors wanted it, it could be applied, of course, to the stock market. They fell victim to the usual conceit of smart people— "We're smart, so naturally we can figure out how to predict the stock market."

I assumed that myself when I first took a job in the investment field. I never expected to work in the financial business, and I had no greed for money. But when I considered it, I thought, "What the heck—I might as well make money. I'm smart, and I'm a mathematician, so, of course, I'll be able to figure out better than other people how to make a lot of money by investing."

That's what Ralph thought. That's what Bruce thought. That's what a lot of fund managers think. But it isn't true.

What They're All Doing

I already knew, in general, before I observed Ralph up close, what all those people spend their time on at investment management firms. Most people at these firms are salespeople. But the people who are actually making the product spend their time trying to pick stocks or bonds or—in the case of hedge funds—to pick combinations of purchases and sales of stocks, bonds, and derivatives.

What they are doing, day in and day out, is data mining. They are beating the data with barrage after barrage of computer programs, Excel spreadsheets, mathematical computations and filters, and backtests upon backtests upon backtests. Sometimes a backtest works. But as I mentioned earlier, it is well known that backtests can be rigged to work by the data-mining process.

So there is a procedure that is supposed to correct for this, called *out-of-sample* testing. This means you find a strategy that works in a backtest during one time period, by trying many, many variations, and then you test it in a different time period.

The fly in this ointment is obvious. You can do out-of-sample backtest after out-of-sample backtest after out-of-sample backtest, too, thus merely moving the data-mining problem back one step. Because of the power and speed of computers and the accessibility of mountains of stock market data, almost all attempts to discipline the process of data mining will be unsuccessful—other than just not doing it.

I've seen people deeply engaged in this process, many times in many offices, though never in close contact hour after hour and day after day for many days at a time as I saw Ralph doing it. When they find a strategy that would have worked historically, they try using it in practice. Half the time it actually works; that is, it beats the benchmark (it would work half the time by sheer chance, too). When it works, they think their hard work and insight have been rewarded with success. They think the success was the product of skill. When it doesn't work, they find some explanation, something that didn't work quite the way it did in the past and needs to be fixed. And they go back to the drawing board to make a minor—or perhaps even a major—adjustment. Or they simply attribute the failure to bad luck. Success, therefore, is the result of skill; failure, of bad luck.

It's a job. It pays very well. And it can be fun the way gambling can be fun, even if it's only pulling the arm on a slot machine time after time after time. It's fun to get a rush when you see something work. It doesn't matter that you'll probably lose money over the time you spend in the casino; you're on vacation, and that's part of the fun and expense. But when you're having fun doing data mining in an office to see whether you can get a rush by doing a successful back-test, you get paid for it with someone else's money.

How the Real Professionals Would Do It

But, you may say, let's face it—Seagull Unlimited was a fly-by-night operation. It was bush league. They didn't even know how to evaluate the return on an investment. It wasn't a large respected firm like Merrill Lynch, or Smith Barney, or Morgan Stanley, or a big bank or mutual fund company. Seagull overpromised and overreached. They weren't prudent, like a big bank or mutual fund company would be or like a good hedge fund manager ought to be. You can't use that as an example. The proof is that Seagull failed. The proof that big name firms do a better job is that they are successful.

Indeed, you have a point. Seagull Unlimited would have had a much better chance of success if it had been a big firm with a big name. It could have gotten investors more easily, investors who trust the company name—just because it is a big name—to mount not just one but several hedge funds. It could then have dropped or merged out of existence the hedge funds that racked up bad performance records and sold like the dickens the ones with good records—never mind whether the records were the result of skill or naked luck. Then, like the Big Bertha manufacturers, it could have reported the results of its surviving funds to the hedge fund database.

The lucky managers of the surviving funds could then have left the bank and gone out on their own and started their own hedge funds, so they could keep all the profits. The venture arm of the big hedge fund company that I talked to—the one that, if you could convince them, would provide seed capital of $20 to $40 million to start your hedge fund—said they mostly funded people who had already managed hedge funds for big hedge fund complexes. Typically, they said, the people whose hedge funds they seeded had been second in command of a hedge fund at a big bank or hedge fund company. They had made a name for themselves in the business and had gotten experience. That's why I had to get another hedge fund company interested in being the manager for Seagull Unlimited's investment strategy—so I could show the venture seeding people that we had an experienced manager on board. It's a cozy little business, but it's not impossible to break into.

The Very Fumarian Moral of the Story

If you have access to enough numbers, you can find any pattern you want. If you are in the investment business, you can gain almost immediate access to literally billions upon billions of numbers: historical prices and performance numbers for thousands of stocks, commodities, and derivatives; trading volumes; economic data—all at tens of thousands of instants throughout any day. You can find patterns very quickly because you can use high-speed computers and fast (though not necessarily correctly applied) statistical analysis programs.

You can produce almost any pattern you want not only from using the historical data but going forward, too. All you have to do is launch a slew of statistics-generating vehicles—whether cigarette brands, mutual funds, or hedge funds. Then you can dump or deemphasize the ones that produce patterns you don't like or don't want to mention.

This kind of abuse of statistics was blatantly obvious in the case of Fumaria. There, statistics were generated and gathered on thousands of cigarette brands and Big Berthas. Emphasis was placed only on the statistics that helped sell a manufacturer's product. We knew something was awry in Fumaria because we know, as an established fact, that smoking does not reduce cancer but causes it.

What has not been widely accepted yet as an established statistical fact—even though it *is* an established statistical fact—is that professional investment service companies do not increase the growth of their clients' wealth but decrease it. This is a *statistical* fact—exactly like the fact that cigarette smoking causes cancer.

Just as you can find a lifelong smoker—or ten or a hundred of them—who never got cancer, you can find hedge fund investors, or actively managed mutual fund investors, whose results—even after fees—were outstanding. This anecdotal evidence does not, however, change the overall statistical evidence—that smoking is detrimental to your health, on the one hand, and that professional investment advice and management is detrimental to your wealth, on the other.

If you think you can beat the odds by investing in the same mutual fund or hedge fund that someone you know made a bundle in—or that advertises terrific historical performance—then think again. You might as well try to stave off cancer by smoking the Fumarian cigarette brand that had the lowest cancer rate last year. The statistical connection between last year's winning mutual fund or hedge fund and this year's winner is no stronger than the statistical connection between last year's cancer-reducing cigarette brand and this year's.

The statistics are crystal clear: market-beating performance has no holding power. You can't count on it to continue, and you can't expect it to continue. Like the low cancer rates for Fumarian cigarette brands, it is a statistical artifact, fundamentally meaningless—the result of random events.

If you give up on trying to beat the market by paying high fees, is there anything left for you, the investor, to hold onto?

Yes, there most certainly is. But be careful—it has been distorted almost beyond recognition by those who are having such a good time collecting your fees.

11

The Simple Rules of Nobel Prize Winners

. . . .

In this chapter and the next, I will explain the Nobel Prize–winning theories that are supposed to form the basis for the advice given to customers of investment advisors and managers.

As we shall see, however, these theories underpin Strategy 1—the simple, low-cost strategy—not Strategy 2, the expensive addition that consultants, advisors, and managers tack on so that they can charge high fees.

Markowitz's Theory: Don't Put All Your Eggs in One Basket

When Harry Markowitz started thinking about investments in the late 1940s, he was a student at the University of Chicago selecting an area in which to write his dissertation. He started to think about applying mathematics to the stock market (a novel idea at the time); his advisor agreed it was a reasonable idea.

Much later, in his Nobel autobiography, Markowitz described how he came up with the seeds of his breakthrough idea—portfolio theory—while reading in the university library:

> The basic concepts of portfolio theory came to me
> one afternoon in the library while reading John Burr

Williams's *Theory of Investment Value*. Williams proposed that
the value of a stock should equal the present value of its future
dividends. Since future dividends are uncertain, I interpreted
Williams's proposal to be to value a stock by its *expected* future
dividends.[1] (emphasis added)

Williams's proposed method was to predict the future dividends a
company would pay, then, based on that, to calculate what the stock's
price should be. By comparing with the stock's actual price, you
could predict the stock's return.

But everyone knows a prediction can be widely off the mark. The
problem with Williams's approach was that it didn't consider the
uncertainty of the prediction. Something more is needed to measure
the risk that the return will actually be far worse than expected.

Markowitz proposed as a measure of the risk the "standard deviation" of return. *Standard deviation* is simply a measure of how
much the return fluctuates—or is anticipated to fluctuate—over time.
The returns of mature companies like electric utilities and large banks
usually don't fluctuate as much as the returns of small startups and
therefore have smaller standard deviations.

Standard deviation is far from a perfect measure of risk; for
example, it counts the "risk" of doing much better than expected
equally with the risk of doing much worse. But its technical advantage is that it lends itself fairly easily to mathematical manipulation.

If you were only picking one stock for your portfolio, you'd want
one with a high expected return but also a low standard deviation—
a low "risk." You might even pick a stock with a lower expected
return than another one if it had lower risk.

But it's somehow clear that you shouldn't pick only one stock. It's
common wisdom that you shouldn't "put all your eggs in one basket."
Now Markowitz had to figure out how to quantify this intuition.

Markowitz found the answer in the statistical measure known as
the *correlation coefficient*. Different stocks tend to move up or down
at the same time, to a greater or lesser degree. The degree to which
they move up and down simultaneously is measured by their correlation coefficient. Two stocks that move up and down together in lock-
step at precisely the same time have a correlation coefficient of one.
Two stocks that seem to move up or down totally independently of
each other have a correlation coefficient of zero. And two stocks that
move in directions exactly opposite to each other have a correlation

Exhibit 11.1   Low Correlation Reduces Risk

Extreme Case: Correlation Coefficient of −1 between Stock 1 and Stock 2

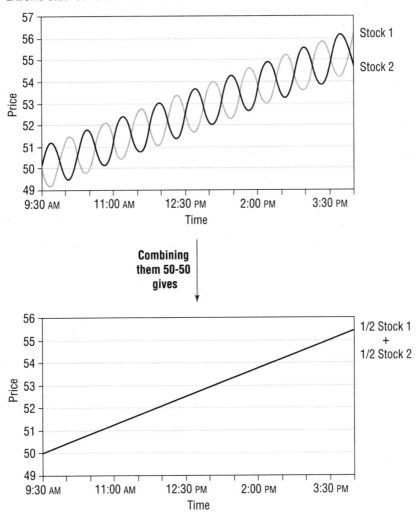

coefficient of minus one. Exhibit 11.1 shows how useful correlation coefficient can be under ideal conditions.

If two stocks had the same expected return but a correlation coefficient of minus one then you should invest an equal amount in each of them. The up-and-down movements of one of them will be cancelled by the down-and-up movements of the other. The combination of the two will have no standard deviation—no uncertainty—at all!

It will be a sure thing that you'll actually get, in the future, exactly the expected return.

Unfortunately, there are no two stocks that have a correlation coefficient of minus one—nowhere near. Otherwise the solution to the problem of portfolio selection would be easy. Instead, it is much more difficult.

Markowitz found that by mathematically combining the expected returns, standard deviations, and correlation coefficients for all the securities in a portfolio (whether they are stocks, bonds, or other investments), you can find the expected return and standard deviation for the *whole* portfolio.

Now that you can find the expected return and standard deviation of a whole portfolio, you can compare the risk/return characteristics of one *portfolio* of securities with the risk/return characteristics of another *portfolio* of securities—not just the risk/return characteristics of two individual stocks.

Then you would choose the portfolio with the maximum return for the risk you want to accept. Markowitz called this process of choosing an optimal portfolio "mean-variance optimization."

For this—and the conceptual framework on which it is based—Markowitz shared the Nobel Prize in economics in 1990.

The problem of portfolio construction was, it seemed, solved. Markowitz's contribution to investment theory was to embed in a mathematical model the age-old intuition that it is better to diversify your investments—not to "put all your eggs in one basket."

Nice, but Can You Actually Use It?

Not only did Markowitz's theory show clearly and mathematically why it is better not to put all your eggs in one basket, but it also appeared to provide a precise algorithm to tell you exactly where to put those eggs. A computerized algorithm—given the expected returns, standard deviations, and correlation coefficients of all securities—would calculate the optimal portfolio.

But where is one to get all those numbers? There are upward of 6,300 stocks of U.S. companies and thousands upon thousands of bonds, not to mention securities of other countries and investment vehicles like real estate investments and commodities.

The set of correlation coefficients between all 6,300-plus U.S. stocks alone comprises about 20 million numbers. And, of course, the algorithm also needs their 6,300 expected returns and 6,300 standard deviations. Where can one get all these numbers?

One way to obtain these numbers is to use the historical standard deviations and correlation coefficients. Analysts running Markowitz's mean-variance optimization algorithm also tried using historical returns to forecast future expected returns, even though historical returns are no good at forecasting future returns.

Armed with this vast quantity of historical data, analysts set about running Markowitz's mean-variance optimization algorithm.

Yes, You Can Use It in Your Sales Pitch

The results were utter chaos. If you only used historical numbers, you'd get absurd results. For example, it might tell you to invest 100 percent of your portfolio in Amazon.com or in Hong Kong stocks. Often these results were plainly opposite to what the theory was supposed to tell you—not to put all your eggs in one basket.

If you are a modern investment manager or advisor, you use mean-variance optimizers now mainly as part of your salesman's pitch. You assert that you use "sophisticated algorithms" and "Nobel Prize–winning technology" to perform asset allocation and portfolio optimization.

But all it would take is a little investigation into the way the process actually works—an investigation that few people outside the industry ever conduct—to find out the truth. If the mean-variance optimizer is even run on a computer at all, its inputs are doctored, and it is run only to obtain a predetermined result. No other form of use is possible—the problem of obtaining meaningful inputs, independent of the desired outputs, is too great.

Taking Markowitz's Theory to Its Logical Conclusion

This may seem a big disappointment. But, often, the ultimate conclusion of a mathematical theory will not be obtained if one tries to apply it too quickly, before the logic has been pursued to its bitter end. In the case of Markowitz's model, people raced to use it to perform calculations that proved in practice to be duds. But it required taking only one little step more with the theory to reach its inevitable conclusion, a conclusion that could be applied in practice with little or no need for complicated calculations.

Nobel Prize winners James Tobin and William F. Sharpe (of whom you will hear again shortly) soon discovered where Markowitz's theory ultimately leads.[2] What his theory says is that if there really are true values for all those expected returns, standard deviations, and correlation coefficients—and if you and other investors knew what they were—then, given your preference for risk, you could calculate the exact optimal portfolio, the one you should invest in.

Note that this portfolio would be *the same portfolio*—the optimal one—for all investors.

If everyone should have the same portfolio, what must that portfolio be? The only way all investors can have the same portfolio is if all of them hold a cross section of the market as a whole—that is, if they all hold the market portfolio.

This is the inevitable end point of Markowitz's theoretical arguments. The end point is not that you should cast your net in hopes of harvesting estimates of upward of twenty million numbers, which you can then feed into a complicated algorithm. That's not taking the theory to its logical conclusion. No, the logical conclusion is simply that if those numbers exist, then *everyone should invest in the market portfolio*. The market portfolio is the one that holds all the stocks in the market in the same proportions as they exist in the market.

Indexing

In the late 1960s and early 1970s, realizing that a market portfolio was the theoretical end point of Markowitz's theories, a few investment professionals at different institutions set about creating portfolios to replicate the market. These portfolios were called *index funds*. The practice of creating such portfolios was called *indexing*.

The initial efforts were motivated more by theoretical considerations—by the argument that the optimum portfolio on a risk/return basis is the market portfolio—than by cost. The first index fund was created by investment managers William Fouse and John McQuown of Wells Fargo Bank for the Denver-based suitcase and traveling gear manufacturer Samsonite Corporation's $6 million pension fund.

Unfortunately, the first fund did not weight the stocks the same as they were weighted in the market. It tried to include all stocks listed on the New York Stock Exchange. To include all of them in a $6 million fund, and to weight them as they are weighted in the market, would have meant investing only a few cents in some stocks, while investing hundreds of thousands of dollars in others. This was impractical. The alternative they fell back on was to equal-weight them, though it departed in a major way from the theory and had other major drawbacks. Yet the Wells Fargo managers found they still had to deal with too many stocks for the relatively small, $6 million portfolio.

Because they realized it would be too difficult to try to replicate the whole stock market without an extremely large portfolio to invest, Fouse and McQuown devised an alternative strategy. The stocks in the S&P 500 index were all large (i.e., their capitalizations—the total values of their shares outstanding—were large). Together, at that time, they constituted about 80 percent of the stock market's value. So to replicate only the S&P 500 would come reasonably close to replicating the entire stock market and would be easier in practice.

Two additional investment managers in the early 1970s, Boston's Batterymarch Financial Management and Chicago's American National Bank, decided to launch index funds. Then in 1974 John Bogle founded the Vanguard Corporation with a not-for-profit structure, dedicating it to the principle that costs should be kept as low as possible, and launched Vanguard's S&P 500 index fund.

After a long start-up period, many (but far from all) investors realized that index fund investing made sense. The realization was fueled in no small part by the performance record that Vanguard's S&P 500 Index Trust built up, beating 85 percent of all mutual funds.[3] Now, Vanguard's S&P fund is one of the two or three largest mutual funds in the United States, with about $70 billion in assets. Because of the now-larger size of mutual funds and new operating efficiencies, Vanguard was later able to start another index fund—the Total Market index fund—finally achieving the ideal of replicating the entire U.S. stock market. (Vanguard has an index fund that replicates the total domestic U.S. stock market and another that approximates the total international—that is, non-U.S.—market.)

An index fund has three all-important advantages: it offers the investor the theoretical maximum expected return for its level of risk; it charges the lowest fees; and because of its low turnover, it keeps commissions to a minimum as well as taxes when investments are in a taxable account.

It's That Simple

I would be the last to say that just because a mathematical theory of investment tells you to do something, like invest in an index fund, you should run right out and do it. That would be an example of the "scientism" justly frowned on by Hayek.

My reason for explaining Markowitz's theory and its logical conclusion is not to argue that it should be immediately applied. Rather, it is to show that Nobel Prize–winning theory is very simple.

The "sophisticated applications" of the theory sold by investment advisors and managers are deliberately overcomplicated, the better to sell you a high-priced product. They turn out to be roundabout ways of constructing for you an indexlike investment portfolio—but at a much, much higher cost than for an index fund.

The foremost reason for investing in an index fund or any similarly well-diversified, low-cost equity investment vehicle is not because of a complicated theory. It is merely that *its cost is low compared with its value.*

Now let's extend the theory by exploring the difficult concept of risk.

12

There's No Such Thing as a Free Lunch

. . . .

I begin this chapter by changing everything I said so far. I said you couldn't beat the market, except by chance—especially after the fees charged by investment managers and advisors.

Now I say, "You want to beat the market? OK, you can." Not only can you beat the market, but it's very easy to do. Here's how. Go out and borrow some money. If you want to beat the market by a lot, borrow a lot of money. Invest it in the stock market.

Consider an example (see Exhibit 12.1 on page 150). Suppose your investment portfolio is $200,000. If you invest that in the stock market, let's say you can expect, in the long run, about an 8 percent return annually. Let's say you invest it for two years in the stock market for a return of 16 percent.

Now assume you can borrow $50,000 at 4 percent interest. Invest that in stocks on top of the $200,000. Your investment portfolio is still worth $200,000—that hasn't changed, because you've got $250,000 invested in the stock market, but you have to subtract $50,000 for the debt you owe.

But now instead of getting the stock market rate of return of 16 percent over the two years, you get a stock market–beating return of 18 percent.

Why? Well, now that you've got $250,000 invested in the stock market ($200,000 of your own and $50,000 borrowed), your 16 percent return will give you $40,000

Exhibit 12.1 The Miracle of Leverage

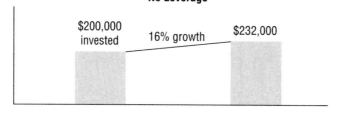

No Leverage

$200,000 invested   16% growth $232,000

25% Leverage
($50,000 borrowed on $200,000)

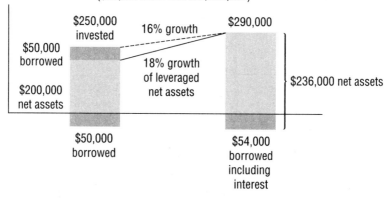

$50,000 borrowed

$200,000 net assets

$250,000 invested   16% growth $290,000

18% growth of leveraged net assets

$236,000 net assets

$50,000 borrowed

$54,000 borrowed including interest

200% Leverage
($400,000 borrowed on $200,000)

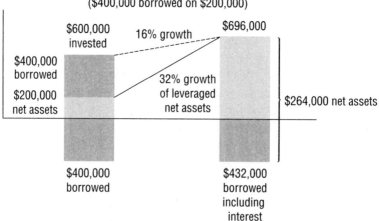

$400,000 borrowed

$200,000 net assets

$600,000 invested   16% growth $696,000

32% growth of leveraged net assets

$264,000 net assets

$400,000 borrowed

$432,000 borrowed including interest

return on the $250,000 invested. But you've got to pay $4,000 interest for two years on your $50,000 4 percent loan. So your net intake is $40,000 less $4,000, or $36,000. On the $200,000 net assets that you actually own, a $36,000 gain is an 18 percent gain.

Is it magic? No, not at all. The word for it is *leverage*. You leverage your portfolio by borrowing. If you can borrow at an interest rate that is lower than your return on investment, you can increase your return. It's not at all unusual. Lots of risk-seeking hedge funds do it. If you borrow even more, you'll increase your return more.

Presto, you're beating the market. And in the long run you really will beat the market (if you're careful not to let your gains get eaten up by costs, of course) . . . provided you can last that long.

The More You Leverage, the Riskier It Is

Wait a minute—what do you mean, "provided you can last that long"?

Well, as we all know, the market goes up and down. You might get 8 percent in the long run, if the market lives up to expectations, but you'll have a bumpy ride along the way. And the more you leverage, the bumpier it gets.

In some years—as anyone with lengthy experience observing the stock market knows—you may experience an unpredictable drop of 20 percent. This is hard enough to take if you're not leveraged. But if you're leveraging $50,000 on your $200,000 portfolio, you'll be down 26 percent, not 20 percent (I won't go into this calculation, but it's not hard)—an even more jarring and unsettling event.

Furthermore, it's just possible that even if you are psychologically prepared to ride out the ups and downs, you may go broke on a down before you get to see the long run. And then there's some uncertainty about the return even in the long run. With leverage, there's more uncertainty; with a lot of leverage, there's a lot more. If the market's return turns out to be disappointing compared with expectations, it will be much worse if you're leveraged.

In short, the more you leverage, the better your long-run return is likely to be; but you take more risk also.

You See, There's No Free Lunch!

As economists like to put it in their jocular way (economics is not called "the dismal science" for nothing), "There's no such thing as a free lunch." What they mean is that if someone offers to take you to lunch, you can bet you'll wind up paying for it eventually. You're going to be softened up with a free lunch, then sold a deal you "can't refuse"—and you'll wind up paying in the end at least as much as the cost of the lunch.

That's what they mean about the lunch, anyway. What they mean about economics is that nothing is free—there's a price tag of some sort on everything. If it isn't a price tag in dollars and cents, then it's a price tag in extra effort, time expended, discomfort, or risk.

So in this sense leverage is a kind of good news/bad news joke: The good news is you'll get a better return in the long run. The bad news is your portfolio may not live to see the long run, because of the risk you'll take.

Of course, you can decide to take virtually no risk at all. If you invest in multiyear certificates of deposit or a U.S. Treasury note, you'll get a guaranteed return of something like 4 or 5 percent annualized, unless the entire U.S. economy—and probably the world's, too—falls apart.

This is the ideal of a *zero standard deviation*—no fluctuation or uncertainty at all in the return you'll get. But your return will be the bare minimum, the so-called risk-free rate.

Sharpe's Insight

Sharing the Nobel Prize in 1990 with Harry Markowitz was William F. Sharpe, a professor of finance at Stanford. His breakthrough, sometimes called the capital asset pricing model (CAPM) or, more broadly, modern portfolio theory (MPT), was that there is a "market price of risk." For each percent of expected return you get above the risk-free rate, you'll have to pay a proportionate amount in increased risk. There's no "free lunch."

You can get this increased expected return—and increased risk— by leveraging the market portfolio. Or you can get it by investing in a diversified nonmarket portfolio with risk greater than the market's. But according to Sharpe's theory, you can't get it by investing in an undiversified portfolio.

That is, if you increase the standard deviation of your return—its riskiness—merely by investing in one highly speculative stock that fluctuates wildly, that won't increase your expected return. Just taking risks with your money doesn't increase your long-run return. You need to invest in specific types of risk—the risk of innovative research, for example, or of trying to build a big production operation. You need to invest in the kind of risky venture that—if the venture proves successful—increases the useful output of society. You need to risk your capital for the purpose of improving productivity and creating wealth. And you need to diversify your risks. Just taking any risk—merely to take risk—doesn't increase your return.

For example, it's no use increasing your risk by "investing" in a lottery ticket or joining a midnight poker game with office associates. In the case of the lottery ticket you will actually reduce your expected return, because the lottery organizers take about half the proceeds. In the case of the poker game, it is a "zero-sum game"; that is, wealth will neither be created nor destroyed, in aggregate. Hence, you can't expect to increase your wealth just by taking the risk of playing (unless you know you are better than the other players).

You can't expect to increase your wealth in the long run by trading currency futures. Trading of currency futures is also a zero-sum game. If one side wins on a trade, the other side loses. The investment by both parties doesn't create wealth. One can expect to win only by being better than the other traders (and few, if any, are).

In other words, just taking risk for its own sake won't increase your return.

If you want expected return—and risk—that is greater than the stock market's, then you must first take the risk of investing in the market, then borrow or leverage that risk. And if you want risk that is less than the stock market's risk, you must combine your stock portfolio with some lower-risk bonds or bank accounts.

Deciding How Much Risk to Take

Thus, in theory at least, you are reduced to a single degree of freedom in the choice of your portfolio: the choice of risk level. If you can take more risk, you'll get a better return than the market in the long run (before fees and taxes!). If you can't take much risk, you'll get a return that is less than the market's.

There is no scientific or precise way to make the risk decision, but historical statistics can provide a guide. Information about how much you're likely to gain over the long run, and how much you could lose in the short run, can help. For example, the historical figures might say that over twenty years with an all-stock portfolio, you have a good chance of getting an 8 percent annual return. But in some year along the way you're likely to lose 20 percent of your assets, all at once.

Can you stand that? If not, then perhaps you'll be more comfortable with a 50-50 stock–bond portfolio that is likely to give you 6 percent a year, but the worst year might be down only 8 percent.

Then it's up to you to choose. How much risk to take in order to increase your chance of reward is one of those existential decisions in life that we wish someone could tell us how to make—but it's up to us, ourselves, alone, to decide.

The Greeks

I would not be doing a complete job covering Nobel Prize–winning investment theories if I didn't talk about the Greeks. No, I don't mean the people who live by the Aegean Sea. I mean the letters from their alphabet. These letters are used frequently in mathematical formulas.

As I pointed out earlier, mathematicians—at least theoretical mathematicians—don't use numbers. We use symbols, symbols that may stand for numbers. As anyone who took high school algebra knows, you begin with letters from the English alphabet—letters like x—to stand for numbers. But after a while you run out of English letters. So you use other alphabets, like Greek and Hebrew.

People in the field that has come to be called financial engineering —MPT plus theories for pricing derivative securities—often speak of "the Greeks." What they mean are the Greek letters, the mathematical details—as in, "We can put the Greeks into that later; let's just explore the intuition right now."

The most important Greeks in MPT are μ (mu), σ (sigma), ρ (rho), and β (beta). Mu is the expected return on a stock or a portfolio, sigma is the standard deviation, and rho is the correlation between two securities or portfolios of securities.

Then there's beta. Beta is the measure of the risk of a portfolio compared with the total stock market portfolio. A total market index fund has a beta of one. The leveraged portfolio in our earlier example —where you borrowed $50,000 to leverage a $200,000 stock portfolio—has a beta of 1.25. A 50-50 stock–bond portfolio has a beta of 0.5.

If a portfolio of stocks has a beta greater than one, it will—by Sharpe's CAPM theory—have an expected return greater than the market's. Therefore, it will—at least in theory—beat the market in the long run (not counting fees!); but it has proportionately more risk than the market, too.

Beta Encapsulates the Risk Decision

The decision what beta to have is the decision how much risk to take, how much to leverage the portfolio, how much to invest in stocks versus bonds.

If the risk-free rate is 4 percent and the expected return on the stock market is 8 percent, then we say the "risk premium" is 4 percent (the market's expected return less the risk-free rate). If your beta is one, then your risk level and expected return are the same as the market's. Hence, your expected risk premium will be 4 percent, like the market's. The expected return on your portfolio will be 8 percent, like the market's. If the market's standard deviation is 16 percent, then yours will be 16 percent also.

But if your beta is two, your portfolio is twice as risky as the market, your risk premium will be twice as high, too. You would have a beta of two, for example, if you borrowed enough to double your investment in stocks. Then your expected risk premium will be twice the market's, or 8 percent, and your portfolio's expected return will be 12 percent—the riskless rate of four plus the risk premium of eight. Your portfolio's standard deviation or "risk" will be 32 percent— twice the market's.

And if your beta is 0.5, or one-half, then you are half as risky as the market. This could happen if you invested half your money in the stock market and half in low-risk bonds. Your risk premium will be only half that of the market—or 2 percent—so your expected return will be the risk-free rate plus 2 percent, or 6 percent all told. Your portfolio's standard deviation or "risk" will be 8 percent—half the market's.

Where, Oh, Where Is Alpha?

Then there's α, or alpha. Alpha is just a little number, a symbol in a formula, a symbol that stands for a number.

But alpha is . . . oh, so much more than that! Alpha is the Holy Grail! Alpha is what every money manager, every investment advisor, every investor seeks. Alpha is what every money manager claims.

But alpha has a dark little secret; a secret that is swept under the rug, unseen and unknown; a secret that nobody ever mentions in good company—though occasionally, it is alluded to fleetingly by those in the know.

Alpha is the percentage by which a money manager or a portfolio beats a risk-adjusted market index. It is supposed to be positive; that is, money management is supposed to add something over and above a market index. But the dark little secret is that alpha is—for the vast majority of money managers—*negative*. Furthermore, when it is occasionally positive, it appears to be no more than a random event, an accident.

In Fumaria, alpha was the amount by which a cigarette reduced cancer below the rate for nonsmokers. It is not likely to be positive very often, and when positive, only by accident.

Articles occasionally appear in technical finance journals—written by prominent and bold authors who have won their stars in the profession and thus the right to speak plainly—with titles like "Is Your Alpha Big Enough to Cover Your Fees?" (Or, ". . . Your Taxes?") The answer is invariably no.

But there's always a little wiggle room left. No, your alpha hasn't been big enough. That just means you've got to work harder or find a new formula. The articles never conclude by saying, "Therefore, the vast majority of you out there should quit what you're doing without success, for such high fees, and go out and seek honest work." The articles don't say, "Therefore, you honest professionals should call up your clients and tell them that because you can't gain for them anything approaching what you cost them, you are taking down your shingle."

It's the Whole Ball of Wax

Having strayed with the Greeks into what may sound like "sophisticated, Nobel Prize–winning" lingo and arithmetic, let me now reiterate that you don't need it. In particular, you certainly don't need to pay someone who knows it or claims to know it, and you don't need to know it yourself—though if you do, perhaps it will make you feel better about making your own decisions.

My main purpose in being thorough describing the theory is to let you know that what I've said is pretty much the whole ball of wax. It's not that complicated, and it's not that important. You've got to make a decision how much risk you can stand to take—how much of your portfolio to invest in stocks—but there's no precise way to do it. In the end you just have to pick a number and take the plunge. You can look up some historical statistics in any one of a number of reputable books, and you can look at any one of a number of Web sites, such as mutual fund Web sites (but don't let that make you invest in the mutual funds if their fees are too high). It's an important decision, and it might be nice to have someone help you, even if they charge for their help. But at fees prevailing in the industry, whatever financial value the help may provide will be eaten up many times over by fees.

So Here's What You Should Do

Pay no attention to the advisors. The Markowitz-Sharpe theory says what to do. It says to first decide on an equity portfolio, which should be a broadly diversified portfolio—that is, an index fund (or perhaps more than one index fund, if needed for broad diversification). Then decide on the division between equities (stocks) and debt instruments—that is, bonds (this could mean, if you're especially aggressive, a negative investment in debt—in other words, borrowing or leveraging).

If you're investing for the long run (twenty years or more) and if you're psychologically able to overlook—that is, to ignore—the ups and downs (particularly the downs), then this division could be 90 percent equities and 10 percent bonds, or even more in equities.

If you're investing for only ten to fifteen years or are squeamish about ups and downs, a 50-50 mix may be for you.

And if you're investing for five years or less or think you'll panic and sell whenever your portfolio goes down, you should probably just forget equities.

Then invest the equity portion of your portfolio in the lowest-cost, most broadly diversified equity market portfolio. The most broadly diversified portfolio includes not only U.S. stocks but also international stocks and real estate.

Here's a good model equity portfolio for you: 60 percent U.S. domestic stocks, 30 percent non-U.S. stocks, and 10 percent REITs (real estate investment trusts).

For the most diversified, lowest-cost U.S. domestic funds, you can choose among Fidelity Spartan total market fund, Vanguard's total market fund, iShares Dow Jones U.S. Total Market Index Fund,[1] TIAA-CREF's equity index fund, and a few others. If you're inclined toward "social responsibility," you could even go slightly off the most broadly diversified option but still have low cost with TIAA-CREF's Social Equity fund.

For the most diversified, lowest-cost non-U.S. funds, you can choose among Fidelity Spartan and Vanguard's total international funds, and perhaps one or two others. And for REITs you can choose among Vanguard, iShares, and others. For the bonds you can use an intermediate-bond fund with a low expense ratio (i.e., low cost), like Vanguard's intermediate-term bond index.

If you really feel you want to have your own personal financial advisor, find a low-cost one that retails the mutual fund investment products of low-cost index fund providers like Dimensional Fund Advisors, in addition to the funds already mentioned.

Revisit the mix every couple of years to see whether your percentages have changed and you want to readjust them to suit your investment horizon—which may have changed—or because you've changed your attitude toward risk. Don't do anything, otherwise.

I suspect, though, that if you do drop in out of curiosity to check out a high-cost investment advisor or manager—even armed with the information I've provided you—they'll make you wonder whether it's true. They'll make you wonder whether you shouldn't hire an expensive advisor after all to recommend to you the best investments. These people are accomplished sales professionals. They're experts at it. And they're so well supported by the Big Investment Lie—the lie that is all around us—they can feel confident in their ability to convince you, even if what they're saying makes no sense and is contradicted by all the evidence.

13

Investment Genius or the Thousandth Coin?

Whenever anyone says that beating the stock market is purely a matter of luck, not skill, it always seems to produce the same response. It's as if people had been scripted to say it.

"Then how do you explain Peter Lynch and Warren Buffett?"

Because of this almost universal script reading, it verges on heresy to suggest that Warren Buffett and Peter Lynch might have been merely lucky. It would be like saying that Abraham Lincoln, without really having any idea what he was doing, sacrificed six hundred thousand American soldiers to grisly deaths by refusing to grant the southern states their request to secede from the Union. Luckily for Abe, it turned out OK in the end.

Once someone is lionized and firmly enshrined in the public legend, it is simply not allowed to say anything that could erode that legend. There is a simple difference, though, between Abraham Lincoln, on the one hand, and Peter Lynch and Warren Buffett, on the other. We can't measure statistically how effective Lincoln was. We can't measure his performance against what might have happened without him or against any benchmarks. We only know the positive results—that slavery in the United States was summarily ended and that the reunified nation grew to become one of the most prosperous and democratic in the world.

We do not know whether any of this would have happened anyway—or perhaps something even better—if it hadn't been for Lincoln. We can't know, and we'll never know. We have no clear theoretical framework even to evaluate the question. Thus, our conclusion that Lincoln's resolve was a decisive force in world events cannot be submitted to any precise test.

It's a different matter with Peter Lynch's and Warren Buffett's investment performance. This is not a question of whether Buffett is a fine corporate manager or whether Lynch was extremely diligent in pursuing his objectives. Both men are firmly ensconced on their pedestals; they will remain there, because of the examples they set of wisdom and hard work. By the same token, the Beardstown Ladies, too, should have remained on their pedestals even after their calculation error made the news.

But whether the Fidelity Magellan mutual fund under Lynch's management or the Berkshire Hathaway portfolio under Buffett's direction performed so much better than the market that it couldn't have been mere luck—or that their performance could have been somehow predicted or anticipated—is a question that can be answered. It's a simple statistical question, with a simple statistical answer.

The Thumbnail Histories of Peter Lynch and Warren Buffett

For those who do not know the stories of Peter Lynch or Warren Buffett, I'll give a brief summary.

Peter Lynch

Peter Lynch started in 1969 as a research analyst at the Fidelity mutual fund company in Boston at the age of twenty-five. He was promoted to director of research in 1974 and then took over management of the Fidelity Magellan fund in 1977. At the time, the Magellan fund had $22 million in assets. Lynch continued to manage the fund until May 31, 1990, when he decided to hand over the reins. By that time, the Magellan fund was valued at $14 billion.

From 1977 to 1983, the Magellan fund racked up spectacular stock market performance. It beat the S&P 500 index by an average of over 20 percent per year. After that, money poured into the fund from new investors who learned of its outstanding performance. Unfortunately, in the years Lynch continued to manage the fund, following the huge influx of new funds from people who noticed how well it had performed, its performance was not spectacular. In 1984–1990, the fund managed only to keep pace with the index. After Lynch retired in 1990, the fund more often underperformed the index than not; but, like Fumarian cigarette brands with once-benchmark-beating cancer rates, its reputation lived on. It continued to be one of the largest mutual funds in the world, earning its managers billions of dollars in fees.

Lynch's legendary performance from 1977 to 1983 set him up for life, and undoubtedly for long after that, as one of the greatest investment gurus who ever lived. Solely because of his spectacular performance during that time (though on a very small asset base), the historical average rate of return over time on the Magellan fund continued to be outstanding. Because the vast majority of the money invested in the fund poured in after that period, however, the average dollar invested in it has not actually outperformed market averages. That fact has been lost in the shuffle of celebrity worship.

Warren Buffett

Warren Buffett's outstanding record has been far more enduring. He has been investing successfully for over fifty years. For most of that time his investment performance can be thoroughly documented.[1]

Buffett started his investment career by buying six shares of Cities Service stock (an oil company) in 1941 at age eleven. After college at the University of Nebraska, he received a master's degree in business administration at Columbia University. At Columbia, he studied with Benjamin Graham and David Dodd, the authors of a highly respected book on fundamental stock analysis. He then worked for two years for Graham's New York investment partnership until Graham's retirement in 1956, whereupon Buffett returned to Nebraska.

Buffett's career history since returning from New York to Nebraska in 1956 is a superb record of investment success. He organized investment partnerships and raised about $100,000 from family and friends to invest in them. He later added additional partners. Between his investments with his partners and his own investments, he accumulated a net worth of over a million dollars in 1962, just over the age of thirty.

In 1962, the Buffett partnerships began to buy stock in a small textile manufacturer in Massachusetts named Berkshire Hathaway. His partnerships soon became the largest shareholders in Berkshire Hathaway and in 1965 took control of the company. In the late 1960s, Buffett dissolved his partnerships and transformed his and his partners' investments to stock in Berkshire Hathaway. Berkshire thus became the holding company for all the partnerships' assets.

Buffett is in virtually all respects a model for most of the practices this book recommends. He believes in buying and holding stocks for the long run. In his investment business he holds costs to a minimum. His investment portfolio is the result of active stock picking, not of passively replicating the market, but the cost for active management is very low. True, he does violate the principle of broad diversification. He holds only a small number of stocks. But this makes sense given his belief that only a very few undervalued stocks exist at any one time.

A measure of how low Buffett's cost is can be found in the way his wealth itself has accumulated. All of that wealth accumulation since the 1960s can be accounted for by the return Buffett realized on his own investments—the same investments he chose for his stockholders. None of his wealth during that time came from overcharging his partners and clients and thus reducing their return. The return Buffett realized was the same return they realized. To the extent he charged them for management, the charge was very reasonable. He accumulated more in total than they did because he had more of his own assets invested in the beginning and because he was invested for a very long time. Buffett's long-term average annual return on investment has been about 27 percent, depending on the time period measured. At that rate, his million dollars in 1962 grew, solely by the miracle of compounding, to about $40 billion in the years since.

Was It Predictable?

It is tempting to say that Buffett is the true exception—perhaps the exception that proves the rule. Buffett seemed to know what he was doing and to exercise skill. He never fell victim to scientism. In fact, he is an ardent advocate against it.

But we still must ask the question: Given all we know about the statistics of all managers' investment performance and about Buffett's performance, was it *predictable* that Buffett's stellar performance would continue? Is it predictable that it will continue now? (His Berkshire Hathaway did, in fact, underperform market indexes in 2003, 2004 and 2005.) Or is it a phenomenon that can only be known after the fact, not before?

Both Buffett's and Lynch's investment philosophies have been in accord with what Friedrich Hayek would have recommended and with what the Beardstown Ladies applied. All three investors—Buffett, Lynch, and the Beardstown Ladies—practiced a stock-picking methodology uninfected by scientism. They all traded using only the tidbits of information that they knew or could gather by diligent observation rather than grand mathematical theories. Then, they let compounding and the long run do the rest of the work for them.

But however laudable Buffett's investment practice is—and it is unimpeachably laudable—our immediate task is to answer this question: Could he have just been lucky? Could he have been just a regular guy from Omaha who merely got lucky—but a guy imbued with the virtues of hard work and thrift, so that he would not squander away his luck?

This is, in fact, the image that Buffett himself cultivates. Could it be that he just got luckier in his stock picking than thousands of other similar guys and gals from Louisville, Weehawken, Jackson, Moline, Fresno, Nashville, Charlotte, Albuquerque, Yakima, Missoula, Bismarck, and hundreds of other places where people try to get rich through investing?

The Statistical Analysis

This question is a statistical question. It has a clear-cut statistical answer. The question can be answered in more than one way. I'll consider each of the ways. I'll focus on Buffett's performance because it has been of much longer duration than Lynch's and is, therefore, far more statistically compelling.

I shall look at Buffett's performance in three ways:

- assuming a naive investor has a 50-50 chance of beating the market each year,

- assuming Buffett's chance of beating the market was greater than 50-50 because his risk was higher, and

- evaluating the size of the margin by which he beat the market.

A 50-50 Chance of Beating the Market Each Year

If beating the market is random and there's a 50-50 chance of doing it, then beating the market average is like conducting a coin-tossing experiment. Any year—any time period at all, for that matter, such as a month—the chances of beating the market are 50-50, like the chances of getting heads on a coin toss.

If you toss a coin over and over, you are likely to get some heads and some tails. The chance of getting ten heads in a row is about one in a thousand (actually, one in 1,024). So if you take a thousand coins and toss each one ten times, it is probable that one of them will come up heads ten times. That coin is the "lucky" one. It doesn't mean it's loaded (though, of course, it could be). It just means that one of the coins was probably going to come up heads ten times in a row, and that happens to be the one.

A statistical analysis would conclude, "The fact that that particular coin came up heads ten times in a row can easily be explained by the hypothesis that all the coins, on all the tosses, had a 50-50 chance of coming up heads."

On the other hand, if you tossed each of the thousand coins fifty times and one of them came up heads forty-nine times, the answer would be very different. The chance of getting as many as forty-nine heads on fifty tosses is only one in twenty-two trillion. Therefore, the same statistical analysis would say, "The fact that that particular coin came up heads forty-nine times out of fifty *cannot* be explained by the hypothesis that all the coins, on all the tosses, had a 50-50 chance of coming up heads. The only reasonable explanation is that the coin is loaded."

The chances of any number of heads or tails can be calculated statistically. Then based on the probability of occurrence of whatever actually happened, you can accept or reject the hypothesis of randomness.

Over the thirty-five years from 1966 through 2000, Buffett's Berkshire Hathaway stock beat the S&P 500 index twenty-three times. The likelihood that could have happened by chance is one in twenty-two. So it would take twenty-two Warren Buffett–like clones, investing for thirty-five years in twenty-two places like Omaha, Nebraska, for one of them to beat the market as often as Buffett did. Obviously, the other twenty-one wouldn't have become as rich or famous.

There were certainly a lot more than twenty-two people during those thirty-five years trying to beat the stock market as often as Buffett did. He happened to be one who actually did it. The hypothesis of randomness cannot be rejected on this basis.

This may be a surprising conclusion, given all the hype and given many statements that are often heard to the contrary. Nonetheless, the conclusion is inescapable.[2]

Risk-Adjusted Chance of Beating the Market Each Year

If you take more risk than the market, you'll have a better than even chance of beating the market. By all the standard measures, Warren Buffett took more than the average market risk. This was because he specialized in what are called "distressed companies"—companies that the market believed were in a bad way but that Buffett thought would recover. Stocks in this category are generally riskier. Buffett's risk was equivalent to investing one borrowed dollar for every three that he actually had. Another way of saying this is that his risk level was equivalent to leveraging by 33⅓ percent—or to having a beta of 1.33.

With the amount of risk Buffett took, his chances of beating the stock market in any given year were not 50-50 but about 54-46. Given that fact, his twenty-three years of beating the market out of thirty-five were even less unlikely. The chances of performing that well become only one in nine.

Risk-Adjusted Chance of Beating the Market by as Much as Buffett Did

The previous two analyses don't really capture the whole feat. Buffett's claim to stock market performance fame is not only that he beat the market in a lot of years but that he beat the market by a wide margin.

Again, standard analysis techniques can assess how likely it is to beat the market as much as Buffett did, given the risk he took. Different analysts will obtain different results, because methods vary and the time period analyzed varies.

I'll present the results of one analysis of the performance of Berkshire Hathaway stock over the thirty-four-year time period of 1967–2000.[3] Merely tracking the market over that time period with 33⅓ percent leverage would have resulted in an annual return of 13.7 percent. Berkshire Hathaway's return was 26.2 percent—a premium of 12.5 percent per year. How likely is it that could have happened at random?

Given the high level of variability, or volatility (i.e., standard deviation), of Berkshire stock, the chance that such a result could have happened by sheer luck is about one in 250.[4] This may make it seem an unlikely result, but remember that there were undoubtedly far, far more than 250 Warren Buffett wannabes trying to beat the stock market during the same time period. It was inevitable, even if there was nothing involved but sheer luck, that at least one hypothetical investor would do as well as the real Warren Buffett.

Anyone Could Do It

Buffett's results were due in large part simply to the miracle of compounding and the long-run benefit of taking risk. Anybody could have done extremely well, at the very least, given Buffett's qualities of fortitude, patience, and thrift. Even without Buffett's skill or luck, whichever it may have been, an ordinary, average investor could have accumulated vast quantities of wealth by applying the same basic virtues that Buffett did. And if you were one of the very few among the virtuous who also happened to be unusually lucky—or perhaps skillful—in picking companies to invest in, you would, like Buffett, have done extraordinarily well.

It's a simple matter of numbers. Buffett worked hard as a young man and saved, selling newspapers as a teenager and investing his earnings in farmland and other small ventures. He then worked for two years for Graham on Wall Street at a good salary for the time, $12,000. He spent little, and he saved and invested. By 1955 at the age of twenty-five, Buffett had accumulated $140,000. His career as manager of his own and others' investments then began for real.

Suppose you—or any Joe in Omaha, or Paducah, or Davenport, or anywhere—were age twenty-five in 1955 and had accumulated $140,000 by working hard and saving. Then for the next fifty years you invested in the stock market, but you took a chance on riskier stocks. Anyone who leveraged his risk as much as Buffett did but, unlike Buffett, merely matched the market over the next fifty years would have realized an annual return of about 15 percent. At that rate you would have watched your $140,000 accumulate to over $150 million.

Say, instead, you practiced the same virtues but rather than having only average luck—or skill, as the case may be—you were that special one in a hundred, or one in a thousand, the thousandth coin. Then, like Buffett, you'd have accumulated tens of billions.

Whether It's Skill or Luck Isn't the Point— It's Whether It's Predictable

I seem to be saying that Warren Buffett was nothing special, just an ordinary guy with good character who got lucky. Why should I try to put Buffett down in this way? Why should I insist that he was merely lucky, that it wasn't skill at all?

That's not really what I'm doing. The issue isn't skill or luck. The issue is *predictability*.

It's entirely possible—and difficult not to believe—that Buffett's performance was due to a keen intuitive insight, accompanied by disciplined analysis, hard work, and a strong sense of value. Its spectacular end results were most certainly due, at the very least, to Buffett's cardinal virtues of thrift, patience, and fortitude.

But could anyone have predicted that Buffett would do so well? And even after he had done very well, could anyone have predicted that he would continue to do so well? Can it be predicted now that he will continue to outperform the stock market by a wide margin? Can it, by extension, be predicted that any money manager will outperform the market?

The answer is simply no. Whether the gift that enables certain people who outperform the market for a time is skill or luck, on the whole the gift does not predictably repeat or sustain itself. The ability to outperform the market might be a skill that is matched only to certain situations, time periods, and events—a specifically tailored skill that is exactly what is needed in certain narrowly defined circumstances. Or it might just be luck. There's no way to tell.

But what is certain is that it is not possible to predict whether this luck or skill, as the case may be, will continue. The chances that market-beating performance will continue are like the chances of heads on a coin toss, no matter who tosses it and what his past history was. Whatever has been the previous result—ten heads in a row or what have you—you still can't predict the next result.

It is absolutely certain that the occurrence of a Warren Buffett, or a Peter Lynch, is no argument that an investor should pay exorbitant amounts to some manager or advisor on the hope of far outperforming the market. On the contrary, Warren Buffett is a shining example of the benefit of keeping costs low.

PART III

HOW YOU ARE SOLD

14

Effective Pitches to Sell the Big Lie

. . . .

When I was a teenager, I had an experience that was very valuable even though I would never dream of doing anything like it again.

I was a door-to-door salesman. I sold magazine subscriptions. Almost everyone has had a magazine subscription salesperson come to the door. It's often a young person, someone in high school or college. It was hard work, but educational and financially rewarding. In one of my summers of magazine sales, I contributed from my earnings about $1,800 in today's dollars to my college education. I was proud of it.

But it was a very strange experience. It was not, I think, a good way to cultivate respect for one's fellow man.

The team was composed of two tiers of salespeople: the managers and the crew. Typically the crew consisted of high school kids, while the managers were college students or at least boys or men older than high school age. Two middle-aged men back at the office assigned us the neighborhood we would work in. Sometimes they gave us a car to use, and they paid us if we made sales.

I started as a high school student, in the summer between my junior and senior years. The job of the crew was to knock on doors in middle- and lower-middle-class suburbs and ask people to check off which magazines they wanted. The pitch was that if they bought one magazine (*The Saturday Evening Post*) for a quarter, they would get three more of their choice for free.

Of course, most people just said they weren't interested. You'd have to knock on at least twenty or thirty doors before you could get anyone to fill out a card.

Most of the kids who showed up to work lasted only a couple of days. They'd get little or no response, and they would give up. The crew and the managers got paid only for making a sale, so if you made no sales you wouldn't get paid.

But every once in a while some kid would show up who was a natural. I never figured out just what characteristics went into making a natural. One of the naturals was a fresh-faced, always grinning, very thin, red-haired boy who would just beam at whoever opened the door and chirp, "Which ones do you want free?" For reasons I didn't really understand, you could see the people were about to say, "I'm not interested." Then something in them would say, "Ah, what the heck—this looks like a nice kid. It's no big deal."

But there were others who didn't grin and in no way resembled the fresh-faced natural, yet they were naturals, too. The only thing the naturals had in common, I think, was that you felt they assumed you would sign up, and they wouldn't quite know what to say if you didn't.

Once the boy on the crew got a prospect to fill out a card, he would chat with the person in a friendly way and then leave, always saying the same thing as he left: "Oh, by the way, my manager might come by to check up on me. Would you please tell him I did a good job?"

I was a long way from a natural, but I stuck with it for the summer. I did OK. After a while you got a sort of an intuition about things. You could tell who was more likely to respond from some of the signs.

One good sign was if a house was set back from the road, so you had to walk down a little longer path to get to the door. This was good because it meant that the lazier magazine salespeople who had been there before—most of these neighborhoods had been hit several times—might not have bothered to go to the door.

Another sign was if someone opened the door and you could see lots of magazines perched in piles on shelves inside. You'd think this would mean they didn't need any more, but really it meant they had no sales resistance. You were in luck.

After my high school summer on the crew, I took a summer off from magazine sales to take another summer job, a job that (I was told) I got only because an uncle, an executive in the company, pulled strings for me. It was the worst job I ever had—very hard physical labor in a sooty, dirty warehouse, at a minimum wage that was reduced because it was a union shop, and I had to pay dues to the Teamsters Union. Though it was at least good physical conditioning, it left me with a hacking cough I couldn't get rid of.

Now I'm the Manager

So the next summer I went back to the magazine sales crew. Now I was a college student and a manager. The education began for real.

When the high school kid got a card filled out and said, "Oh, by the way, my manager might come by to check up on me. Would you please tell him I did a good job?" what he really meant was "My manager definitely *will* show up, and he will try to convert you to a four-year magazine subscription at a price higher than you want to pay."

I was now the manager, and that was my job—to start with the high school kid and the little card with three magazines checked off, and wind up getting the prospect to sign a very legal-looking green contract to pay every month for four years. Nobody really wanted to do this, so you had to use sales techniques. Learning these techniques on the job was an experience and a half.

The main problem was that the prospect was looking for an opening to say, "No, I don't want it." You had to get those openings closed before the prospect could say no.

After a large number of failures, you would realize that the places in your pitch where the prospect said, "No, I don't want it," were pretty much always the same. So you had to figure out something to say at each of those places to keep them from saying that.

For example, there was one place in my pitch where I could always be sure the prospect would say, "I don't want any prescriptions." No, that's not a misprint—they almost invariably said, "I don't want any prescriptions." These weren't the brightest and most literate people we were going after. So they usually said "prescriptions" when they meant "subscriptions."

We had been told by the bosses not to say, "This is not a subscription," because it *was* a subscription. Lying outright was outside the bounds. So, no problem, I simply learned to say at that point, "This is not a prescription."

To my initial astonishment, this worked. It got them past the opening, and I could continue. There was a slightly sheepish look they got when I said that. I'm sure what was happening was that they had a fleeting suspicion they had used the wrong word, and I was lightly mocking or patronizing them—which was true—but they were too embarrassed to dwell on it. So in a state of slight flusterment they let me continue. (A foreshadowing, I think, of what happens when a prospect sees an investment consultant, and the consultant talks about modern portfolio theory or sophisticated algorithms—which, of course, the prospect wouldn't understand.)

The second opening—the cause of my losing many a sale near the very end of my pitch until I figured out how to get past it—was when I drew the little legal-green contract out of my valise for them to sign. You could almost see the dotted line (like in the cartoons) suddenly shoot from the prospect's eye to the little contract, even though I was casually trying to bring it only very gradually into view. They would say something like, "I'm not signing any contracts!" and that would be the end of that.

What I discovered worked, I do not to this day understand. If I said with a little laugh as I casually and confidently drew out the contract, "This is for your protection so you don't get sued," all difficulties were almost invariably avoided. It beats me why. No one asked, "How on Earth does this protect *me*?" No one said, "Like hell it's for my protection—it's for the company's."

The salesperson's motto, I discovered, is "Whatever works, works."

The Sales Business of Investment Services

The investment services business is first and foremost a sales business. It focuses by far the largest part of its effort on determining what sales pitch the customer will buy and delivering that sales pitch. It uses a trial-and-error process, just as I did when I tried to close magazine subscription sales. Eventually it finds the best ways to package its products, the best lines to deliver, and the best arguments to make to convince prospects to sign up.

In the process, it finds out what sounds good to prospective clients, not necessarily what is strictly and precisely correct. If there's a little confusion in the communication process—if the advisor/ salesperson says something that could be intended to have one meaning ("This is not a prescription—ha, ha, just kidding") but could be interpreted by the prospect to have another meaning ("This is not a subscription"), well, if it works, if it puts the client at ease, if it makes the client feel comfortable, well, OK. It's a better presentation than I gave when I was seventeen years old and closing magazine subscription sales at people's front doors, but it's the same principle.

The methods used by the salespeople in the investment services business are so standardized that it's worth putting them in a list:

Sales Techniques to Sell Investment Services

1. Use facile figures.
2. Talk technical word salad.
3. Look respectable, earnest, and sincere.
4. Exploit the client's will to believe.
5. Move on—quickly—past objections.
6. Project that savvy look.
7. Be well prepared to co-opt counterarguments.
8. Have a new line—and a new product—always ready.
9. "Speak in tongues"—bleed the language of its meaning.
10. Emphasize your "sophisticated technology."

Use Facile Figures

One reason why it's so difficult to pin down the truth and chase off a lie in the investment business is the sheer volume of available statistics. Almost anything can be claimed using a carefully selected subset of those statistics. It's not even important to select your statistics carefully. Who is going to bother to check? Remember how many years the Beardstown Ladies "got away" with an incorrect statistic, one that could have been checked easily? And there are not enough in the way of "truth-in-advertising" laws (as there are for the pharmaceutical industry) to prevent the investment services business from presenting rigged statistics as fact.

Talk Technical Word Salad

Because there is so little constraint in the form of scientific review of sales claims and presentations, consultants and salespeople I have known in the investment field engage in astounding monologues of what I call "technical word salad," spiraling and self-elaborating fantasies piling technical words and statistics on top of more technical words and statistics, frequently making no sense at all—but the layman doesn't know that.

This process of verbal spiraling and self-elaboration is reminiscent of that wonderful old children's book by Dr. Seuss, *To Think That I Saw It on Mulberry Street.* This is a book written in the 1930s about a boy named Marco who ambles home from school and sees a droopy-looking horse and wagon wending its way down Mulberry Street.

Marco thinks he might tell his father about it, who will ask him what he saw on his way home. But then Marco thinks that's not really enough to tell about, maybe he'll dress it up a little. By the time he is approaching home, with wings on his feet, he has elaborated the story in his mind to the point where the vehicle and its accoutrements would do a dozen Cinderellas and their fairy godmothers proud.

As Marco runs in breathlessly to tell his father about the coach and four with the brass band and so forth that he saw on Mulberry Street, his bubble suddenly bursts. He sees his father with a stern look on his face, a strict authority figure Marco had almost forgotten about. When his father asks what he saw on his way home from school, Marco says, "Just a plain horse and wagon on Mulberry Street."

In the investment field, for lack of an authority that can effectively quash manufactured statistics and absurd tales of sophisticated technological and mathematical methodologies, the tale self-fantasizes on and on, without bounds.

Look Respectable, Earnest, and Sincere

This process is speeded along its way by the Big Investment Lie. Nearly everybody has bought into it to one degree or another. We all accept that these people—professional investment advisors and managers—are not sleazeballs trying to skin us for hundreds of thousands or millions of dollars for a worthless product. They are earnest, educated, and intelligent professionals who have our best interests at heart. As such, they tend to be given very wide latitude for making mistakes, uttering misstatements, and even saying things that aren't quite the whole truth, for the sake of a sale.

Exploit the Client's Will to Believe

We ourselves, the investors, would like very much in our heart of hearts to believe the Big Investment Lie. Just as people would like to believe that someday their ship will come in or they'll win the lottery, they would like to believe that the Big Investment Lie is true. They would like to believe that someone out there, somewhere, can make them rapidly rich through investing. I have suggested that the relationship between the investment advisor and the client is a mutual agreement to believe in magic. It is worth something to people to have such a relationship even if the reward is psychic, not monetary. People often have such relationships with their psychiatrists. But what they will pay investment advisors and managers for a relationship is ten or twenty times, or more, what they will pay a psychiatrist.

Move On—Quickly—Past Objections

Because of this general acceptance of the Big Investment Lie, the alacrity with which the industry can leap from each apparent failure to a new success is truly astonishing. Wall Street firms have somehow repeatedly survived nearly unscathed from revelations that should leave a firm's reputation in ruins.

Airlines and airplane manufacturers suffer a loss of business if one of their planes crashes or suffers a serious malfunction. But when it was found that (among other misadventures) consultants at Merrill Lynch advised the public fund of Orange County, California, to invest in highly risky securities, resulting in an enormous drop in the fund's value and the county becoming unable to make payments (but huge fees for Merrill Lynch), it hardly seemed to dent Merrill's advisory business. And later, when it was found that Merrill and other Wall Street firms recommended that clients purchase securities that its own brokers thought were wildly overpriced, it still did not seem to jeopardize their business. The firms just increased the onslaught of advertising in two-page magazine spreads, television commercials, and billboards, adding more layers to the Big

Investment Lie: "We know how to make money in investment and you don't."

Project That Savvy Look

The fact that many prominent research studies, accepted authorities, and even news stories contradict this line doesn't seem to matter much. The Big Investment Lie is a part of the ambient cultural environment. The investment advisory community needs only to put the face and suit of a savvy-looking investment professional on a billboard or in a magazine spread. A mere glimpse seems to hypnotize investors into seeking the advice of that man (or woman) and his firm.

Be Well Prepared to Co-opt Counterarguments

And if some simplifying approach gains credence—if some investment methodology or philosophy seems to work well, is embraced by many experts, provides good results, and dispenses with expensive professional advice and management—then the investment services business finds a way to co-opt that approach, making it a part of a new, modified, better-than-ever sales pitch that somehow manages to say with renewed vigor, "You need our help now more than ever." It takes that simple approach, spins it, makes it its own—but with an added twist—and tells you that you need to hire us to help you do it.

Have a New Line—and a New Product—
Always Ready

Mark Twain was the author of many folksy, funny, and spectacularly apt sayings. One of the best is "A lie can travel halfway around the world while the truth is getting its boots on." This saying applies to nothing so well as to the marketing of professional investment services. Each time the truth laces another loop on its boots, the Big Investment Lie catches a jet and flies halfway to China.

The profession once implied it could help you, the investor, pick stocks. The truth slowly laced an eyehole, and that line lost steam.

Then the profession said it could pick mutual funds for you, the ones that pick stocks best. That's a tough sell to anyone who has heard that index funds beat more than 85 percent of mutual funds or that the most recommended funds are often the ones that perform worst later. Then the industry said what really matters is not your specific investments but "asset allocation," and you need us to do that for you. The steep market decline of 2000–2002 made investors wonder why asset allocation didn't protect them against it. Then in an attempt to create a new distraction the industry discovered the biggest bonanza yet, for which it could—incredibly—charge much higher fees: hedge funds that imply they can somehow both make you rich quick and protect you against a decline.

"Speak in Tongues"—Bleed the Language of Its Meaning

In a business where providers offer a product whose touted benefits don't quite square with what the providers know to be true, it helps to bleed the language of its meaning. Nebulous terminology like *wealth preservation*, *asset allocation*, and *value-added strategies* will help. If the language of a business is vague—almost as if people were speaking in code—it magically serves several useful purposes:

- It allows customers and prospects to draw the conclusions they would like to believe, conclusions only implied in an encoded way by the salesperson without having to state them outright.

- It cows customers and prospects, making them think it is all mystifying and beyond them.

- It allows the sales process to seem a soft sell, hardly a sales pitch at all, because the benefits of the product are not blurted out aloud the way you might sell a bar of soap but only hinted at indirectly and in passing (and also somehow telegraphed by the plush quality of the salesperson's office—though why the salesperson's outlays for an expensive office should suggest any benefits to the client is unclear).

- It affords the salesperson (aka advisor or consultant) deniability, both as regards his or her own ethics and as regards the client, when the results are later revealed not to be what may have been implied or suggested.

- It allows the business to sport an aura of "refinement" (and by contagion to make the client feel more refined, too) by not speaking directly about the client's greed for money, which is, of course, the reason the client or prospect is here.

- Perhaps most important, the veiled language (and the pretense that lust for money is not a factor) allows the salesperson to gloss over fees quickly, so that the client or prospect examines the costs only superficially if at all—both for fear of insulting the salesperson's obvious refinement and for fear of exhibiting his own greed, the secret of which the advisor is so accommodatingly and carefully protecting.

- Finally, it keeps the advisor out of trouble by not making any specific claims or guarantees.

Emphasize Your "Sophisticated Technology"

Almost every presentation by a typical professional investment advisor or manager is likely to be strewn with mentions of "sophisticated technology" and "sophisticated algorithms." These seem to be virtual code phrases, passwords of the industry.

Why this should be is not at all clear. Many fields these days use "sophisticated technology" and "sophisticated algorithms." (An *algorithm* is a step-by-step prescription for calculating a mathematical formula.)

For example, many fields of engineering use much more sophisticated mathematics than the investment services profession. Partial differential equations and their solutions are basic tools in engineering and science. The chief "sophisticated" tool of the investment profession—statistical regression analysis—is so commonplace that it is contained in virtually every piece of commercially available calculation software for the personal computer. Microsoft's Excel spreadsheet program, for example—which comes packaged with the standard Microsoft Office suite of programs comprising Word, Outlook, Excel, and PowerPoint—has the ability to do basic regression analysis. Medical and pharmaceutical research employ far more sophisticated statistical analysis tools than any used in the investment field.

True, the explosion in the field of financial derivatives and their pricing since the early 1970s has given rise to a more mathematically oriented doctorate of finance degree—based in large part on the mathematics of Kiyosi Itô, the once-obscure Japanese mathematician whose work I read in preparing to write my thesis. Outside this activity, the most "sophisticated" technique used—and the most sophisticated with which most people in the financial world are familiar—has always been regression analysis. Yet the term *sophisticated* technology has been used for decades—and continues to be used all too frequently—by people in the investment world who have had no brush with Itô or any mathematics like his.

Why, then, the profusion of claims for "sophisticated technology"?

The obvious answer is that hucksters for investment services have discovered that these words have tremendous sales value. People seem to be impressed by proclamations of "sophisticated technology," and they are softened up to be sold expensive investment advice and management services.

In fact, the "sophistication" sales pitch seems to work better when delivered by someone who really knows little or nothing about the "sophisticated" mathematics of which he speaks. That way, he remains in awe of it. Someone who actually uses it or attempts to use it will know the things I have mentioned in earlier chapters—that it is difficult to apply the mathematical methods meaningfully because the data inputs required are totally unreliable if available at all, and they have to be pulled out of thin air.

When I gave talks to investor lunches in the late 1990s and early 2000s as the chief economist of an investment services firm, I was frequently paired on the dais with a representative of a money management firm. My host—the person throwing the lunch for his investor-clients and prospects—would typically be an investment advisor who was a client of my firm. My firm also provided access to individually managed accounts (with a minimum investment of $100,000), managed by professional money management firms. These firms were happy to provide luncheon speakers, and our advisor-clients were happy to have them.

When I was paired with a speaker from a money management firm, I would go through a kind of internal exercise to prepare myself to button my lip. I wouldn't know beforehand whether I would enjoy the other speaker's talk or find it difficult to stomach.

Some of the speakers were quite good. They would give talks peppered with funny jokes, reasonable thoughts, and, occasionally, good information.

Sometimes, though, the speakers were—for me—nearly unbearable. One time I was paired with a young man representing a money management firm that had soaring performance in the "bubble" of the late 1990s. The firm was run by a man who flew around the country in his expensive jet. It went through the now-familiar fin-de-siècle cycle of spectacular performance for a while (attracting a fawning following and enormous quantities of investment dollars, making its owner fabulously rich) followed rapidly by terrible performance, wiping out all the former gains.

The young man gave a very sincere and excited talk. The talk consisted almost entirely of a recitation of how many computers his firm had; how big they were; how many gigabytes—or possibly terabytes or petabytes—of storage they had; how many megahertz or gigahertz they ran at; and so forth.

So what did that have to do with money management and investment, I wondered? It was quite plain to me that the young representative had absolutely no concept of what these computers were actually doing.

I myself shuddered to think what they were doing: beating and torturing data, day after day after day, hour after hour, applying "sophisticated algorithms" in the belief that this would lead to superior investment performance. And, by chance, it actually did for a while, inflating the firm's fortunes and its owners' and employees' heads.

The young man was a true believer—because he had a high-paying job, because his firm was successful and admired (at least for a while), and because he was overawed by technology. Such true believers are great salespeople. At least they seem to sell well to other people who, like them, have no idea what they are talking about.

The Asset Allocation Scam

I want to look in depth at the most recent two legs of the Big Investment Lie's amazing journey: asset allocation and hedge funds. Let's take up asset allocation to end this chapter; hedge funds deserve a chapter all their own.

An article written by three coauthors, Gary Brinson, Randy Hood, and Gil Beebower, appearing in the July–August 1986 issue of the *Financial Analysts Journal*—an often-technical journal of the finance and investment profession—became one of the most cited articles ever in the investment field, to the surprise of its authors. (I'll call the article BHB, for the initials of the authors' last names.)

The article looked at the investment performance of ninety-one large U.S. pension plans over the ten-year period of 1974–1983. It used several simplifying assumptions, but its chief results have been substantially uncontested. They are not unexpected.

The result was merely that most of the fluctuation (i.e., the variability or volatility) in investment returns was due to "strategic asset allocation" or "investment policy"—that is, chiefly to the way the portfolio was divided between stocks and bonds.

In view of the theories and virtually all the empirical evidence to date, the BHB result was not in the least novel or surprising. The division between stocks and bonds pretty much determines the risk being taken in the portfolio. So, of course, it will have a major influence on how much the portfolio's returns fluctuate.

But the investment profession immediately transformed this simple and unremarkable result into a new approach to investment advice and management, an approach that used an exhibit that seems to have a mesmerizing effect on people—the pie chart.

It was all the consequence of slight word changes in the findings of the BHB article. The study says nothing more than that the average stock–bond allocation over time matters more to a portfolio's volatility, its riskiness, than anything else—something of a plain-horse-and-wagon finding.

But this result was transformed by the Marcos of the business into a much more elaborate asset allocation decision. Now the advisor tells you that you must allocate not only between stocks and bonds but among a larger number of "style" categories. Of course, the advisor can tell you how to do that right. The universe of stocks is taken apart into "styles," such as large growth, large value, small growth, small value, and the like, and percentage allocations to them are recommended using . . . a nicely colored pie chart!

The end result of the allocation is that you'll get essentially the same well-diversified mix of stocks as an index fund. But an index fund is too simple and might make you wonder why you need the advisor. Besides, when an advisor recommends an index fund, he gets no kickback from the fund (unless it's a phony higher-cost "index" fund with worthless bells and whistles added). But if each of your style categories needs a separate fund that specializes in that unique style, well, that's starting to look a little more complicated and interesting. That's starting to look like what I saw on Mulberry Street.

15

How Investors Delude Themselves

Investors are alarmingly prone to self-delusion, and most investment advisors and managers are only too happy to take advantage of that fact. It might just be part of our makeup.

In the near future, brain researchers will discover that the urge to get rich quickly originates in the same region of the cerebral cortex as the urge to have an orgasm. The same behavior patterns accompany both, the same attitudinal changes: a tendency to have less concern with speaking the truth; a tendency to overlook or forgive others' disregard for the truth; a marked increase in the level of gullibility; a decrease in the capacity to notice flaws; a singleness of purpose, accompanied by diminishment of the ability or will to think rationally.

I have seen people in this condition more times than I can count. Sometimes they came to me seeking objective comment or knowledgeable counsel. But it often turned out that—though they appeared to seek it—neither objectivity nor wise counsel was what they really wanted. They wanted someone to ratify their urge to *go for it*.

This makes (at least temporarily) willing victims of those who are in the throes of—or can be put into the throes of—the urge to get rich quickly. Some of those who exploit them do it coldly and calculatedly. But more often, those who exploit them do it while they themselves are in the throes of the same urge.

This leads to a remarkable number of manic-depressive incidents, even in ordinary psychically healthy individuals. In the cold light of day, the get-rich-quick scheme one bought into while that particular region of the cerebral cortex was in command looks different than when one was liquored up with greed.

Everyone knows the sensation—the priming of the neuron by some stimulus; the neuron that, when stimulated, unfurls a banner in the head, lit up in dancing bright neon, a banner that says, *I could get rich!*

When that banner lights up, everything is in a fever. Adrenaline is pumped; the pulse quickens. The victim says to the seducer, "Tell me more!"

It rarely turns out as exciting as one thought it would. And all too often, a decision is made that one will regret for a lifetime.

Tweaking the Neuron at a Conference

The analogy (and it may prove more than an analogy, if my forecast of the results of brain research is correct) has a great deal of applicability. The financial writer Jane Bryant Quinn has labeled trash investment advice books "investment porn." Like titillating romance novels, they entice with the promise of stimulating the get-rich-quick neuron.

Getting that neuron fired or titillated can be fun. Every year in the late 1990s and early 2000s, I would give a fairly routine talk on market and economic conditions, at a conference my firm held for about five hundred of its investment-advisor clients. The conference was in a cavernous conference center, amid a sea of parking lots near the Dallas–Fort Worth airport. It was deliberately held in this uninteresting locale because it was the easiest place for everyone to fly into, and because there were few nearby activities to distract attendees from the conference.

To help relieve the dreariness of the statistical subject matter, I opened with a little numerical bagatelle I had prepared.

The year 1998 was a peculiar one for the stock market. Most of the late 1990s were peculiar years, but 1998, especially, stands out.

In 1998, the S&P 500 index, the most commonly cited broad U.S. market index, rose 23.4 percent. Thus, the average stock—based on capitalization-weighted averaging—rose 23.4 percent. (*Capital-*

ization weighting means weighting each stock by the aggregate dollar value of its shares.) The NASDAQ index, containing most of the Internet and tech stocks, rose 39.6 percent—almost 40 percent.

Yet, in spite of these spectacular rises in the averages, the *median* of all stocks *lost* 11 percent, and the median NASDAQ stock lost 15 percent. In other words, though the rise in the *averages* was in the 20+ to 40 percent range, at least half the stocks dropped by more than 10 percent.

A similar phenomenon occurred in 1999 also—in some ways even more pronounced: the NASDAQ rose 85.6 percent, while its median stock rose only 2 percent.

What was happening was that a few go-go stocks (like those called "the magnificent seven": Microsoft, Cisco Systems, Intel, Lucent, AOL, Dell, and IBM) were increasing in price by leaps and bounds, while old-economy stocks—that is, most stocks—were in the dumps. (Note, incidentally, the precipitous *declines* of several of these "magnificent" stocks only a year or two later.)

Whatever mechanisms were in play in the market to cause these phenomena, they seemed to lend a special pizzazz to a numerical exercise I tried. The year 1998 proved best for this, but 1999 (and, to a little lesser extent, any other year) would have been nearly as good.

My company subscribed to the stock and mutual fund data services of Morningstar, Inc., a company known largely for its mutual fund rating system. Morningstar's data include monthly rates of return for the six thousand or so U.S. public stocks.

I decided to single out the best-performing stock each month of 1998 and see how a portfolio would have done if it made all twelve—just twelve—perfect decisions that year. Every month, at the beginning of the month, it would—presciently—put all its assets into the stock that would perform best that month.

I titled the PowerPoint slide I created for this lighthearted introduction to my talk "*If only I had invested in* . . . The Down-Home Ladies Stock-of-the-Month Investment Club." (At that point I, like everyone else, thought of the Beardstown Ladies' investment club as synonymous with stock market statistical dreamland.)

My Down-Home Ladies investment picks turned out very well. If they started with only a dollar to invest at the beginning of January 1998 and invested it in a company called AmerAlia—whose stock rose 233 percent in January—they would have had a little more than $3 at the end of January. Then the Down-Home Ladies would have taken their $3 and invested it all for February in a company called

BrandEra.com. BrandEra.com rose 192 percent in February. So the Down-Home Ladies had $10 at the end of February. They took this and invested in Telenetics in March, netting a 400 percent rate of return and ending the month and the quarter with $49.

They struck gold in April, investing their now $49 in Computerized Thermal Imaging. Computerized Thermal Imaging was a bonanza in April (more about Computerized Thermal Imaging later). The company returned a spectacular 16,686 percent increase in price for the month, rocketing the Down-Home Ladies' $49 to $8,180.

They then proceeded to invest in May in Spatialight for a 6,600 percent positive return; in June, in Earthcare for a 58,771 percent return; in July, in Westmoreland Coal (*coal?*) for a 533 percent return; in August, in Covalent Group for a 167+ percent return; in September, in Telenetics (again) for a 198 percent return; in October, in the Stonepath Group for an 869 percent return; in November, in Books-a-Million for a 937 percent return; and finally, in December, in Everlast Worldwide for a 688+ percent return.

These investments had a wondrous effect on the Down-Home Ladies' already-fabulous $8,180 at the end of April. At the end of May, these investors had accumulated $548,082; at the end of June, $322,661,382; at the end of July, $2,041,639,897; at the end of August, $5,444,373,738; at the end of September, $6,246,702,670; at the end of October, $157,365,562,060; at the end of November, $1,632,307,968,694; and at the end of December—at the end of this *annus mirabilis*—$12,863,726,144,271, more than $12 trillion.

Of course, this schedule of investments became only hypothetical at some point. At the end of August, the Down-Home Ladies would have had too much money to put it all in Telenetics in September, because the company didn't have that much stock outstanding. So they might have had to be satisfied in the end with a mere hundred billion or so. Not bad for starting the year with a dollar.

I thought, frankly, this was a rather silly introduction to my talk. But my audience, to my amazement, commenced to howl with laughter and appreciation somewhere around July. They didn't stop howling and laughing until long after December.

Evidently I had tweaked that get-rich-quick neuron. I had made it look so *easy* to turn one dollar into twelve trillion. All you would have had to do was buy the right stock twelve times in that one year. No day trading in and out minute by minute or hour by hour, day after day. It would have been so easy. That old neuron was just itching to turn back the clock and dive in.

My second exhibit—which I almost skipped because I thought the joke had probably been used up by now—presented the flip side. It showed the investment performance in 1998 of the "Now-You-See-It-Now-You-Don't Investment Club." This club, being very well heeled, started the year with $100 million. By choosing the worst stock each month (including Computerized Thermal Imaging in May, which dropped 99 percent that month after its 16,686 percent rise in April), the Now-You-See-It-Now-You-Don't club managed to turn the $100 million into 1 cent by the end of the year.

To my surprise, the audience howled and laughed again—not quite so loudly as the first time, but they still did.

My joke example of the Down-Home Ladies' Investment Club was a lesson of a kind. It was a lesson not only in the miracle of compounding but also in the power of hindsight.

Stimulating the Neuron and Starving to Death

For some reason the get-rich-quick neuron doesn't come into play when contemplating buy-and-hold, long-term investing. One can get as rich as a little Buffett by hard work, thrift, saving, and forty years of buy-and-hold stock market investments (like Buffett)—being careful to give little of it away to investment advisors and managers. But it doesn't excite the neuron. People want to get rich *quickly*. They want to *beat* the stock market. So just to give their neuron hope, they blow it by paying huge amounts to investment advisors and managers who will give it that hope.

This is reminiscent of an experiment I'm told was carried out during the heyday of behavioral psychology. At that time, many psychologists thought all psychology could be explained by doing experiments with rats in cages and mazes.

The typical routine was to put a rat in a cage with a lever it could push. If the rat pressed the lever, a pellet of food was delivered automatically. It took a rat placed in a cage a little while, during which it tried various random actions, until the rat realized that pressing the lever produced the food. This was called "learning." A rat that knew to press the lever to get food was called "educated."

One experimenter, who knew where the pleasure center of a rat's brain was, decided to try something. He put a second lever in an educated rat's cage. He then wired an electrode into the rat's brain to deliver a little shock to the pleasure center. Pressing the second lever would deliver the shock.

The rat spent a little time in random action until discovering what the second lever did. When the rat discovered this, it spent all its time pressing the second lever that delivered a shock to the pleasure center and starved to death.

I have not been able to corroborate this story and suspect it of being apocryphal. But I believe it. For many people (maybe rats, too), just living, even living comfortably, isn't enough, when you could get rich and have your neuron fired all the time (or so they imagine).

Everyone seeks to better him- or herself. This is fine. But because of the lure of golden cakes and golden crumbs, too much of this noble pursuit is perverted into attempts to get rich quickly by beating the stock market. It was the unfortunate end of Seagull Unlimited, the company I joined briefly and described in Chapter 10. They wanted to do something intellectually stimulating and technologically productive. But they wound up in a farcical effort to beat the stock market. They did it because their investors demanded it; because they could—for a while at least—get someone to pay for it; and because, in the end, it went to their heads.

The Donahue Story

Many of the get-rich-quick schemes can be identified before the fact—by someone with just a little knowledge—as being, in all probability, hopeless. But many cannot. Some—quite a few—succeed for a while by dint of sheer luck, only to fail later, after establishing an apparent record for consistent success. These are the ones that make some people in the investment industry (like hedge fund managers) really, really rich.

I had brushes with several investment schemes that, to my educated and skeptical eye, seemed almost certain to fail. But there was always that small chance they would succeed. So I would give people, when asked, my opinion couched in probabilities. I would say that something seemed highly unlikely to succeed or that there was a 95 percent chance it would fail. In all of these cases, to the best of my knowledge, the scheme did indeed fail—even when it had the backing or buy-in of very wealthy, influential, or supposedly sophisticated investors.

For example, in 1990, my friend Paul, the president of an out-standing international nonprofit organization based in Colorado, had an employee who was enamored of an investment he had learned about.

The employee—I'll call him Fred—told me that the investment fund, run by a man named Jim Donahue, earned an investment return every year, like clockwork, of 25 percent. Furthermore, Fred said, a 25 percent return was guaranteed by the manager.

I told Fred that a 25 percent return each and every year was highly unlikely. I told him that high returns like that usually came with a lot of volatility, so that you'd get a very high return one year and a very low one the next—even if it averaged out high over time. I said that, usually, to get a steady return that was the same year by year, you had to settle for a low one.

I also asked him, if the 25 percent return was guaranteed, with what was it guaranteed? For a manager to guarantee a 25 percent return, he'd have to have a gargantuan pot of money set aside separately to pay investors if the target wasn't achieved.

I smelled the strong scent of rat.

I hoped I had adequately discouraged Fred from putting his money into Donahue's investment fund. But it turned out he did it anyway. He really didn't want advice; he wanted me to tell him to *go for it*.

In this particular case, it didn't take long before I could have said—if I had wanted to—"I told you so." The story broke shortly thereafter, on August 23. A complete account was given in a November 19, 1990, story by Sandra D. Atchison in *Business Week*. The story is characteristic of such incidents in all its details. It begins by telling of a man named Warren E. Phifer who put $300,000 into a limited partnership managed by Hedged-Investment Associates Inc. on the recommendation of a friend,

> a friend who spoke glowingly of consistently high returns as well as the integrity of Hedged President James D. Donahue, an elder at Cherry Creek Presbyterian church in suburban Denver. . . .

> Phifer discovered at an Aug. 23 meeting in Denver that his nest egg was gone.
>
> Before an audience of hundreds, a tearful Donahue admitted in a videotaped message that he had lost "almost all of the total assets of the fund." . . .

It's little consolation that Phifer is part of an elite group of stunned investors that sounds like a Rocky Mountain Who's Who. . . .

Most investors were beguiled by what seemed to be a surefire money machine guided by high-powered computers. . . .

Donahue's early track record was remarkable. Hedged-Investments boasted an impressive eight-year run of annual returns of 23% to 34%. . . . Donahue marshaled three mainframe computers to collect split-second market information on stocks. . . .

Donahue, 56, had the background to make it work. Acquaintances describe him as a low-pressure, likable computer fanatic [with] a master's degree in mathematical statistics from Stanford University. . . . In 1974, shortly after the Chicago Board Options Exchange opened, he devoted himself to applying statistical theory and computer techniques to stock options, even publishing a reference work, Option Strategies. . . .

Hedged was never audited, a fact Donahue freely admitted. . . . Investors also wonder whether the fund got too big to maintain the high returns that drew in so many investors.

For a while Donahue's investments seemed to work beautifully. But as investors learned later, at some point certain big bets he made failed miserably.

Few investors believe that they'll see their money again.[1]

This little story has all the earmarks of the typical manic-depressive investment saga: the "high-powered computers"; the "sophisticated statistical models"; the earnest mathematical-genius manager with impeccable credentials; the stellar historical record; the unaudited performance figures; the postmortem suggesting it would have continued working if the fund hadn't grown so big, or hadn't taken on extra risk, or . . . ; the supposedly intelligent and sophisticated investors who bought into it (including major institutional investors as well as individuals, and at least one prominent consulting firm, who had been recommending Donahue's Hedged-Investments Associates to its institutional investor clients).

You would think this tale would be cautionary, but it repeated itself a few short years later and twenty times as big with Long-Term Capital Management, whose story I'll cover in the next chapter. And many similar stories came in the years following the Donahue fiasco.

Such stories continue at the rate of at least dozens per year. The public never hears of most of them.

Donahue's strategy just happened to work for a while, making him believe that his "sophisticated statistical models" run on his "high-powered computers" actually had intrinsic validity. By extension, he came to believe that he himself was possessed of investment genius. Therefore, not only would his "sophisticated" models continue to work, but any investment idea he came up with would work.

This is how it happens. Random luck is interpreted as innate skill. The same skill that created that outstandingly lucky result—it is assumed—will continue to produce outstanding results in the future.

The Original Ponzi Scheme

The most fascinating of get-rich-quick schemes was the one that gave many subsequent scams their generic name. Prior to the incredible history of Charles Ponzi, the phrase for such hoodwinks was "robbing Peter to pay Paul."[2]

Charles Ponzi was born Carlo Ponzi in northern Italy. He sailed to the United States in 1903 at the age of twenty-one, a poor but aspiring immigrant. Like so many immigrants of the era, Ponzi had been told that in the United States, "the streets are paved with gold."

Ponzi was a good-hearted, cheerful man with an eagerness and confidence that drew people in. Unfortunately, he also had a penchant for building castles in the air, dreaming constantly of ways to become rich. In the course of his misadventures in the New World, he ran afoul of the law twice and spent four years in prison in Canada and the United States.

Finally, in 1919, having set up a small office for himself to pursue business ideas, he found one that seemed ideal.

In the early 1900s, as now, citizens living abroad sometimes had a need to send a package enclosing a self-addressed, stamped envelope. But in their countries of residence, there was no way to purchase a stamp of their homeland. (This is still the case, as I discovered living in Portugal in the first half of 2005. I could not purchase a United States postage stamp in Portugal unless I was an employee of the U.S. government.)

To remedy this situation, government representatives of a number of countries agreed to issue international postal reply coupons. These coupons could be purchased in any country and redeemed in another country for postage stamps. The cost of the postage stamps in foreign currency was fixed, while the relative values of currencies fluctuated.

Ponzi saw in this what would now be called an "arbitrage" opportunity. He could buy postal reply coupons in a country with a weak currency—like Italy—and redeem them for stamps worth much more in a country with a strong currency, like the United States. The profit was built in. Ponzi saw so much profit in it that he offered investors a 50 percent return on investment in forty-five days. Offers to invest included in capital letters "50% RETURN GUARANTEED IN 45 DAYS."

Ponzi's sales pitch was so infectious, and the promised return so good—and people were so gullible—that his efforts to recruit investors (and commissioned salespeople to recruit more investors) were wildly successful. By the mid-1920s, thousands of people were constantly mobbing his School Street office in Boston, clamoring for the opportunity to invest. Ponzi's enterprise was taking in more than $1 million a week in new investments—at a time when the annual salary of the president of Harvard was $6,000.

In the meantime, Ponzi—always faster to sell a product than to work out the details—discovered he was unable to actually execute the currency arbitrage plan. It was difficult to obtain international reply coupons from abroad. Once obtained and in the United States, they could be redeemed for stamps; but it was not clear how they could be converted to cash. Furthermore, U.S. postal inspectors turned their suspicious gazes on the whole scheme.

It is doubtful that Ponzi ever arbitraged a single international postal reply coupon. Yet, investors who asked for their investment and their 50 percent return in cash were cheerfully paid from the funds deposited by the thousands of new investors. But most—seeing how good the return was—simply reinvested.

This situation haunted Ponzi's private reflections in the summer of 1920 and gave him a growing ulcer. Nonetheless, he suddenly found himself with millions in cash, together with boundless ambition and self-confidence.

Ponzi began, wishfully, to think of himself as being like Christopher Columbus, his countryman who boldly set sail for India on a wildly uncertain expedition only to discover a new country on the way; or like Edmond Dantès, Alexandre Dumas's count of Monte Cristo, who—wretched but unconquerable—escaped from prison to discover buried treasure and become rich.

Ponzi made very serious efforts, helped by his huge reserves of cash, to unearth buried treasure—buying a company, taking over a bank, trying to find a way to make at least the 50 percent return he had promised his investors. He tried to plan a new, much bigger export–import company that would own steamship lines, sell $100 million in stock, pay off Ponzi's original investors, and then settle for a more staid but still excellent future return on investment.

Had Ponzi found, for example, a Computerized Thermal Imaging, with its 16,686 percent one-month return, or had his export–import company gotten off the ground and raised $100 million in capital, he could have reached his goal. His desperation, his urgent need to take big risks to fend off the inevitability of total failure, paradoxically made a big success—though not likely—more likely than for other investors.

For some people, it actually works. Some of the great investors and businesspeople who are now lionized by history were those who took big risks, got lucky, and won. Most who didn't get lucky are forgotten. Ponzi was among the most unlucky of all. Not only did he not win, but he had his name engraved, right at the top, in the annals of conniving swindlers.

Ponzi's efforts to salvage the situation failed, almost (but not wholly) inevitably. The house of cards fell apart. Instead of being remembered as an extraordinarily bold businessman, who amassed huge amounts of money and invested it in a winning enterprise, he is remembered as the man who gave his name to the "pyramid" scheme—the technique of promising investors a big return and then paying them off with money from later investors, without actually doing any real business to justify the return.

The character of Ponzi himself is memorable and extraordinary. But the characters of his many thousands of willing and eager gullible investors are extraordinary, too. Once again, we see that if a return can be shown to have been produced historically, however briefly or in selected circumstances, people are taken in. They do not look under the tent to see how someone could possibly obtain the kind of return they are claiming. When their get-rich-quick neurons are activated, people's rational faculties become supine.

And nothing—and I mean nothing—stimulates those neurons like hedge funds.

16

How Hedge Funds Operate and Are Sold

. . . .

A few years ago, I was the chairman of the investment subcommittee of the board of an important and creative nonprofit organization near Aspen, Colorado. The investment subcommittee was part of the finance committee, so it often met as part of a finance committee meeting.

As chairman of the investment subcommittee and the person most knowledgeable about investments, I recommended a fairly high allocation to stocks for the nonprofit's small endowment of about $8 million (since it would be invested for the long run). I recommended passive funds—that is, indexes—for the actual investments. After some discussion, we agreed on a stock allocation, and the others agreed to the index recommendation. We chose for part of our index investment a broadly diversified, low-cost, indexlike "socially responsible" mutual fund.

I sent the committee a write-up with the usual caveats about the stock market. The caveats said that the stock market will almost surely produce a good return in the long run, but it will experience unpredictable declines along the way, some quite steep.

Sure enough, along came the bear market years of 2001–2002. In spite of my caveats, some members of the finance committee began to say that we've got to get professional investment management. I said it was not worth the cost, and it wouldn't have saved us from the bear market. But I agreed to interview money management candidates anyway, as long as we could insist on very low fees.

The nonprofit's chief financial officer interviewed one big-name firm and wrote them off, while I interviewed another and wrote them off, too. The people from these firms that we interviewed were transparently all sales pitch, no substance. (How do they ever get hired?)

The nonprofit's chief financial officer had been solicited by a new, independent one-man Aspen money manager who previously worked for Merrill Lynch. The CFO seemed to like him. When I interviewed the money manager, I was appalled by what he said. But I knew the pickings are not good in the investment management field. One must steel one's self to suffer through the sales pitch.

This man said he agreed with me wholeheartedly about the use of index funds. But he thought one must vary the allocation to them over time and vary the allocation to stocks and bonds to "follow the trends" in the market. So apparently, his methodology was that if stocks had gone up recently, you invested more in them, and if they had gone down recently, you invested less. He seemed not to know that "the stock market can turn on a dime and always does."

This sounded like a selling maneuver to me: agree with what the prospect says, and then say the prospect just needs something else in addition to make it really right. But for the sake of keeping the peace, I went along. At least I got part of what I really wanted (other than not having to hire an investment manager at all). We prevailed on the manager to reduce his fees to an unusually low—for a money manager—35 basis points, or 0.35 percent. I figured it was the best result I could get without expending all my political chips with the rest of the finance committee.

Lo and behold, the money manager performed quite poorly compared with what our fund's performance would have been without him. Of course, this did not have to happen. His result from trying to vary the investment mix would be expected to be random. He could equally well have accidentally performed better. But in fact he performed poorly. Then we had to pay him his fee too, about $30,000. This was $30,000 the nonprofit would now have to raise somehow— and raising money for a nonprofit isn't easy.

Our money manager naturally gave an excuse for the poor performance. One of the skills that a successful (i.e., yacht-owning) investment manager or advisor needs is the ability to explain away poor performance. He said—without reason—that his strategy would perform well in down markets, while we had just experienced an up market. This was nonsense—nonsense that was made up essentially on the spur of the moment. Investment managers and advisors are allowed to get away with this sort of thing time and again.

But our money manager at least won a small amount of my respect when the chairman of the finance committee next spoke up and said we should put 10 percent of our investment in hedge funds. The money manager offered a tiny bit of resistance to this proposal, seemingly on knowledgeable grounds (he had read a cautionary piece about hedge funds in *The Economist*)—though I could tell he was also trying to gauge where the political power on the committee lay and with whom he should agree in order to keep his job.

I finally used up all my political chips by putting my foot down on hedge funds. If the money manager was an unnecessary cost, hedge funds would be an unnecessary cost twenty times over—for a service that careful analysis could not show to be worth anything at all. That was beyond my capacity to endure, whatever the political cost.

The Investment Reserved for "Sophisticated" Investors

This leads us to the matter of hedge funds. The anecdotal evidence— and the fact that only wealthy, so-called sophisticated investors are allowed into them—has made many people believe that hedge funds are the stars of the investment world.

As we've already seen, hedge funds are indeed the stars in terms of fees reaped by investment managers. Nothing like it can be seen in any other field. It's no wonder that well in excess of ten thousand hedge funds have been launched in recent years (it's hard to be sure how many there were because they are not required to divulge records). The lure of hedge fund management is that if you are successful at it, you can become a hundred-millionaire many times over. Most of the funds that were launched are now defunct, but many that survive make billions of dollars for their managers.

The genesis of hedge funds is traced to Alfred Winslow Jones in 1949. The practice of "hedging," however, started long before Jones launched the first hedge fund.

How Hedging Works

Importers and exporters, for example, have long hedged currencies as a matter of course. The practice is more than a hundred years old. If you are an American company and you've agreed to buy manufacturing equipment from a seller in Europe, you could be exposed to currency exchange risk. You can "hedge" away this risk in the futures market.

For example, suppose the shipment will be delivered and paid for in six months. The payment, by agreement, will be half a million euros. If your company does business in dollars, you are exposed to the risk that the dollar–euro exchange rate will change for the worse in six months. Given that risk, you don't know for sure how many dollars it will cost you. But you can hedge against this risk by trading forward— by agreeing now to buy half a million euros in six months for a predetermined number of dollars. There are markets for this sort of trade, the forwards and futures markets. That way you know how much you'll have to pay in dollars when the time comes—the risk is eliminated.

What you've done is to match one trade that has an element of risk—the exchange of euros for the equipment—with another trade, the forward currency trade, a trade that by itself would also have an element of risk. When the two trades are engaged in simultaneously, it cancels risk.

What Hedge Funds Are

All "hedging" operates on this principle. But not all "hedge" funds do. The term *hedge funds* is now applied to all funds that avoid oversight by regulatory authorities because they are not offered to the general public.

Funds that are offered only to wealthy, so-called accredited investors—those who are presumed not to need government protection against their own folly—can avoid most regulatory requirements. An accredited investor is one who has at least $1 million or has had income of at least $200,000 for each of the last two years. In recent times, that definition encompasses literally millions of investors. Hedge funds used to be the province of the very rich. Now millions of gullible investors can invest in them.

There are many hedge funds that use countervailing trades— trades whose risks offset each other—as importers and exporters do.

But there are also other funds that simply take extra risk. Even many of the funds that use countervailing trades to offset risk actually take on extra risk; they do it by using leverage—that is, by borrowing.

A Hedge Fund Prototype

The original hedge fund model of Alfred Winslow Jones is still typical of many hedge funds today. These funds are called *market-neutral funds*.

Jones believed he could pick winning and losing stocks—and, who knows, maybe he could. This was back in the 1940s. A lot fewer people back then were scrutinizing markets. Information was less widely available than today. Maybe it was easier for some people to do a superior job guessing the future price of a stock.

In any case, Jones's problem, it seems, was that the whole stock market goes up or down and has a tendency to carry all stocks with it —be they winners or losers. Jones wanted to separate out his predictions for individual stocks from the movement of the whole market. He also wanted to magnify the gains he believed he could get from picking winners and losers.

The answer was to simultaneously sell the losers and buy the winners. He did this in such a way that he was "market-neutral"; that is, he sold as much in predicted losers as he bought in predicted winners. The means of selling predicted losers is "short-selling"—you borrow shares of stock from someone else and sell them, but you owe it to the person you borrowed from to replace the shares.

You may be able to see that this is, by its nature, a highly leveraged way of investing. In fact, it would seem you don't even need to put up any capital at all—what you receive from the sales pays for what you pay for the purchases. As a result, you would be "infinitely" leveraged. That is, with no capital invested at all, your return would be infinitely great if your investments gained (a positive gain divided by zero capital investment) and infinitely negative if they lost.

But there are margin requirements that require you to at least place on deposit a minimum amount of capital. Still, it is a much more risky position you are taking than if you simply bought stocks and paid for them. If you've guessed right, your return on capital will be enormous. If you've guessed wrong, it will be enormously negative.

As the story goes, Jones's return was enormously positive. A 1966 article in *Fortune* said his performance had beaten the best-performing mutual fund over five years by 85 percent, after fees (about 9 percent annually). We can only assume this was not a Beardstown Ladies statistic—that is, that the number was actually correct. But if it was correct, it was a lot more likely to occur than the stock market performance claimed by the Beardstown Ladies, because Jones used so much leverage. Leverage multiplies your chances of getting either extremely good results or extremely bad ones. That's why so many hedge funds (almost 20 percent of them[1]) go out of business each year. It's also why some hedge funds reap fabulously high returns, making all investors salivate.

But just because some hedge funds at times reap very high returns is no reason to think hedge fund investing is a good idea. Hedge funds have the same twin problems mutual funds and other investment vehicles have: average performance worse than market averages, and no predictability of performance. Some hedge funds perform at times spectacularly well, and some perform spectacularly poorly, but there's no way you can tell beforehand which will be which. And hedge funds are saddled with a drag on performance that is much worse than that of mutual funds—incredibly high fees.

A Typical Hedge Fund Story: Long-Term Capital Management

A near-complete education in the pitfalls of hedge funds can be obtained by reading *When Genius Failed*, an excellent book by *New York Times* columnist Roger Lowenstein about the rise and fall of the big hedge fund Long-Term Capital Management (LTCM).[2]

The tale is not primarily of outlandish salesmanship but of its fraternal twin in the investment services business, scientism. We have met scientism before when we became acquainted with the ideas of Friedrich Hayek. It is the fallacy of believing that mathematical models have as much validity in economics and finance as they do in the physical sciences.

The Geeks versus the Jocks

"Science"—that is, the use of the scientific method to test hypotheses and validate theories—has had a very uneasy relationship with the main business of the investment services industry, which is sales and marketing. About thirty years ago, employees in the investment services business who actually tried to seek the truth about the statistics being quoted in the business were patronizingly called "rocket scientists" by the marketing people. They were trotted out on display as Exhibit A to buttress the claim that the firm used "sophisticated" mathematical methods; then they were shunted into a back room to keep them from contradicting the outrageous claims being made by sales and marketing.

This caused a competition, marked by envy and simmering conflict, between the "geeks" and the "jocks" in the industry.

The jocks—the salespeople—had for a long time clearly had the upper hand. They hired the geeks—the "rocket scientists"—seemingly just to put them on show, as if they were weird alien sideshow attractions. The jocks paid the geeks much less well than they paid themselves. They treated the geeks as if they weren't quite with it, as if they hadn't caught onto the basic principle of life that it's all a power game in which what's most important is who can sell what to whom, by whatever means—not some kind of scientific thought experiment in which everybody sits around contemplating navels and trying to figure out what is really true. They made young people who had spent years in universities, living cheaply and studying some subject in great depth, feel like—in the jocks' view—they had just been screwing off.

The geeks—like so many underrated people who quietly nourish a grudge—believed it was all topsy-turvy, that actually they were much more important than the jocks and some day they would prove it.

As we all know, that day came for plenty of geeks in many professions over the thirty years that followed. It came also in the investment profession. But it is questionable whether the geeks in the investment profession really were as superior as they thought they were—or as superior as they convinced many other people that they were.

Geekdom Falls Prey to Scientism

What the geeks had were mathematical models of finance. Those who make and use mathematical models in the social sciences, however—particularly in economics and finance—constantly forget what Hayek knew. They forget that the models bear no resemblance to scientific models. They do not model the financial and economic worlds with anything approaching the accuracy of mathematical models of the physical world.

In the financial and economic fields, real-world complexities are assumed away in order to create mathematical models. These are not just minor complexities; they are often the most important phenomena. For example, the academic fields of economics and finance assume away, for the sake of reducing some economic or financial pattern to a formula, these complicating factors: transaction costs, taxes, fees and expenses, and price jumps.

As a result, mathematical formulas derived by ignoring these factors are of no more than theoretical interest. Economists generally admit to this and agree to it; then they go right out and apply the formulas anyway, for the simple reason that someone will pay them to do it.

If these people happen to be lucky enough to experience some success—success that they think is due to their learned application of mathematical formulas—their self-confidence and hubris can become almost unbounded.

That is what happened to the brilliant investment managers of LTCM, geeks all.

What LTCM Thought It Had

The LTCM partners were like old-time stock pickers (and current active investment managers), but with a difference. The stock pickers think they can predict the future price of stocks better than other people. The LTCM partners thought they could predict future standard deviation or riskiness better than other people.

They thought the recent introduction of a plethora of derivative products created an opportunity for people who understood risk measures better than anyone else—using mathematical formulas—to make money by arbitrage.

Arbitrage is a way of taking advantage of a small pricing discrepancy. Back around 1985, there was a "gray market" in the United States for European automobiles because the dollar was worth so much more than European currency. Consequently you could buy a car in Europe for much less in dollar terms than it could be bought in the United States. Some people went to Europe, bought cars for European money, shipped the cars back to the United

States, and sold them there for a profit. These people were doing arbitrage.

Arbitrage can also be done at your desk with a PC without leaving your office, if you're dealing not in physical products but in financial products. If you find out that you can—for at least a brief moment—trade dollars for euros, then the same euros for yen, then those yen back for dollars again, and make money, you can arbitrage the currency rates by executing all the trades at once. Because there are so many eagle eyes watching for such opportunities, the opportunity is small and usually doesn't pay enough to be worth the trouble, but sometimes it is there.

LTCM partners thought they could find these opportunities because they could measure things so well with their formulas, then leverage to the sky to make as much money as possible on them, and produce a fantastic rate of return on investors' money.

A Problem Common to Mathematical Models in the Real World

But as with the Markowitz formula, it turns out that the formula isn't much good without some numerical assumptions to put into it. And you've got to get those numerical assumptions somewhere.

The LTCM partners, like most practitioners of scientism, had to pull some assumptions out of the air.

The main assumption they pulled out of the air was that the market was overestimating risk. They had a sensible core reason for this belief: they thought that when new financial instruments are introduced, market participants initially view them as more risky than they really are. LTCM, because they could quickly assess the risk of a financial instrument in combination with other financial instruments, could estimate the "true" risk of that instrument or combination of instruments. (Sound familiar? It's not that much different from stock pickers who believe they alone can estimate the "true" value of a stock.)

The result was that most of LTCM's bets—though the partners thought they were diversifying them—really went the same way. They bet on market risk levels—standard deviations and point spreads between more and less risky bonds—to come down. Then they borrowed tens of times more than the money they actually had in capital to leverage their commitments to these bets.

The Familiar Manic-Depressive, Boom–Bust Cycle

For a while—for several years—the risk levels did come down, LTCM's bets did extremely well, and the fund had extraordinarily impressive paper gains. Investors clamored to be cut in.

Then a time came when LTCM's partners were wrong, and they were disastrously wrong all at once. In August 1998, concern about global risk went sky-high when Russia effectively defaulted on its debt obligations. The value of LTCM's holdings plummeted.

Remember how we said in Chapter 12 that with leverage, "in the long run you really will beat the market . . . provided you can last that long"? Well, LTCM couldn't last that long. (Besides, because its partners weren't just buying simple shares of stock, even in the long run they couldn't be sure of beating the stock market.)

But to make matters worse, LTCM had borrowed billions from several of the largest banks in the world. Some of these banks already were having their own financial problems due to the roiling markets (some of those problems were caused by doing the same kind of arbitrage trading that LTCM was doing). The banks were getting worried.

The concern got so serious that officials of the U.S. Federal Reserve organized a meeting of the lender banks to bail LTCM out, in order to keep its failure from causing dangerous tremors in the entire global financial system. LTCM acquired—to its now-busted partners' dismay—the unique fame of being almost the only hedge fund more well known for its decline than for its glory days.

It's the Story of Every Hedge Fund

The story of LTCM can easily be thought of as the story of every hedge fund. All hedge funds are not alike, of course—far from it. But the LTCM story is probably typical, at least of highly leveraged hedge funds doing exotic trades. (The others—those that are, relatively speaking, plain vanilla—have even less justification to charge the outlandish fees they levy.)

All hedge funds, like all actively managed investments, are doing the same thing. They are trying to find financial securities whose future prices they think they can predict.

The price of a security can depend on several factors at once. For example, it can depend on the prevailing interest rate, on the health of the company that issued it or on whose fortune it depends, and on investors' beliefs about the future price and risk of that security.

Many hedge fund managers believe they can predict the price's dependency on one of those factors but not on the others. So they try to "hedge" against the risk of the factors they can't predict and leverage the factors they can predict.

For example, LTCM's partners thought they could predict investors' future beliefs about the riskiness of securities, but they didn't believe they could predict interest rates. So they hedged against interest rate changes by buying one bond, while selling an equal amount of another one. The bond they bought was the riskier one and therefore had the higher risk premium (they thought that premium would come down), while the one they sold was the less risky one. This way they took no position on the general level of interest rates, only on the "spread" between the prices of the two bonds.

The LTCM partners were (irrationally, if the truth be spoken) convinced they could predict risk better than other people, just because they had complicated mathematical models to calculate risk.

Most hedge funds do something similar in principle though it can take many forms. For example, some hedge fund managers, specializing in what is called merger arbitrage, believe they can predict whether two companies will merge and/or whether the price of the merged company will have a higher or lower price than the separate companies before the merger.

Almost every type of hedge fund tries to isolate a price or price relationship that its managers think they can predict, and then hedge out the risk of other price changes or price relationships they think they can't predict. This does not hedge against risk in general. It only hedges against the risks the manager thinks he or she cannot control. But it frequently entails leveraging the risks that the manager thinks can be controlled. Therefore, risk is frequently magnified. That was the case with LTCM.

LTCM's partners thought they could predict the market's beliefs about the level of risk prevailing in the market. They leveraged that belief to the hilt. For a while they seemed to be right. Then they were dramatically wrong, losing all their previous gains, all in the space of a few short weeks.

Big Unpredictable Ups and Downs Are
Inevitable for Leveraged Hedge Funds

But the order in which they were right, then wrong, could easily have been reversed. That order is reversed for many hedge funds, probably about half. That is why nearly one in five hedge funds fails every year and why most of them fail even to get started. Had LTCM's history of being right, then wrong, been reversed, the fund never would have gotten off the ground.

The boom–bust pattern of LTCM was not in the least unusual in the history of hedge funds, even though LTCM seems to be almost the only fund that got a bad name for it. In the 1980s and 1990s, two hedge fund managers, Julian Robertson and George Soros, became famous for the same thing LTCM did in the early 1990s: racking up extremely high returns. But at the end of the 1990s, Robertson's funds (valued at $23 billion in 1999) dropped more than 75 percent in eighteen months. Robertson gave the excuse that his philosophy was made impossible by an "irrational market." Soros's empire ended in a similar fashion at about the same time.

Both managers—lionized still, even now, as investment geniuses—apparently didn't know how to deal with the soaring market for technology in the late 1990s. Not only did they fail to benefit from the boom, but they were so wrong in their investments that their funds were ruined by it. Unlike the unfortunate Nobelists and mathematical geeks of LTCM, though, Soros's and Robertson's reputations seem to have survived on the strength of their earlier successes—and, of course, on the fact that they are still personally rich and have turned their wealth to admirable philanthropic pursuits.

While it is quite clear that both Soros and Robertson fared very well in their personal finances from managing their hedge funds, it is less clear how well their investors actually did.

For example, Soros closed his Quantum fund after making all the wrong bets in the inflated high-tech market of 1998–1999. According to an article in *The Economist* of May 4, 2000, Soros's fund lost hundreds of millions in 1998 and $700 million in March 1999 by selling tech shares short, on the (eventually correct) assumption that the market was overpriced. But then his fund started to dabble by buying into the tech market instead, doing very well in 1999 after all. The result was $5 billion in profits, of which Soros's Quantum fund kept half. The next year when the market for high-tech dropped, the fund lost $2.5 billion. Soros closed his funds and quit the business. So what did the investors keep? Not much, it would seem.

Robertson's funds had their biggest losses in the eighteen months after achieving their highest level of assets: $23 billion. This must mean that a very large quantity of investors' money rode the roller coaster down to the bottom. Earlier investors in the funds' heyday got great returns, but there weren't so many of them then, and they didn't have as much invested. So how well did the average investor do over the years the fund was in existence? Not all that well, in spite of the reputation. To do well you had to be in at exactly the right times. Just being invested in a "good" fund is not enough—you have to be invested at the right time. And how is an investor to know that right time, in advance?

However much hedge funds—or any other investments—may claim that they use "sophisticated quantitative methods," those methods are no more than computational accessories to develop the predictive beliefs of the managers. But the evidence—the evidence that probably none of them can actually predict anything at all—is always the same. Somehow, on average, the whole lot of them fails to outperform a passive stock portfolio.

Why People Buy into Them

Hedge funds became the next major leg of the Big Investment Lie's trip around the world when the stock market tanked in 2001–2002. Investors who should have been reasonably happy with their big gains of the 1980s and 1990s, and who should have been adequately warned that stock market declines will happen, now turned in droves to believing that the Holy Grail must be found elsewhere. When it comes to searching for the Holy Grail in the investment world, you can always find someone ready to guide you for a big fee.

Hedge funds are not supposed to advertise, and they don't. But the ambient culture of the Big Investment Lie nurtures and amplifies any sales promotion that the industry or a subindustry can put into currency. Word of mouth transmits it. It is breathed in admiring tales by self-interested parties in the hedge fund world such as newsletters, researchers, hedge fund database compilers, financial advisors, and lapdogs in the journalistic and academic professions.

The Big Investment Lie is helped by the fact that those who happen to have made a killing in an investment, be it a hedge fund or a day-trading binge—like those who make a killing in Las Vegas—enjoy telling people about it. It makes them look smart. Those who took a dive usually don't talk about it. Hence, the anecdotal evidence is highly skewed. In a field in which both big gains and big losses are likely to occur simply because of the high leverage, it is much more common to hear about big wins than big losses. This makes fertile ground for the right marketing pitch.

A Marketing Pitch of Sheer Distortion

The marketing pitch used to sell hedge funds is a mixture of Nobel Prize–winning terminology and technical word salad. The will to believe on the part of investors is so great that, it seems, almost anything would work—except, of course, the plain truth.

Recall Chapter 11's discussion of the work of Nobel Prize winner Harry Markowitz. The most important things in stock investing, he found, are the risk or degree of fluctuation (i.e., standard deviation), the correlations between stocks, and the diversification of risk that can be obtained by combining stocks having imperfect correlations. This all led to the conclusion that the combination of all stocks in the market—an index fund—is the optimal portfolio.

All three of these concepts—a lower standard deviation, diversification with low correlations, and index funds—have been co-opted by the hedge fund industry as part of its stilted marketing pitch. In all three cases, the terms are misconstrued and misapplied, then presented to the gullible investor as brilliant constructs derived by theoreticians from modern portfolio theory.

Hedge fund purveyors tout hedge funds as having a low correlation with the stock market. By and large they're right. But it's not the kind of low correlation that Markowitz showed is important.

Constructing an exotic security that has a low or negative correlation with stocks is easy. Just having a low correlation with the market is not in itself a virtue. It has been sold as a virtue because the recent spurt in hedge fund sales occurred as a reaction to the market's decline in 2000–2002. People's memories are most sharply etched with the last regrettable event that occurred. As if somehow to go back and relive it again and do the right thing this time, they thrash about for strategies that would work if it recurred.

Hedge fund marketing exploits this irrational tendency. The implication is that hedge fund managers are smarter than mutual fund managers because they are paid better, and they can go against the market if they want to. They would never let a decline occur like the one that happened when the market dropped in the early 2000s (never mind that much worse declines did happen to the supposed best and brightest in the hedge fund industry—the LTCM group, George Soros, Julian Robertson, and many others). They would use low correlations to hedge against it. Of course, this means they would have to see the decline coming ahead of time—and all investment advisors and managers, in all times, have been no better than the average Joe at seeing declines coming ahead of time.

As if low correlations with the market were not enough, the most enterprising fee chargers in the entire business—fund-of-hedge-fund providers—say you need a combination of hedge funds with less-than-perfect correlations to hedge further against the risk of only one hedge fund (a risk they say is already low). And, of course, you need to pay more for this.

In one notable case, a fund-of-hedge-funds packager went further with the spurious Markowitz MPT analogy and created what they call an "index fund" of hedge funds. The fact that this has absolutely none of the characteristics of an index fund of stocks, beneficial or otherwise, doesn't seem to bother anybody. Just using the term *index* is enough to convince gullible investors that it's the safest way to invest in hedge funds—and invest in hedge funds, it seems, they must, exorbitant fees be damned.

17

How Consultants and Money Managers Sell to Institutional Investors

Let's look at how it typically works in the institutional investor market—the large employee benefit, endowment, and foundation funds.

Big institutional investment funds (their assets can be in the tens of billions of dollars or more) almost always retain a consulting company. The consulting companies, which specialize in the institutional investment consulting business, can be large and extremely profitable. For example, the president of the consulting company Wilshire Associates (with whom I once debated at a University of Chicago conference) had in his youth worked on computer programming for the U.S. space program. At the age of sixty—perhaps feeling nostalgic for space projects—he reportedly spent $20 million to buy himself a ride on the Soviet Mir space station. His institutional investment consulting business must not have done too badly!

Consulting firms perform various research studies for their clients, such as—for example—running asset–liability models, which project the future assets of a pension fund compared with its liabilities. (A pension plan's liabilities are what it will cost later to make the promised payments to retirees.) These models can help the fund's managers determine how likely it is they'll have enough to cover benefits and how much they might need to add to the fund in the future.

Picking a Money Manager

The consultant's central role, however, lies in manager selection and evaluation—that is, in deciding who will get the lucrative job of investing the funds. The consultant's role in this process bears no small resemblance to the way Fumarian consultants helped HMOs choose cigarette brands to recommend to their members. Data are sliced and diced in thousands of ways, characteristics of management at managers' firms are analyzed, and results that have the look of being carefully researched are produced.

The procedure a consulting firm uses to help a fund sponsor search for and select money managers is approximately as follows. The consulting firm must first determine the fund sponsor's specific preferences, such as for a money manager based in a certain region of the country. Then, the consulting firm sends a questionnaire to a number of money management firms that may be candidates. These questionnaires are usually tediously long and detailed, requiring money management firms to give detailed information about their finances, their employees' education, experience, and length of service; their methodology and organization for selecting securities, markets, and sectors to invest in; and on and on. As a result, many money management firms simply toss the questionnaires in the wastebasket, unless they have reason to believe they are serious candidates and must fill out the questionnaire to comply with the necessary paperwork.

The consultants then narrow the field down to a few candidates. How do they do this? Not just based on past performance, because the consultants usually don't really believe it matters. They often even caution their clients to the effect that "past performance is not necessarily indicative of future performance." But they review past performance nevertheless and jettison the managers whose past performance was below average. Why do they do this, if it doesn't matter, and if a manager who was below average in the past is as likely as one who was above average to perform well in the future? Obviously, because it's hard for their clients to fully believe it. The tendency to believe past performance is a predictor of future performance is too deeply ingrained.

Consulting firms do not select managers based on past performance alone. The evidence that it doesn't help predict their future performance is too strong. So consulting firms must come up with other criteria.

Asset Allocation Again

Just as advisors have done with individual investors, institutional investment consultants have dealt with this problem in part by adding "style allocation" to "asset allocation." The consultant first goes through the exercise of asset allocation with the client, to determine the overall allocation to stocks and bonds and perhaps small investments in real estate and "alternatives" (which can include investment in private companies and hedge fund investments).

After asset allocation the consultant recommends a style allocation. *Styles* are subsets of the whole stock market. "Large growth" is a style, meaning stocks in companies that are large—have large capitalization; that is, the total value of their outstanding stock is large—and have high price-to-earnings ratios and a history of rapid growth. Other styles are large value, small growth, small value, and emerging markets.

A "search" is often performed just to find a money manager who uses a specific style—a style the consultant has determined the client ought to have. A different money management firm may be selected to manage each style.

A rather odd criterion that consultants have chosen to evaluate and select money managers is to steer clear of money managers who exhibit "style drift." The money manager is supposed to declare a management style as a discipline and stick to it. Evidence that the manager has not stuck to its style suggests lack of discipline and is presumed bad. Computer programs can be run to check whether the manager's investment history over time shows that it stuck closely to its style.

But the more the manager is exhorted to stick closely to its style, the more it must resemble an index fund. There are index funds available to invest in all the stocks of a given style. Being passive investments, these index funds carry low fees. So to force investment managers into a mold in which they are not supposed to exhibit style drift means to make them more like index funds. So why should they charge higher fees if they're just running closet index funds (not to mention that they probably don't add any performance above index funds anyway)? Active managers who win out in the search are often the ones who are best at weasel-wording answers to such questions. (On occasion passive managers do win, however.)

Furthermore, a style allocation in which the manager of each style must not exhibit style drift—and therefore resembles an index fund manager for that style—will *in toto* resemble a total market index fund, but at much higher cost. (Not a few institutional investors finally decide the whole charade is not worth the trouble and cost, and they just invest in broad-based index funds.)

After the field has been narrowed down to a few candidates, the surviving money management firms are invited in to meetings with the fund managers and consultants. These meetings are major events for the money managers. They prepare for them assiduously, because success can mean many millions of dollars in revenues.

For a multibillion-dollar institutional fund, the whole process costs millions of dollars. The money comes from the pockets of the corporation's employees and investors. The data clearly show that the corporation's employees and investors get no monetary value in return for this outlay.

Principal–Agent Theory Applied to Institutional Investors

The explanation why *individual* investors—those who invest their own money—pay exorbitant amounts to advisors and managers may be because they are irrational. But for *institutional* investors, an irrationality explanation isn't needed. A branch of classical economics explains why perfectly rational, self-interested institutional investors would "fall victim" to these irrationalities.

The branch of economics is called *principal–agent theory*. The principal–agent problem occurs whenever the "agent" in charge of managing an asset is not the same as the "principal" who owns it.

For example, when corporate managers (agents) are different from the corporation's stockholders or owners (principals), the principal–agent dilemma becomes a problem. The corporate managers cannot necessarily be trusted to act in the interests of the owners. And when those who have charge of an investment pool, such as the staff of a pension or endowment fund, are not the ones who own or invest in it, the problem arises again.

We might naively assume that the principal and the agent are on the same team and therefore have the same interests at heart. But economic assumptions—and reality—are colder than that. People are faced with different incentives, even if they're on the same team. They react differently. In other words, it's every man for himself.

One statement of the principal–agent problem is as follows:

The central dilemma investigated by principal agent theorists is how to get the employee or contractor (agent) to act in the best interests of the principal (the employer) when the employee or contractor has an informational advantage over the principal and has different interests from the principal.[1]

For the principal, the asset is *his* golden cake. For the agent, it's someone *else's* golden cake. The more golden crumbs the agent can shave from the cake and keep for himself, the better off he'll be. And the agent usually has an advantage in this incongruity of interests. The agent has more information than the principal does. The agent is in the thick of things while the principal isn't. The agent is in a position to manipulate the information that the principal sees.

A corollary of principal–agent theory is that the agent will complicate the information so it is difficult to evaluate the agent's effectiveness. The agent doesn't want the principal—his boss—to evaluate him based on his results; that's too risky. He would rather be evaluated based on his behavior, not his results. That way he—and the peer group of professionals he belongs to—can define the terms of the evaluation, by claiming that certain behaviors are deemed appropriate by the profession. They can even create professional societies and certifications to define accepted behavior, and their bosses will have to go along with it.

Fareed Zakaria, in his book *The Future of Freedom*, laments the fact that agents these days are just looking out for their own interests. He argues that there was a time in America a few generations ago when staunch community members—lawyers, counselors, and advisors—were virtually synonymous with the public trust. These noble servants were often from the "aristocratic" class. Their education—at the best schools, from boarding schools on up—trained them to be trustworthy public servants first and foremost.

Ah, wouldn't it be wonderful if consultants and advisors truly had only the interests of their clients, employers, and the public trust at heart. But economics is too cynical to believe that anyone acts in a 100 percent economically disinterested manner. Self-interest always comes into play and alters behavior—frequently very subtly, yet decisively.

Principal–agent theory looks at the situation from the standpoint of the agent's self-interest. It notes that the agent will have an incentive to resist the principal's information-gathering efforts. That gives the agent more control over the golden cake and more opportunity to shave off golden crumbs.

Agents Have an Incentive to Be Incomprehensible to Their Bosses

One way to resist the principal's information-gathering efforts—in the apparent name of best professional practice—is to join a community of agents (and their consultants) who all use impenetrable, difficult-to-understand jargon and pursue objectives couched in this jargon.

Every institutional fund has a staff that oversees its investment. For example, the Harvard endowment fund, with assets of about $20 billion, has a staff of more than a hundred. CalPERS, the California Public Employees Retirement System, with almost $200 billion in assets, has a much larger staff. All told, there are tens of thousands of employees who oversee very large pieces of golden cake. The job of these staff members is to manage and monitor the investment of the funds and to obtain the best investment result at lowest risk.

These staff members—the keepers of the golden cakes—consort regularly with investment consulting companies and investment management firms. The revenues earned by the consultants and managers come from scrapings off those golden cakes, awarded to them by the pension funds' and endowment funds' staff members.

Not surprisingly, much of the language of the staff members—the golden cake keepers—and their hired consultants and managers, is impenetrable to outsiders. In particular, it is largely incomprehensible to the owners of the golden cakes—the corporations and their employees and pensioners who own the pension funds, and the nonprofits that own the endowments. These principals are left with little alternative than to assume that the staffers (and their coterie of consultants and managers) know what they are doing.

A Lavish Hedge Fund Conference

To see what kind of discourse takes place nowadays among players in the fast-flying hedge fund industry, I went to an invitation-only hedge fund conference in Geneva, Switzerland, in April 2005. It was a two-day conference at the luxurious Hôtel Président Wilson, on the shores of the beautiful Lac Léman.

I had been at many similar conferences during my years in the investment business. But hedge funds had only recently enjoyed a large enough market to spawn a string of conferences of their own. I had not attended one before. I wanted to see whether the talk was any different from the talk I'd heard at conferences in the past.

About three or four hundred people attended—mostly men, by about a five-to-one ratio. There were hedge fund managers, actual or potential hedge fund investors (institutional investors like European pension funds), and the usual army of consulting companies and computer software providers. About five of these companies, which had ponied up very big bucks to cover the costs of the conference, advertised and demonstrated their wares at well-appointed booths.

Most of the attendees saw the conference as an opportunity to network in the pursuit of tons of money.

But I saw the principal–agent problem in action.

I knew, before I went, the results of the most careful research that had been done on hedge funds. So I saw the forest for the trees. I knew the big picture—that hedge funds are a poor investment on average; that beating the average is an out-and-out gamble, because hedge fund performance is unpredictable. The truth of this big picture could not, of course, be mentioned at the conference. It would undermine the whole purpose.

Being thoroughly shielded by tacit agreement from this inconvenient reality made for a very pleasant conference. It felt like we were bathing in an abundance of golden crumbs. The air was filled with a sense of wealth—at the very least, intimacy with wealth.

The discussions were all couched in technical jargon. Virtually all presentations were layered thick with the mathematical-sounding argot of the academically oriented investment world. The language is an elaborate extension of Markowitz's mean-variance analysis developed in the early 1950s and Sharpe's analysis of the pricing of risk developed in the 1960s.

The Same Old Flawed Pseudomathematics

Many—perhaps the great majority—of the talks presented mathematical formulations that couldn't really be put into practice, at least not meaningfully, because the numerical assumptions that the formulas need either are not available or have no validity to predict their future values. But this didn't seem to bother anyone.

To my mild surprise, the substance of talks and discussions at the conference was almost exactly the same as at conferences I had attended years, even decades, earlier. The same investment concepts were constantly tossed around—the same continual mention of alphas and betas; the same repeated use of regression analysis as the "sophisticated" mathematical technique of choice.

There was no secretiveness whatsoever (other than the nominally invitation-only nature of attendance, but invitations had been distributed quite liberally). All information presented was open to inspection. Presentations were in the standard PowerPoint slide show format now ubiquitous at conferences. A compact disk containing all the PowerPoints and much more information, too, was given to each attendee on arrival.

But the apparent openness was illusory. Everything was so jargon laden and formula encrusted that most people outside the profession (and many—probably the majority—inside the profession, too) could hardly understand a word or a Greek character of it.

A Pea Soup of Jargon

The conference was run by a French academic institution that is heavily supported by the hedge fund industry. The academic institution provided many of the speakers. They also spent a fair amount of time touting a hedge fund performance measurement product they were about to launch.

The jargon at this conference was so thick you could cut it with a knife. Nothing was ever said in relatively simple language if it could be said in mathematical-sounding lingo. Managers who run index funds were call "beta factories." Managers who try to beat the market were called "alpha specialists."

This jargon, of course, obfuscates the information that is passed on to the principals, the owners of the golden cakes. Truly assessing the performance of a hedge fund is made more difficult by the fact that the industry classifies hedge funds into at least ten different categories. It uses at least five different measures of risk, all difficult to calculate.

The Pitch

Two key hedge fund industry claims were often repeated or alluded to at the conference. These claims comprise the chief arguments made by the industry to convince institutional investors to invest in hedge funds. The claims are (1) that hedge funds add to performance by exposing an investor's portfolio to new risks and (2) that these new risks increase portfolio diversification, because they are uncorrelated with the portfolio's existing risks.

For example, a paper written by one of the employees of the hedge fund conference's academic sponsor states:

> The variation of returns may be linked to exposure to risk factors other than market risk. The most salient exposures are to changing levels of implied volatility, credit risk, changes of the yield curve, commodity and currency risk, equity market returns and equity style factors. Exposure to these risk factors actually varies greatly for different hedge fund strategies. For example, Equity Market Neutral hedge funds are typically exposed to changes in the value premium, the small cap premium and implied volatility, while CTAs [commodity trading advisors] are exposed to changes in currency and commodity prices. In the literature, there is a consensus that the exposure to such alternative risk factors is the principal source of hedge fund performance.
>
> The low correlation of hedge fund returns with equity and bond returns can be linked to their exposure to these different risk factors.[2]

But there is no reason why most of these added risks should add anything to performance. They are of the no-expected-value-added types of risk, like the risk of playing in a poker game or of trading currency futures. For example, there's no reason why exposure to the risk of the fluctuating "small cap premium and implied volatility" should add anything to your expected return. Therefore, there is no reason why these strategies' low correlation with stocks and bonds should be beneficial.

These claims are an ignorant (or, perhaps worse, deliberate) corruption of the Nobel Prize–winning theories. As I pointed out in Chapter 12, for an investment risk to be capable of enhancing long-run return, it must be an investment in a venture that can create wealth.

Hedge Fund Industry Participants
Control How They Will Be Evaluated

The industry had founded a new professional association and a new certification, the Chartered Alternative Investment Analyst^{SM} or CAIA certification. (*Alternative* is a word used for a broad class of unconventional investments, the majority of which are hedge funds.) The academic institution running the conference advertised itself as "the exclusive official CAIA association course provider for Europe."

True to the corollary of principal–agent theory, the conference put much more emphasis on the *behavior* of the participants in the industry than on their *results*. If you use alphas and betas a lot in your speech patterns, if you get a CAIA certification, and if you go to a lot of conferences like this one, your bosses and clients can only assume your results must be—or will be—good. You've managed to change the way they evaluate your performance to one you can control.

The actual providers of the golden crumbs were in evidence on panels. Several were in charge of pension investments for large European companies. These providers' largesse in doling out pieces of golden cake for the scraping was the chief target of the other participants.

In spite of the negative results of broad studies of hedge funds, institutional investors have been getting into them apace. One reason (or excuse) given to get into them is because of a few anecdotal experiences of good hedge fund performance. Another is because of frustration over the recent inability to predict stock market peaks and precipitous declines like the one of 2000–2002.

But the cynical, economically cold explanation is that hedge funds provide a golden opportunity for agents and their cronies—the consultants and managers they hire—to cash in big on the principal–agent problem. Hedge funds have been getting away with very large scrapings of golden crumbs from golden cakes. The justification offered for these large scrapings is that they are only scrapings from the winnings and that the hedge fund business is very technical, requiring extremely smart and well-paid people.

The Golden Cake Providers Are Easily Seduced

The principals' immediate agents (those who are in charge of, e.g., pension fund investments for large companies) may feign reluctance; but they, as individuals, can only gain from a dalliance with hedge funds. They can only gain, that is, given that the community of hedge fund providers and consultants provides them cover, by polishing the legend that hedge funds are a technological miracle and a great investment.

As long as the professional hedge fund community can provide the golden cakes' agents with that cover, making hedge fund performance measurement arcane and offering plausible explanations when poor performance cannot be concealed, the agents will prosper in their careers. The agents will seem more technically aware to their employers for consorting with these speakers in alpha-and-beta tongues. They will have an excuse to hire more staff and, therefore, to have their own compensation increased.

And they will, of course, be treated to a variety of lavish and ingeniously devised perks by their compatriots-in-arms—the hedge fund managers and consultants—whom they are making rich.

18

Derivatives: The Good, the Bad, and the Ugly

. . . .

I will talk about derivatives because there actually can be a place in some people's—and some institutions'—portfolios for certain kinds of derivatives, especially if they are almost paranoically concerned about the possibility of losses. But as most of the public is at least vaguely aware, some uses and forms of derivatives can also be quite dangerous. In this chapter, I will explain the beneficial uses as well as the bad uses.

In the last thirty years, a segment of the financial market that was once very small has come to account for a large portion of the trades. Derivative products called *options* and *futures*, which are derived either from individual stocks or from stock indexes, or from commodities like oil, have proliferated and are traded very actively.

Most of these contracts are more like insurance contracts than investments. (Of course, for those who offer the insurance, it is an investment.) They are called *derivatives* because their values depend on the value of some other indicator—such as the price of a stock, a stock index, or a commodity.

Derivatives can have their uses in the investment world—at least in principle—mostly as forms of insurance. The most common forms of derivatives are futures, call options, and put options.

A *futures contract* is a contract to purchase something at a future time at a predetermined price. An example of a futures contract is the currency future. For example, you could purchase a currency future for $900 to receive 100,000 Japanese yen in a year. The contract obligates you to pay $900 in a year and receive 100,000 yen.

A *call option* is an *option*—not an obligation—to buy. For example you could pay $50 for the option to buy 100,000 yen in a year for $900. In a year, you can decide whether to exercise your option or not (but you'll be out the $50 in either case).

A *put option* is the reverse of a call—it is the option (not the obligation) to *sell* something at a future time for a predetermined price.

These instruments, under certain circumstances, can have practical uses in an investor's portfolio, particularly to hedge against the risk of a fall in the portfolio's value.

I'll explain this application in a little while. But first let's look at some of the simpler uses of derivative products.

Using Derivatives to Hedge against Currency Exchange Risk

Suppose you are a U.S. citizen and plan to take a long trip to Japan in a year, but you're on a tight budget. You are willing to spend $10,000 in Japan but no more than that. At anticipated yen–dollar exchange rates, it looks like you'll be able to do it.

But you are a little concerned that if the dollar weakens more than expected in the coming year, your cost could exceed ten thousand dollars. You can "lock in" or hedge the cost of your trip in yen by purchasing $10,000 worth of yen futures. These futures will guarantee you a predetermined yen–dollar exchange rate at the time of your trip.

Who will sell you these yen futures? Why, quite possibly someone from Japan planning a trip to the United States in a year, who doesn't want to take a chance that the dollar will strengthen.

Actually, you'll buy your yen futures on a currency market like the Chicago Mercantile Exchange, and you won't know who sold them to you. It could be a currency futures broker who will do it on speculation and for the broker's fee, rather than a Japanese tourist who wants to come to the United States.

There is a little cost to this hedge and a little risk (of a sort). The cost is the brokerage commission. The risk is that the dollar will actually strengthen and you won't reap the benefit (this could be called a "regret cost").

It's really your choice whether you want to hedge the currency risk. Hedging costs a bit, but it insures against the risk of a currency move that is detrimental to your pocketbook. But it also reduces the chance that you will accidentally benefit.

Corporate Currency Hedging

Small export–import companies frequently hedge currency risk because big currency exchange losses could ruin them. But big companies often don't bother with currency hedging. They regard it as an unnecessary cost, because they assume that currency exchange losses and gains will cancel each other out in the long run.

In the mid-1980s, I was working on a derivatives-based method of hedging against downside risk in stock market investing. It occurred to me that the same method could be used by a corporation to hedge its currency risk.

To confirm that this would be a concern for big companies, I checked out a few corporate annual reports. I was surprised to discover that in 1985 the Coca-Cola company had lost $500 million in international currency transactions.

This was the same year that Coca-Cola became a laughingstock for launching the "New Coke." Its reasons for launching it were sound. Coke had an edge in the market over Pepsi. But every time Coca-Cola researchers conducted a blind taste test with randomly selected subjects who sampled unmarked glasses of Coca-Cola and Pepsi, they said they liked the Pepsi better.

The difference between Pepsi and Coke was that Pepsi was sweeter. So the Coke people decided they'd better make Coke sweeter, or they would lose market share to Pepsi.

It was said that Coke spent $10 million, a seemingly exorbitant sum (but it was probably much more than that), on market research and refurbishing bottling plants to change to the New Coke.

When it was launched, people immediately rebelled against it. They said they liked the old Coke better—confounding the taste tests. Ultimately Coke reissued "Classic Coke" and let New Coke slip away quietly. Later, they discovered that although people said they preferred New Coke in blind taste tests, when the taste tests weren't blind— that is, when people were told what brand they were drinking—they said they preferred Coke. It was brand name reliability that mattered, not the taste of the first sip.

At any rate, Coke's wasted expenditure on the New Coke might have been less of a laughingstock if people realized how small it really was to the company. It was dwarfed by the $500 million the company lost on currency transactions.

The previous year, Coca-Cola had *gained* $500 million on currency transactions. To the company, gain or loss on currency transactions was a randomly fluctuating wave going on somewhere in the background in its financial statements. It was a wave that averaged out to zero in the long run, not something the company needed to do anything about.

TIGRs and CATs, Oh, My!

One of the earliest widely marketed niche financial products, created from another financial product, was launched in August 1982 by Merrill Lynch and almost simultaneously by its competitor Salomon Brothers. Merrill Lynch called its product "TIGR"s (for Treasury Investment Growth Receipts), while Salomon called its "CATS" (for Certificates of Accrual on Treasury Securities). This illustrates how competitive the market is for equivalent financial instruments and how quickly they become competitively priced.

Other investment banks followed suit and issued their own similar vehicles shortly afterward. Eventually, in 1985, the U.S. government got into the act, calling its investment vehicle "Treasury STRIPS" (for Separate Trading of Registered Interest and Principal Securities).

The niche market for these TIGRs, CATS, and STRIPS consisted of families with young college-bound children. If you bought a TIGR or CATS or STRIPS for your kid, you could lock in the cost of college.

It was a good idea, and it was launched at the right time. Interest rates were at a historic high. Costs of education were climbing fast. Lots of people had young children. An increasing percentage of them were planning to send their kids to college. They weren't sure how they could afford it.

If you wanted to send your eight-year-old daughter to a four-year college when she reached eighteen, it might be projected to cost you $45,000 in ten years. Lo and behold, if you bought, let's say, a

$20,000 TIGR, you would be guaranteed to have $45,000 in ten years. (This really *was* a guarantee, backed by U.S. Treasury notes.) If your child wasn't even born yet and you planned to send her to college in twenty years, it might cost you as little as $10,000 to guarantee her future education.

The way they did this was interesting. Merrill Lynch bought U.S. Treasury notes maturing in, say, ten years. These notes paid interest payments of about 8 or 9 percent, plus repayment of principal (the original investment) at the end. Then Merrill reissued them, split into two pieces—one that paid only interest with no repayment of principal at the end and the other that paid only principal at the end but no interest payments. The latter was its TIGR. You buy one, you get a big payment in ten or twenty years, but no interest payments before that. But it costs you much less. Someone else pays for, and gets, the interest payments.

You might think these vehicles, these CATS and TIGRs and STRIPS, were a godsend to parents of college-bound children. You might think they were a financial miracle that you should have known about, but never would have unless you had a good investment advisor. Therefore, you might think, you need an investment advisor to sort through all the endless variations in investment vehicles and find the one that's right for you.

But remember that all investment vehicles (and there are so many of them) are competitive with each other, and the cash flows are fungible. They are, therefore, all—for the investor—really near-equivalents, except for risk.

As it turned out, lots of other investment vehicles (ones you knew about) would have been fine, too. They would have been even better, as it turns out, for the purpose of sending your child to college.

If you had bought a TIGR or CATS in August 1982 for $20,000, it would have matured ten years later for $45,000. But if you had invested that same $20,000 in a diversified stock index fund with low fees, you would have had $100,000, not $45,000. If you had invested it in a diversified long-term mutual bond fund, you would have had $65,000.

It was a period when all investments grew rapidly—perhaps not surprisingly, given the high return on a risk-free investment. The guaranteed 8 or 9 percent on the TIGRs and CATS was good, but most other investments were even better. That's the way the cookie crumbles. The investments compete with each other, and they tend to be near-equivalents except for risk.

Hedging with Options against a Fall in the Stock Market

Many people are understandably loath to invest in stocks because their downside appears unlimited. True, no contractual obligation requires that an investor in a stock be paid anything at all, ever. The investor relies on her portfolio of companies to grow in the long run. The investor trusts that the companies' shares will increase in value and be marketable later, or that the companies will pay dividends.

A diversified portfolio of stocks is almost certain to grow, pay dividends, and be saleable for a higher price later. But some people are still uncomfortable that there's no guarantee it will be worth anything at all.

Equity-Linked Contracts

A simple options strategy can allow such a giddy investor to invest in the stock market yet be guaranteed not to lose money—at least not much of it.

This strategy has been offered to investors numerous times over the last twenty years. It caught on in a big way in its first incarnation in the mid-1980s, dubbed "portfolio insurance," though principally among big institutional investors. The market for options was unfortunately not well enough developed at that time, so the strategy had to use so-called synthetic options—a method that uses futures to mimic options—but the synthetic options strategy was not foolproof. It suffered a serious blow in the 20 percent one-day market decline of October 19, 1987, and the subsequent market volatility.

The method is now typically embodied in what is called *equity-linked contracts*.[1] They work something like this.

If you buy a diversified stock portfolio, but you also buy a put option on a broad market index like the S&P 500 as insurance, you can virtually guarantee that the value of your portfolio won't drop below some predetermined minimum.

But the put option will cost you. That will eat significantly into your gains. An individual can do this without an advisor or money manager or packager—and thus without incurring unreasonable fees. But the opportunities are limited (puts are offered on the open market only for a few fixed exercise prices and a few expiration dates). Thus, packaged products available through advisors can be more suitable. But their fees—as is normal in the investment services profession—are high.

The Bond-Plus-Call Hedge

A variation on this strategy that does the same thing, and that packagers often use, is very easy to understand.

The strategy is to buy a "risk-free" bond—say, a U.S. Treasury STRIP—maturing in, for example, three years. If you have $50,000 to invest, you can buy notes that mature at $50,000. This might cost you, now, about $45,000.

That leaves you $5,000 out of your $50,000. Invest that in call options on the S&P 500. If the market goes up, the call options will go up much more. You'll reap a good profit (though probably not as much as if you'd put it all in the market). If the market goes down, well, in three years at least you'll still have your $50,000.

Doing this sort of thing is called *shaping the risk*. Instead of just submitting yourself to a portfolio that goes up and down with the market, with the ups and downs distributed in what is called the *bell curve*, you could decide how many and what size "ups" you'd like, for how many and what size "downs."

There's no free lunch, of course. If you try to limit your downs, you'll give up something on the ups. But because of the huge variety of derivative instruments, you could tinker with this to your heart's content. You'll also give up something on brokerage costs (and a whole lot more than that if you do it through an advisor or money manager). But if you really think you know what shape of risk entices you, you can satisfy your desire.

Needed: A Lower-Cost Hedge against Downside Stock Market Risk

A demand exists in the market for a lower-cost long-term hedge against downside stock market risk. If, say, a ten- or twenty-year insurance contract were available (like a put option) at reasonable cost, there would be a strong market for it.

Such contracts are now available from large investment banks, but only for large amounts and only at exorbitant cost. If a low-cost long-term put option (or call option) could be developed, to go along with an investor's low-cost long-term stock index fund, it would be a boon to investors. Costs could and should be lower than they are now, but—in the same way that experimentation with index funds finally got their characteristics right and their costs down—some experimentation with new equity-linked products and new ways to create products will be needed.

Are Derivatives Dangerous?

Thus, derivatives can have their uses, and there are many other uses in niche markets in business, foreign exchange, banking, and others. In large part, though, they're used by—and created by—the game players, people like those I played cards with in college, matching wits with each other. As in my nightly college poker games, some win, some lose.

This is unlike investing in stocks directly, where the money can be used to create a valuable product and turn a profit without reducing anyone else's wealth. The best kind of investment creates wealth: more for everybody, less for no one.

A running debate has been taking place recently among those who think financial derivatives are dangerous to the financial system and mere "speculation" as opposed to investing. Warren Buffett is on the side against derivatives. On the pro side, the chief argument is that derivatives enhance "liquidity." That is, they provide more and more ways to make cash flows fungible. By doing this, they increase comfort that the financial system offers opportunities for investors to bail out or change their risk posture. By making investors more comfortable, it increases the overall availability of investment capital where it is needed.

There is something to this argument. The United States has been the hotbed of innovation. It is also the place where willingness to take investment risk is highest. Complicated ways to invest or to shape the risk of investing abound. This may have helped make capital to fund risky innovation more available. Perhaps, the innovation rate is high in the United States because there are so many ways for investors to take or to hedge risk.

Anyone who wants to take extra risk in investing, and can afford to, should by all means be encouraged to do so—if she can do it without becoming a ward of the state if she fails. Risk capital is good for the economy. Financial instruments to encourage and facilitate risk taking that can create wealth, and to reward it, are, therefore, good for the economy.

But as we well know now, financial derivatives can have their darker sides, too. One is exemplified by headline news stories about firms (like Barings) that went under because of rogue traders who took big positions in derivatives without the full knowledge of their bosses. Very big bets can be placed by professional traders using derivatives while hardly batting an eyelash. Then, if markets go in the wrong direction, their bets can lead to very big losses.

And, as we also well know now, derivatives can be used for financial and accounting legerdemain to mask the true state of a company's financial affairs. Enron's extraordinary creative accounting is a case in point.

The Black-Scholes Formula

One of the most surprising developments in the financial world in recent years has been the widespread acceptance of an arcane mathematical formula. The Black-Scholes option pricing formula—one of whose derivations comes from the body of theory developed by that once-obscure Japanese mathematician, Kiyosi Itô—has blazed through the financial world like wildfire. Although the Black-Scholes formula is difficult even to write and requires a programmer with esoteric mathematical knowledge to program, it is in constant use every day in many financial institutions. It has been enshrined on widely available handheld calculators along with buttons to calculate mortgage rates, annuities, and the like.

It is beloved by financial mathematicians and would-be mathematicians because of its compactness—the "elegance" so prized by the mathematical mind. It is also embraced because of the assumptions of its derivation—a hypothetical arbitrage between a share of stock and an option on that share of stock.

But mostly it is beloved because it quantifies, however inexactly, the price and risk of a large number of financial instruments. Before the advent of the formula, these prices and risks could not be quantified at all.

The thirst for quantification, in an effort to provide objectivity in the business and academic worlds, has become so rabid that any means of quantification, no matter how inaccurate, is thought far better than no quantification at all. Amid this perceived need for quantification, especially of prices and risks, the Black-Scholes formula meets the need better than most such formulations.

If you work at an investment bank and you contemplate a new financial derivative, the first thing you'll do is calculate its estimated price using the Black-Scholes formula—or a similar formula derived using the Itô calculus or a binomial approximation method. It may not turn out to be the price the market places on it, but it gives you some idea what can be charged for it.

Conversely, if you see that the market is bidding some financial derivative at a certain price, you can work backward and deduce what the market thinks is the underlying risk. Again, it's an imperfect measure, but it gives you some idea.

The Black-Scholes formula has been used to price a number of other things, too, like the value of stock options offered to an executive or an employee of a startup. The formula is used by energy companies to price contracts for future energy needs. It has become a required tool in the tool chests of many financial executives and risk managers in various fields. Once the formula was created, its invention became the mother of necessity.

It Won't Help You Beat the Stock Market

The formula does not, of course, help predict the future. Hence, it doesn't help determine whether one investment will work out better than another. And it doesn't necessarily enhance the ability to avoid risk. On the contrary, it has enticed some too-smug people—infected with scientism—to make monumental errors of risk assessment. (For example, witness the downfall, covered in Chapter 16, of Long-Term Capital Management—a firm that included prominently among its partners the two Nobel Prize–winning creators of options pricing theory and one of the Black-Scholes formula namesakes.)

Most financial derivatives are for people who have a specific financial need or a risk that can be hedged—like the traveler from the United States to Japan and the traveler from Japan to the United States who exchange currency futures with each other. Most financial derivatives are not primarily for investors, other than the inveterate game players.

Investors can trade financial derivatives if they think offering the needed risk hedge can make them money—just as they might become Lloyd's of London "names" and provide risk capital to insure oil tankers. And they might use them to hedge their own investment risk. But by and large, financial derivatives, like all other investment vehicles, follow the expected no-free-lunch rule: you get what you pay for. If you take more risk—in the long run and on average—you'll get more return; otherwise you probably won't.

The Many Pitfalls between Sales Reality and Real-World Reality

Remember I said earlier that derivatives can have their uses, at least in principle? Well, it turns out the little qualifier "at least in principle" should not be overlooked. Execution of an idea that is good "at least in principle" isn't always quite what you thought it would be.

An experience I had in 1999 proves this point. As the chief economist for an investment services firm, I was looking for ways to provide attractive, beneficial investment vehicles for our clients and our clients' clients—the investors. (My firm's direct clients were financial advisors.)

The market at the time was rocketing upward. It had been for many years. Returns over 20 percent annually had become almost the norm. Some inexperienced investors were coming to expect them.

A debate was raging about whether we had entered a new age of innovation and efficiency, an age in which information exchange was so easy that economic growth rates would be permanently elevated.

Some intelligent observers thought yes. They thought the stock market would keep on rocketing. But others thought things were not all that new and different. They thought there was no reason to expect high growth rates forever. They concluded the stock market was dangerously overvalued.

It was hard to know which view was right. No one wanted to reduce their stock market investments, because they would be so sorry if the market kept soaring.

But no one wanted to get caught in the collapse either, if the naysayers were right.

I thought the ideal solution to this dilemma was the strategy mentioned a few pages earlier: hedging stock market investments with an index put option or, equivalently, combining an index call option with a risk-free bond. This would give investors a piece of the upside if the stock market continued its steep upward trend, but it would limit losses if the market fell.

This strategy was already offered by another investment provider. I thought we could just lease their product from them and offer it to our investment advisor-clients.

Our Lawyer Weighs In against It

When I discussed this with the other partners of my firm, I was surprised to find that our lawyer, the general counsel, was firmly against it. His reason provides a lot of insight—and he was probably right.

The lawyer said we had hundreds, probably well over a thousand, of investment advisors who were our clients, not all of them very bright. We couldn't trust them to explain something to their customers as complicated as downside stock market protection. One or more of them would explain it incorrectly, or the customers wouldn't understand it. Something would go wrong, and we'd get sued.

In short, if there was a possibility our clients—the investment advisors—wouldn't understand it and their customers wouldn't understand it, we'd better not offer it, no matter how good an idea it might be for investors. The only thing they could be counted on to understand was that they were hiring us to beat the market. We were stuck with the Big Investment Lie for a sales pitch and a product, and nothing else. The Lie was so thoroughly embedded in the context of our business that any departure from it—even for the good of the investor—was dangerous to our firm's health.

It Wasn't What It Seemed, Anyway

Then I discovered that the downside protection wasn't really what they said it was.

The hedge was being implemented by the New York investment arm of a large European bank. A longtime colleague of mine had, in fact, worked as a consultant to the New York investment firm and had been involved originally in planning the strategy.

He and I went to New York to visit the company. We knew that the brokers selling the package claimed it limited your possible losses to 10 percent at most.

We asked the investment management folks exactly how they guaranteed the lower limit. Their answer was unclear. We couldn't get a better answer, so we asked to look at the data on their investments —how much they had invested in what, at what times.

After poring over the information (which I felt the investment managers hadn't really wanted to give us), we found out what was really going on.

The strategy was supposed to protect each investor, using a put or putlike instrument, against having his portfolio lose 10 percent or more of its value over three years.

But it didn't treat each investor separately. It just lumped them all together. Then it divided the portfolio between two managers. The first one managed an actively managed portfolio of stocks.

The second manager bought put contracts on the Chicago Board Options Exchange at seemingly random times. The timing—and the amounts of the puts, their exercise prices, everything about the puts—had nothing whatsoever to do with any individual investor and what that investor had at risk, and for how long.

The result was that whenever the investor bet on stocks in his portfolio, the put-buying arm of the investment management firm would make a countervailing bet against those stocks—and add it to the investor's portfolio.

In short, the "hedge" was simply to neutralize the investor's stock investments. It merely canceled out his stock investments—by buying stocks with one hand and, in effect, selling them with the other. The investor could have done this much better on his own by merely reducing his allocation to stocks. Then, he wouldn't have had to pay the high fees.

What was sold as a "highly sophisticated" hedging strategy was nothing of the kind. It was dumber than dishwater. What was sold as "a plan customized to your objectives" was not the least bit customized—it was the same stupid strategy for everybody.

The sales pitch, and possibly even the original intent, can be one thing; the actual implementation is another thing entirely. Often, it turns out that once an investment concept is sold to investors, implementing it isn't so easy. So the investment manager just does something—anything. The investor never knows the difference. It's much too hard for anyone—even a knowledgeable professional, let alone an investor who pays little attention—to find out what's really going on.

In my experience, far more often than not, it's not what they say it is.

19

The Modern Slippery Slope
of Business Ethics

. . . .

In the eighteenth and much of the nineteenth centuries, the vast majority of people worked on farms. Then the industrial revolution and mechanization took most of the labor out of farm work. In the industrialized Western world, farm laborers became factory workers. In the end, less than 5 percent of the workforce in the developed world now works on farms.

More recently, after farm workers became factory workers, factory jobs in America and Europe moved to regions of lower-cost labor in the Far East and South Asia. America became more and more the land of service industries and white-collar professions.

Now, even service labor such as computer programming, data entry, and telephone-based technical assistance is moving to countries like India and other lands where knowledge workers can be hired at lower cost. America is, consequently, fast becoming the land of financial engineering and marketing engineering.

Is the pursuit of these new professions as respectable as it seems, even granted their high income levels and status? Are they leading to a general degradation of the business ethic in the United States and Europe? Where, in the next phase, will this progression lead?

Anyone who has read a history of the high-flying telecommunications companies of the late 1990s, like Kurt Eichenwald's comprehensive account of the rise and fall of Enron, *Conspiracy of Fools*, will see that the business of many companies was chiefly to engineer their financial reports to make their profits look high. Enron was, in fact, widely admired by corporate America for its financial legerdemain.

Is it possible that America has begun to exhaust—except possibly for its continued ingenuity in the high-tech field—its ability to out-perform workers in other countries and therefore to justify higher wages? How long can the connivances and borderline deceptions that often characterize "marketing engineering" and "financial engineer-ing" continue?

The Path of Deception

Let's trace some of the practices to which these new arts have led.

One example is the exploding use of "rebates" in product mar-keting. Rebates are a way to artificially engineer buyer perceptions and payments, to tweak more money from customers while maintain-ing good "optics"—that is, the appearance of low cost.

The whole practice depends on a consumer class that can be deceived—or induced to deceive itself—in small ways, sometimes even in large ways.

If a product is sold for $99.95 but carries a rebate of $20, it can be advertised for a price of $79.95. The optics, therefore, are good. But as a blogger on the Tech Observer Web site put it in speaking about a Dell Computer rebate:

> The merchant advertises the product at the "after rebate" price, but you actually pay the "before rebate" price. Then, you have to touch your right ear with your left hand, while standing on your left foot, face South and hop up and down three times. If you do even one of those things wrong, they refuse to give you your rebate, even though they've advertised the product at the post-rebate price.

The seller hopes that many, perhaps most, of the buyers will dis-cover that the process of obtaining their rebate is not worth the trou-ble and won't bother. In the meantime, the seller retains the use of the $20—the "float"—on which they can earn interest, until months after the sale when some buyers actually receive and cash their rebate checks.

Designing and implementing these rebate programs requires smart people who do careful research, analysis, and strategizing.

But is this activity productive? Is it really respectable to engage in intense and deliberate planning to take financial advantage of consumer weaknesses, irrationality, and misconceptions? Does it not even border a little on the fraudulent?

Then there are the credit card, phone card, mortgage, and installment plan offers that advertise in huge print a low rate, then mention (because regulations require it)—in very fine print—additional costs that negate the benefits of the rate quoted in large print.

Many package deals—for telephone service, for example—are engineered so they are low in cost if the user stays within the complicatedly defined boundaries of the package, but they become far more expensive with any minor departure. This makes, once again, for good "optics"—the quoted rate is low. But a large percentage of users wind up paying much more than the face price. These deals are deliberately engineered to look cheap but to cost on average far more than advertised, thus enhancing the seller's revenues.

The problem is not only that these minor deceptions could be considered mildly unethical by a stickler. Of more concern is that they are now well within the bounds of accepted business practice.

Pushing the Outer Edge of the Envelope

The real problem is the slippery slope. When these kinds of deceptions become ordinary business practice, go-getters in middle management, under pressure to produce higher revenues, will push the edge of the envelope. They will try to milk even higher revenues from their customers in hopes of winning stars for their profit numbers from their bosses.

For example, I had an experience recently that, given the current business environment, may well have resulted from some middle manager pushing the edge of the envelope of "mildly" deceptive practices.

I sold a condominium that was bought with a floating-rate mortgage from CitiMortgage, part of the Citibank financial conglomerate. The mortgage was to have no prepayment penalty on sale. (According to the mortgage agreement, there would be a prepayment penalty if the condominium were refinanced but not if sold.)

As anyone who has bought or sold a house or a condominium knows, you have to go to a closing at which the buyer and seller supposedly read and sign an enormous number of documents. Almost no one actually reads them—it would take hours. Even the form that is sometimes included, in which you vouch for the fact that you have read the forms, is signed but unread.

As I was leafing through the forms and not reading them and signing at the bottom, something suddenly caught my eye. It leaped out at me—I must be lucky to have a good eye for such things. I was being charged a prepayment penalty of $2,500.

I frankly did not remember the exact terms of the mortgage (they were complicated, like so many financial arrangements these days), but I thought this was not right. I would have known that there would be a prepayment penalty.

Fortunately, I had a mobile phone with me and had used a mortgage broker to get the mortgage. The mortgage broker was in. While the closing agents tapped their feet with impatience, I called my mortgage broker and asked him what the terms of the mortgage were. He told me there was to be a prepayment penalty only if the mortgage were refinanced, but not if the condominium were sold.

I relayed this to the closing agent and the real estate agents. They looked very annoyed at the inconvenience. It was too late to alter the forms. I extracted absolute assurances from them that the closing agent would retrieve the $2,500 from CitiMortgage.

Weeks later I received a check. But it could so easily have slipped by me—and fattened the CitiMortgage division's bottom line.

The Faithlessness of the Modern Business Environment toward the Customer

Given the environment of marginally deceptive practices, this is almost par for the course. "Mistakes" like this one are somehow hardly ever made in the consumer's favor. It is conceivable, of course, that it was an honest error. But I strongly suspect it resulted from at least a partially deliberate effort to squeeze more revenue for the department of some middle manager at CitiMortgage. In this case, in my opinion, it did not border on fraud but *was* fraud. Yet it is debatable whether it is more fraudulent than the rebate practice or the practice of advertising low rates and negating them in the fine print.

The Exaltation of Quantification

In the environment of business that has evolved, the "bottom line" is all that matters. It is considered the only possible measure of what is good and desirable. Other measures, such as whether business is being conducted in a manner that is upstanding and ethical, suffer from being "unquantifiable."

The exaltation of "quantifiability," and the concomitant reduction in status of the nonquantifiable, has a long history.

On October 4, 1957, the Soviet Union shocked the United States. by being the first to launch an artificial orbiting satellite they called *Sputnik*. The United States, perceiving itself locked in a nuclear arms struggle for survival with the Soviet Union, was appalled and frightened. It seemed an indication that the Soviet Union was ahead of the Untied States technologically.

America's federal government poured millions and billions of extra dollars into research in physics, aeronautics, nuclear energy, astrophysics, and other sciences in an effort to regain the upper hand. It was a bonanza for researchers and industries in the hard sciences.

But not for the soft sciences. Researchers and academicians in fields like psychology, sociology, economics, and even business all got a bad case of "physics envy."

The solution for researchers in those fields was to make them look like the hard sciences—to use a lot of mathematics and to demand "quantification," "measurability," and "verifiability." These may be laudable pursuits, but they don't meet every objective.

Prominent people who demanded quantifiability, like Robert S. McNamara, president of Ford Motor and then U.S. secretary of defense, exerted great influence by insisting on supposedly hard-nosed quantification-based reporting and management.

Single-Minded Pursuit of Bottom-Line Quantifiability Breaks Fiduciary Bond with Customers

Qualities like ethical uprightness, professionalism, and good service are not very quantifiable. Financial attributes like revenues and profits are. One result of this exaltation of quantification is that professional workers who used to be highly respected for the services they provide (e.g., schoolteachers) are now less respected, for the simple reason that, due to their sources of income, they cannot be paid very well. This leads many people who would otherwise be excellent schoolteachers to pursue financial or marketing careers instead, not only because of the higher earnings—because money isn't everything—but because of the higher social status accorded them.

Meanwhile, people with a much lower level of ethics—including many mutual fund salespeople and managers, hedge fund managers and their associated flacks, and providers of investment advice—are more highly respected, for the dubious reason that they make more money because they are better positioned to scrape golden crumbs off golden cakes.

In the late 1950s, a writer named Vance Packard wrote a series of best-selling books with titles like *The Hidden Persuaders* and *The Waste Makers*, about how companies connive to extract more money out of consumers. For example, in *The Waste Makers*, Packard tells how a company decided to color its potato peelers white, because that way they were more likely to be thrown out with the potato peels. The consumer would then have to buy another potato peeler.

But these little tricks are small potatoes, as it were, compared with how the investment advice and management business tucks away costs so they become almost invisible (to all but the least casual observer) and overemphasizes benefits.

For example, the prospectus for a popular "index" fund of hedge funds mentions only in a barely noticeable passage that it pays the managers of the hedge funds anywhere from 15 to 25 percent of gains. (Of course, the managers do not pay back any percentage when they lose.) This is in addition to several percent of assets as management and "index" fund fees, plus certain other unrevealed costs that have been found by recent studies to be very substantial. As pointed out in Chapter 3, what with the ups and downs generally experienced with hedge funds, as with all risky investments, the fees could easily prove to eat up the bulk of any long-term investment gains.

Many, undoubtedly the vast majority, of people who engage in these practices regard themselves as upstanding, moral participants in the business life of the twenty-first century. Their code demands that they do everything they can to make a buck—to increase the quantities on their bottom lines. Only law restrains them. If they do something that the law (perhaps creatively interpreted) does not demand but that reduces their profits, their shareholders or investors could even sue them.

Ethics Is Something You
Practice outside Business

The result is a curiously exaggerated division between business and ethical life. Businesspeople who earn fabulous amounts of money deceiving the gullible look forward to establishing nonprofit foundations with their riches to fund altruistic services for the downtrodden.

In a typical account of cleansing beneficence, *Los Angeles Times* writer Kenneth R. Weiss wrote of retired hedge fund manager David Gelbaum in an October 28, 2004, piece subtitled, "David Gelbaum has shunned publicity while giving millions to preserve California wilderness and teach youths about nature":

> He has given more money to conservation causes in California than anyone else. His gifts have helped protect 1,179 square miles of mountain and desert landscapes, an area the size of Yosemite National Park. . . .
>
> Over a decade of steadily growing contributions—including more than $100 million to the Sierra Club—this mathematician turned financial angel has taken great pains to remain anonymous.
>
> In manner and appearance, David Gelbaum has maintained a low profile for someone who can afford to give away hundreds of millions of dollars.
>
> At age 55, retired from the rarefied world of Wall Street hedge funds, he lives in Newport Beach with his wife and two of his five children in a large home where visitors on occasion have mistaken him for the gardener. . . . He drives a Honda Civic hybrid, wears jeans and T-shirts to business meetings and helps the kids clean up at the wilderness camp-outs he sponsors. . . .
>
> His donations, which according to public records and other sources total at least $250 million, have preserved hundreds of miles of wildlife corridors across mountains and deserts, tying together once-isolated national parks and wilderness areas. One conservation deal, land trust experts say, is the largest single purchase of private land ever handed over to the U.S. government for one purpose: to leave it alone.

As to the source of funding that enabled this largesse:

> His business success, he said, "was all a matter of chance."

A plethora of tales like this one helps account for the galloping growth of nonprofits in the last two to three decades. The nonprofit online newsletter *Nonprofit Leader's* January 2004 issue says, "Employment growth in nonprofits and philanthropy has outpaced government, business, and industry over the last five years. Nonprofit employees now outnumber the civilian employees of the entire federal government and the 50 state governments combined." According to the *Chronicle of Philanthropy*, "The growth in nonprofits is mind-boggling. In 1977, 739,000 nonprofits existed, employing 5.52 million people and raising $111.1 billion a year. In 1999 nonprofit organizations spent nearly $785 billion accounting for 8.5% of the nation's gross domestic product."

As the concentration of huge amounts of wealth in the hands of golden crumb scrapers increases, nonprofit budgets—swollen by ethically laundered funds—grow exponentially.

Is This the Best Way to Donate to Good Causes?

Is it sufficient satisfaction to know that even if we are taken for large amounts of our money by investment advisors and managers who only occasionally succeed if lucky, at least a lot of the money is going to good causes—given them by people who spent careers telling white lies to magnify their bank accounts, while nursing pent-up desires to become philanthropists?

This certainly seems an unnecessarily backhanded way to contribute to altruistic causes. It does, though, help us to forgive managers like George Soros or Julian Robertson, many of whose investors lost money while paying enormous fees, but who adequately atoned by putting substantial portions of their gains to beneficial social uses.

It does not, however, constitute sufficient reason to give our money away again in the future to investment managers and advisors who (we can only hope) might use some of it for high-minded social missions—missions that, if we are lucky, we ourselves might approve of.

Wouldn't it make more sense to withhold excessive payments to the golden crumb scrapers and to use them ourselves for the social causes we ourselves deem most worthy, or even—should we harbor fewer guilty feelings than the superwealthy—for our own benefit?

Because the golden crumb scrapers are able to exercise so much beneficence, it is very difficult to blow the whistle on them. I was, for example, exploring the Web site of a nonprofit organization recently, an organization doing excellent work. On its site were two or three icons identifying their funding sources. One was a brokerage firm I have spoken of in this book in a negative light, though not by name.

I felt a pang of regret that I was badmouthing this company and its many similar competitors so mercilessly in my book. Their support was enabling a worthy nonprofit, one with high ethical goals and effective methods, to exist.

In a way the brokerage was acting as a collector and redistributor of charitable donations. As any giver to charitable organizations knows, however, one must scrutinize the recipient's overhead rate. If the organization receiving the funds uses 90 percent of the donations for fat salaries, it's not a good deal. Only 10 percent of your donations go toward the nonprofit's charitable goals, while the rest enriches the staff.

In the case of the brokerage firm and numerous others like it, far less than 10 percent helps deserving nonprofit organizations. Far more than 90 percent goes to enrich—extraordinarily handsomely— the collectors of the funds. Hence, it makes no sense to make your charitable donations through a company like that, no matter how well its greenwashing efforts serve to polish its name.

If it is not your intent to use investment advisory and management firms as a very leaky conduit for your charitable donations— and if it is not your intent merely to enable some well-clothed people to live the high life—then you must ask yourself whether the fees you pay to them reap for you, yourself, a benefit at least equal to the charge.

The answer is an unequivocal no.

To Sum Up

The reasons why investment advisors and investment managers (with rare, very low-cost exceptions) do not provide benefits anywhere near worth the costs can be summarized in a couple of sentences.

First, the investments these service providers furnish do not, on average, earn more money for you than you could earn without their help—even if you have no "expertise."

Second, you cannot determine in advance which managed investment vehicles will be above average and which will be below average —and neither can anyone else.

These are statistical facts as irrefutable as the fact that smoking causes cancer. Anecdotal evidence—individual cases of mutual funds or hedge funds that rack up huge gains over some time period—do not invalidate the statistical evidence, any more than individual cases of heavy smokers who don't get cancer invalidate the evidence that smoking causes cancer.

What You Can Predict

The only things that can be predicted are fees and taxes. Fees and taxes can be very, very large; they can be predicted; and they can be reduced enormously by anyone who merely tries. Efforts to predict anything else are doomed to fruitlessness.

That is what the statistical facts prove.

As I have tried to make clear, it's not just a matter of statistical evidence. No, there are good and cogent reasons why it should not be worth paying much, if anything, to try to beat the stock market. They are the same reasons why it would not be worth much, if anything, to hire an expert consultant to save you money on a mass market personal computer. The experts have *already* caused the prices of personal computers to reflect their values. The experts' opinions can be consulted in newspapers, in magazines, on the Web, and on television. But more than anything, expert opinions can be consulted in the computers' prices themselves. The computers that are priced higher have—in the experts' opinions and in the combined opinions of consumers—better features, better speed, better reliability, better technical support, or a combination of these benefits. Those that are priced lower have less. You don't need to pay an expert to know that.

The "Experts" Are Putting One Over on You

What, then, of all the "expert opinion" you see and hear incessantly if you read the voluminous and often overexcited financial press, or watch financial coverage on television, or seek out (or be inundated by) advertisements and sales pitches for investment services in magazine and TV ads, word-of-mouth recommendations, cold calls, and invitations you might receive to elegant dinners involving advisor-sponsored "investment seminars" or "retirement planning" discussions?

Hard as it may be to believe, all of it doesn't amount to a hill of beans. "Experts" may say things that sound knowledgeable. They may speak of the Internet bubble, but when the stock market was "bubbling," they were recommending hot-performing high-tech mutual funds all the same. They'll speak of how important asset allocation is for the performance of your portfolio, but they won't mention that they can't "asset allocate" any better than by merely investing in a cross section of the market. They'll say that stock groups belonging to certain investment styles are "going up" or have historically gone up, but they won't tell you that what has happened recently or historically bears no relation to what will happen next. And they will say things we haven't even thought of, because they found that they work well in sales pitches. You can ignore it all—there's nothing there.

The Hedge Fund Spiel

And what of the highly educated, jet-setting people who offer and manage the newly fashionable hedge funds, and what of those highly educated, jet-setting people who invest in them? Don't they have truly sophisticated formulas and mathematical techniques? Don't they have arguments that have the ring of truth?

We know, for example, from Nobel Prize–winning developments that it's good to have investments with low correlations to each other. We know—again from Nobel Prize–winning theories—that you can only get higher return by taking risks.

So the hedge fund spiel is that they expose you to nonmarket risks with low correlations to the market. They say you can't get these risks with an ordinary mutual fund or stock portfolio, but you can get them with hedge funds.

But they forget to mention that Nobel Prize–winning theories don't say you get better return just by taking risk. The theories invoke a very specific risk—the risk you take by investing in (by straight-out buying) shares of risky companies.

If you invest a percentage of your assets in a pool to bet on how many people will jump off suspension bridges in the coming year, it will be a risky investment, and your results will have a low correlation to the market. (As John Kenneth Galbraith pointed out—in spite of all the rumors—no one actually jumped off a building on Wall Street the day of the 1929 market crash.)

Does that mean it would be advantageous to your investment portfolio to "invest" in bets on the number of bridge jumpers? No; taking risks with low correlations to the market is not an end in itself. The Nobel Prize–winning theory says you will be rewarded only for diversified investment risk that is correlated with earnings-producing or interest-paying ventures. Using it by analogy to justify any other form of investment risk is a gross misapplication of theory.

The hedge fund spiel is therefore—there is no other way to say it—a lot of nonsense. The spiel arose in response to investor angst caused by the 2000–2002 drop in stock and mutual fund values. Investment professionals perceived a niche opportunity for a sales pitch and pounced on it, developing for the occasion—as is the habit of investment management and advice sales professionals—a sophisticated-sounding body of technical word salad.

The hedge fund phenomenon is a patent-medicine remedy worse than the disease it's sold to cure—namely, the unpredictable ups and downs of equity mutual funds. It is worse for the simple reason that its fees are yet higher—in most cases much, much higher.

The Statistical Legerdemain

And what of the "proprietary trading systems," "proprietary forecasting models," and the like—always proprietary, making them impossible to examine—that are incessantly claimed to produce above-market returns?

They are nothing but patterns the historical data finally confessed to—after suffering beating upon beating upon beating until some system or model was constructed that would have worked in the past. They're like the Fumarian cigarette someone found to "prevent cancer" (whose smokers got less cancer than nonsmokers): the result of exhaustively mining the data—trying thousands upon thousands of times to produce the numbers you'd like to advertise, until at last you succeed—but not meaningful or predictive at all.

Anyone can find some stock market strategy that would have produced superior returns in the past, provided they work at it hard enough and long enough. It doesn't mean there's any reason or cause behind it. And it certainly doesn't mean it will continue producing superior returns in the future.

I've already answered throughout this book the obvious question: "Then what *do* you do?" You have to have a way to monitor and select investments. It can't be done haphazardly. You can't just select investments without quantifying, measuring, documenting, showing due diligence. The method we have now may be imperfect, but it's the best we've got.

The problem is that the method we have now—or that our advisors have for us—is not only imperfect but no good at all. It serves no purpose but to project the image of quantification, measurement, documentation, and due diligence—and to line the pockets of a gigantic image-projecting service profession. It's all appearance, no substance.

I'll now summarize in a new "ten commandments of investing" the very simple rules that will allow you—whether you are an individual investor or an institutional investor, a rich investor or a lower-middle-class investor with a 401(k) plan—to earn back for yourself the enormous wealth you might otherwise have squandered on bogus expertise.

Conclusion: The Ten New Commandments for Smart Investing

The Ten New Commandments for Smart Investing sum up this book's message and tell you all you need to know about how to be a smart investor.

I'll state the Ten New Commandments and then restate them with an explanation of each one, recapping what has been said in the book and adding additional information.

The Ten New Commandments for Smart Investing

1. Follow a wealth-building strategy, not a gambling strategy.
2. Stop searching for the Holy Grail: give up the futile quest to beat the market.
3. Stop believing that past investment performance predicts future performance.
4. Don't be duped by the false claims of investment managers and advisors.
5. Fire managers and advisors who charge more than barebones fees.
6. Don't pay anyone to pick stocks for you; there's no reward for the cost and risk.
7. Avoid hedge funds like the plague.
8. Know the risks of investing; take only the risk you are comfortable with.
9. Keep fees and taxes as low as possible; they can swamp your investment returns.
10. Invest only in true low-cost index funds.

These commandments divide naturally into three categories:

- Commandment 1 is the basic premise: you are investing to build wealth, not to gamble;

- Commandments 2–7 show you how to avoid wasting huge amounts of money gambling; and

- Commandments 8–10 show you how to build wealth through investing without gambling.

The Basic Premise: You're Building Wealth, Not Gambling

Commandment 1: Follow a Wealth-Building Strategy, Not a Gambling Strategy

As I have explained, most investment advisors try to sell you a combination of two strategies: a sound, wealth-building strategy of diversified investments in the stock and bond markets; and a second strategy overlaid on top of that, a gambling strategy with no expected reward to the investor—but the advisors and managers receive enormous payments.

You can implement the wealth-building strategy easily by yourself, so never buy into the gambling strategy.

How to Avoid Wasting Enormous Amounts of Money Gambling

Commandment 2: Stop Searching for the Holy Grail: Give Up the Futile Quest to Beat the Market

The quest to beat the market is the gambling strategy that you pay so much for. If you think you must try to beat the market then do it yourself by picking a few stocks you believe in; don't ever pay anyone to do it for you. And be sure your whole portfolio is diversified enough so that if your picks turn out to be wrong, you'll still have a broad market investment base to support you.

Commandment 3: Stop Believing That Past Investment Performance Predicts Future Performance

There's absolutely no reason whatsoever to believe that investment results of the recent past will help you predict future performance. You're wasting your time analyzing the performance of any mutual fund, investment manager, or individual stock in the past year, three years, five years, or ten years. It will tell you nothing about what will happen next.

Commandment 4: Don't Be Duped by the False Claims of Investment Managers and Advisors

Almost all of the "expertise" that investment advisors and managers offer you is wrong. Don't listen to them.

Commandment 5: Fire Managers and Advisors Who Charge More Than Barebones Fees

Because advisors and managers have very little, if anything, to offer you, there is no reason to pay them any more than absolutely necessary. You can pay only the bare minimum by investing in the lowest-cost, most widely diversified investment vehicles, such as index funds—which are, in fact, the most "sophisticated" investments you can get.

Commandment 6: Don't Pay Anyone to Pick Stocks for You; There's No Reward for the Cost and Risk

Not only do you receive nothing for your payments if you pay someone to pick stocks for you, but you will also assume additional risk, because you will depart from an optimally diversified cross section of the market, with little or no expected reward.

Commandment 7: Avoid Hedge
Funds Like the Plague

Hedge funds are the most expensive scam on earth. Don't consider them for an instant.

How to Build Wealth through
Investing without Gambling

Commandment 8: Know the Risks of Investing;
Take Only the Risk You Are Comfortable With

You must choose the risk you are comfortable with—no one can do it for you. Another person can serve as a sounding board, but he or she cannot tell you how to do it.

You choose your risk by selecting a percentage mix between a diversified portfolio of equity investments and a low-risk portfolio, such as intermediate- or short-term bonds or money market funds.

You can choose anything from 100 percent bonds to 100 percent equities. You can even go above that to a leveraged portfolio in which you borrow in order to invest even more than 100 percent of your assets in an equity portfolio.

The decision depends on three factors:

- The number of years to your investment horizon—that is, how many years it will be, on average, until you withdraw the funds

- Whether you feel you will have as much as you need even with a slow growth rate (implying a high fixed income commitment) or will need a higher growth rate to achieve your goals (implying a higher equity commitment)

- How comfortable you will be with fluctuations in the value of your assets. If you are comfortable with large fluctuations and believe you will not panic, this implies a higher commitment to equities (if your investment horizon is long enough); if you are uncomfortable with large fluctuations, this implies a higher commitment to fixed income.

Several mutual fund companies have begun offering "life cycle" funds that change their allocations to stocks and bonds depending on how long it will be until the investor's retirement. The table on page 258 summarizes the allocations for three mutual fund companies, TIAA-CREF, Vanguard, and Fidelity.

These allocations can serve as a reasonable guide, but they only address the first of the three factors listed. If you are less comfortable with market fluctuations or feel you will have enough money in the future even with a relatively low growth rate of assets, your equity commitment could be lower. But if you are very comfortable with market fluctuations and believe they will not cause you to waver from your plan, and/or you feel you will need higher than a relatively low growth rate of assets to achieve your goals, you may wish to increase the allocations to equities.

Many free Web sites offer additional information to help you make the risk decision about how much to allocate to stocks and how much to fixed income. For example, the Web sites for the three mutual fund companies cited in the table provide good information if you feel you need it to help you make the stock–bond allocation decision.

Sometimes the information takes the form of probabilities of long-run and short-run rates of return, based on the frequency of occurrence of various rates of return historically.

For example, suppose you are trying to decide between 50 percent and 100 percent equities. Suppose also you have decided that the choice hinges on how likely it is you can get at least an 8 percent return, with little chance of losing more than 10 percent in any year. You might use the table below to help you with your decision.

This table says that with 50 percent equities, you have only a 30 percent chance of getting an 8 percent return. But with 100 percent equities, you have a 57 percent chance. Improving your probability of an 8 percent return with 100 percent stocks, however, entails greater risk of unsettling fluctuations. Each year, with 100 percent stocks, there is a 23 percent chance that your portfolio will lose more than 10 percent. The risk is only 5 percent if your portfolio is 50 percent stocks and 50 percent bonds.

Equity %	Expected Long-Run Return	Probability (%) That the Long-Run (20-year) Return Will Be 8%	Probability (%) That in Any Given Year the Short-Run (1-year) Return Will Be –10%
50	7	30	5
100	9	57	23

Life Cycle Investment Allocations for TIAA-CREF, Vanguard, and Fidelity

Years to Retirement	Approximate Investment Horizon	TIAA-CREF		Vanguard		Fidelity	
		EQUITY	FIXED INCOME	EQUITY	FIXED INCOME	EQUITY	FIXED INCOME
-10	0	—	—			20%	80%
-5	5	—	—	35%	65%	28%	72%
0	10	35%	65%			50%	50%
5	15	50%	50%	—	—	50%	50%
10	20	55%	45%	53%	47%	59%	41%
15	25	60%	40%			70%	30%
20	30	65%	35%	64%	36%	72%	28%
25	35	70%	30%	—	—	82%	18%
30	40	75%	25%	80%	20%	83%	17%
35	45	80%	20%	—	—	85%	15%
40	50	—	—			88%	12%
45	55	—	—	90%	10%	90%	10%

NOTE: From TIAA-CREF.org, Vanguard.com, and Fidelity.com. The investment horizon assumes twenty-year spend-out after retirement, withdrawn on average ten years after retirement.

You, alone, can weigh the meaning of this information for your portfolio and your risk decision. This information can help you decide whether the reward of higher levels of investment in equities is worth the risk.

Note, however, that if you think you would feel more comfortable seeing an advisor to help you make the decision, you must be extremely careful about the fees. Advice from the typical advisor will wind up costing you at least 2 percent per year and probably more. As you can see from the "Expected Long-run Return" column of the table, this amount is more than the difference between the expected return on a 100 percent equity portfolio and the return on a 50 percent equity portfolio. In other words, any benefit the help can possibly provide you will be more than wiped out by the fees.

Commandment 9: Keep Fees and Taxes as Low as Possible; They Can Swamp Your Investment Returns

I showed how true this is at the end of Chapter 4. I'll recap that analysis here.

I asked you at the end of Chapter 4 to consider two investors, John and Mary. Both of them had $250,000 to invest.

Mary decided to put 80 percent of her money in broadly diversified index funds. The other 20 percent she put into low-risk short-term bonds.

John went to an investment advisor and incurred the extra fees and taxes that entails.

I concluded that Mary will most likely wind up after thirty years with about 1.2 *million* dollars more than John—about 137 percent more money than he will have.

That, in capsule form, is the harm that fees and taxes can do to your portfolio.

Commandment 10: Invest Only in True Low-Cost Index Funds

True index funds mirror the securities in the market as a whole. (I include in the term *index funds* exchange-traded index funds, or index ETFs.) If Company A's outstanding stock is worth ten times as much as Company B's, then a true capitalization-weighted index fund will have ten times as many dollars in Company A stock as in Company B stock. Not only is this the recipe for optimal diversification in theory, but it also means that your portfolio will rarely have to buy or sell stocks to maintain its index weightings. The same is not true of equal-weighted "index" funds that contain an equal dollar amount in each security. These funds have to be frequently reweighted to adhere to their equal-weighted prescription, incurring significant gains taxes and commissions in the process.

There's no reason to buy several index funds to represent different segments of the market when you can simply buy the broadest market index fund that already includes all of these segments. Buying all the segments separately will not improve your diversification as opposed to buying a single total market index fund, into which they are all already bundled.

You may, however, want to buy separate index funds to represent the U.S. domestic stock market, the international (non-U.S.) stock market, and the liquid real estate market as represented by REITs. The non-U.S. market is larger than the U.S. market. Hence, broad diversification suggests a mix weighted toward the non-U.S. market, such as 40 percent in the U.S. market, 50 percent international, and 10 percent REITs. But many U.S. investors will prefer to weight U.S. domestic stocks more heavily. For them a reasonable mix in their equity portfolio might be 60 percent in a U.S. domestic index fund, 30 percent in a non-U.S. index fund, and 10 percent REITs. The objective is to achieve greater diversification than you would by only investing in a domestic U.S. stock fund.

Genuine broadly diversified, low-cost U.S. domestic market index funds have fees in the neighborhood of 0.1 percent, and certainly not more than about 0.2 percent. Broadly diversified international (i.e., non-U.S.) funds may have fees in the neighborhood of 0.2 or 0.3 percent. If a fund charges much more than this, it is not a true low-cost index fund.

This is all you need to do—there is no more. Any other advice and assistance you get, if you pay the normal fees for it, will deplete your portfolio far more over time than it will gain you.

It is my hope that this book will make a substantial contribution to a massive information campaign that will finally debunk—once and for all—the grand lie that is being told to customers of investment advice and management services, often with the customers' willing, even exuberant cooperation.

It is time to blow the whistle, once and for all, on the Big Investment Lie.

Notes

Introduction

1. Michael C. Jensen, "The Performance of Mutual Funds in the Period 1945–1964," *Journal of Finance* 23, no. 2 (May 1968): 389–416, Papers and Proceedings of the Twenty-sixth Annual Meeting of the American Finance Association, Washington, D.C., December 28–30, 1967.

Chapter 1. The Beardstown Ladies versus the Professionals

1. Amy Rauch-Neilson, "The Beardstown Phenomenon," National Association of Investors Corporation, Better Investing Community, October 2001, http://www.betterinvesting.org/articles/bi/16/371.
2. Ibid.
3. Ibid.
4. Tom Gardner, "Cash-King Portfolio Report," *The Motley Fool*, Fool.com, March 5, 1998, http://www.fool.com/CashKing/1998/CashKing Port980305.htm.
5. A careful analysis based on the publicly available data strongly suggests that the Beardstown Ladies did not perform as poorly as the published Price Waterhouse figure suggests and that they may have done very well indeed. Price Waterhouse found that the Ladies' performance had been only 9.1 percent over the ten years 1984–1993. But the Price Waterhouse audit also revealed that over an extended, fourteen-year period, 1984–1997, the Beardstown Ladies' average performance was 15.3 percent. Media stories also reported that senior partner Betty Sinnock's error was that she had misread the 23.4 percent return as being for ten years, while it was actually for the two-year period of 1992–1993. These facts lead to the following conclusions:

   • By simple arithmetic, the Price Waterhouse data imply that the Beardstown Ladies' annual return in 1994–1997 was 32.4 percent.

This is calculated by removing the ten-year return from the fourteen-year return. In the same period, 1994–1997, the S&P 500's return was only 23.0 percent. Therefore, according to Price Waterhouse, the Beardstown Ladies beat the market in those four years by 9.4 percent annually. They even beat Warren Buffett, whose Berkshire Hathaway in those years returned an average of 29.6 percent.

- It is reasonable to assume the 23.4 percent the news stories say the Beardstown Ladies actually realized over the two years from 1992 to 1993 was an unannualized return not an annualized return. Therefore, their annualized return was 11.1 percent. The S&P 500's return over those two years was 8.8 percent. Hence, in those two years, the Ladies beat the market by 2.3 percent annually. (If the 23.4 percent was in fact an annualized return not an unannualized one, then the Ladies beat the market by an incredible 15 percent annually in those two years.)

Therefore, for the six years of 1992–1997, the Beardstown Ladies beat the market by an average of 6.9 percent. This would have put them in the top 5 percent of mutual funds and probably in the top 1 percent.

What about the preceding eight years, in which they achieved—based on the other data—only a dismal 8.6 percent compared with the S&P's 16.5? The answer is probably that the Beardstown Ladies took much less risk than the market in those years, particularly in the early years of their club. Hence, they realized a lower return than the market. In those years, I suspect, they had a low allocation to stocks and thus low risk. It is not appropriate, therefore, to compare them in those years directly with a stock market index. A stock market index is 100 percent stocks and has higher risk.

Their lower allocation to stocks in the early years is what would be expected when an investment club gets started. At first, money is deposited monthly by the members in the club's bank account while they discuss what stocks to buy. They invest slowly while the cash mounts up. The allocation to stocks is small, so most of their money receives only the low bank rate of interest.

It is worth pointing out also that unlike the go-go funds that frequently capture the notice of the media and investors for charging out of the gate with big wins and then plummet later after they have been bloated with new investor dollars, the Beardstown Ladies had their mediocre performance in the early life of their fund when there were few dollars in it and then performed well later when it was well stocked with assets—a far superior sequence of events.

6. The total revenues of the investment management and advice industry are difficult to estimate but clearly exceed $200 billion a year.

Mutual fund management fees are approximately $70 billion (from the Morningstar mutual fund database). Hedge fund management fees are estimated to be at least $70 billion (Edward Chancellor, "Hedge Funds Today: So Much Money, So Little Talent," *Wall Street Journal*, August 24, 2005). Institutional investment funds' assets, including pension and endowment funds, are a little less than twice that of mutual funds (The Conference Board, *The 2005 Institutional Investment Report: U.S. and International Trends* [New York: Author, September 2005]), but their fees are lower; their total management fees can be estimated as at least another $70 billion. In addition, all the fees collected by investment advisors and consultants must be counted, totaling in the tens of billions. Compensation of those staff personnel of pension and endowment funds whose job it is to select investment managers should also be counted.

7. Adolf Hitler, *Mein Kampf* (Boston: Houghton Mifflin/Mariner Books, 1998).

8. See Chapter 7; also M. M. Carhart, "On Persistence in Mutual Fund Performance," *Journal of Finance* (March 1997): 57–82; Eugene Fama, "Market Efficiency, Long-Term Returns, and Behavioral Finance," *Journal of Financial Economics* 49 (1998): 283–306; Burton G. Malkiel, "Returns from Investing in Equity Mutual Funds 1971 to 1991," *Journal of Finance* 50 (1995): 549–72; Richard Roll and Robert J. Shiller, "Comments: Symposium on Volatility in U.S. and Japanese Stock Markets," *Journal of Applied Corporate Finance* 5, no. 1 (1992): 25–29; G. William Schwert, "Anomalies and Market Efficiency," in *Handbook of the Economics of Finance*, ed. George M. Constantinides, Milton Harris, and René M. Stulz (Amsterdam: Elsevier/North Holland, 2003); Burton G. Malkiel, *A Random Walk Down Wall Street* (New York: Norton: 2003).

9. John C. Bogle, "The Mutual Fund Industry 60 Years Later: For Better or Worse?" *Financial Analysts Journal*, January/February 2005.

Chapter 2. The Extraordinarily High Cost of Investment Advice

1. John Kador, *Charles Schwab: How One Company Beat Wall Street and Reinvented the Brokerage Industry* (Hoboken, NJ: Wiley, 2002).

Chapter 3. The Outer Limits: Hedge Fund Fees

1. Chancellor, "Hedge Funds Today," A10.

2. Riva D. Atlas, "Hedge Funds Are Stumbling but Manager Salaries Aren't," *New York Times*, May 27, 2005.

3. Jane Mayer, "The Money Man," *New Yorker*, October 18, 2004.

4. Iain Jenkins, "Determining the Fees," *Hedge Fund Intelligence*, September 2004, http://www.hedgefundintelligence.com/ar/reports/2004_09/determining_the_fees.htm.

Chapter 4. Taxes Down the Drain

1. Morningstar Principia database, periods ending December 31, 2005. The high-cost equity funds are those with top-quartile expense ratios, plus commissions and amortized front loads; the low-cost equity funds are those with fourth-quartile expense ratios.
2. This assumes investment vehicle fees and taxes range between the 10th and the 90th percentiles in the Morningstar Principia database for mutual fund fees and taxes, and that the advisor's fee ranges between 0.6 and 1 percent (including 12b-1 fees remitted back to the advisor by the mutual funds).
3. Mary pays more taxes than John pays in the low-tax scenario because Mary accumulates more wealth to pay taxes on.

Chapter 5. Why Do We Give Golden Crumbs to Rich People?

1. Roger Lowenstein, "Exuberance Is Rational," *New York Times Magazine*, February 11, 2001.

Chapter 6. Why Investment Professionals Can't Predict Markets

1. John Cassidy, "The Price Prophet," *New Yorker*, February 7, 2000.

Chapter 7. The Abject Failure of Professional Advisors and Managers

1. M. L. Bachelier, *Théorie de la spéculation* (Paris: Gauthier-Villars, 1900).
2. The term *random walk* is used for discrete processes—that is, processes that move in discrete steps. *Brownian motion* is the continuous form of the random walk—that is, processes whose steps are infinitesimal in size.
3. Louis Bachelier, "Theory of Speculation," in *The Random Character of Stock Market Prices*, ed. Paul H. Cootner (London: Risk Publication, 2000), 17.
4. Alfred Cowles III, "Can Stock Market Forecasters Forecast?" *Econometrica* 1, no. 3 (July 1933): 309–24.
5. Ibid., 323.
6. Paul H. Cootner, ed., *The Random Character of Stock Market Prices* (London: Risk Publication, 2000).
7. M. G. Kendall, "The Analysis of Economic Time-Series—Part I: Prices," in Cootner, *The Random Character of Stock Market Prices*, 85.
8. Eugene F. Fama, "The Behavior of Stock-Market Prices," *Journal of Business* 38, no. 1 (January 1965): 34–105; Irwin Friend, F. E. Brown, Edward S. Herman, and Douglas Vickers, "A Study of Mutual Funds: Investment Policy and Investment Company Performance," Report of the Committee on Interstate and Foreign Commerce, House Report No. 2274, 87th Congress, Second Session

(August 28, 1962); William F. Sharpe, "Mutual Fund Performance," *Journal of Business* 39, no. 1, pt. 2, suppl. (January 1966): 119–38; Jack L. Treynor and K. K. Mazuy, "Can Mutual Funds Outguess the Market?" *Harvard Business Review* 44, no. 4 (July–August 1966): 131–36.

9. Jensen, "The Performance of Mutual Funds in the Period 1945–1964," 405.

10. S. J. Brown, W. N. Goetzmann, R. G. Ibbotson, and S. A. Ross, "Survivorship Bias in Performance Studies," *Review of Financial Studies 5*, no. 4 (1992): 553–80.

11. Mark M. Carhart, "On Persistence in Mutual Fund Performance," *Journal of Finance 52*, no. 1 (March 1997).

12. Schwert, "Anomalies and Market Efficiency."

13. Fama, "Market Efficiency, Long-Term Returns, and Behavioral Finance."

14. Ibid., 304.

15. Josef Lakonishok, Andrei Schleifer, Robert W. Vishny, Oliver Hart, and George L. Perry, "The Structure and Performance of the Money Management Industry," *Brookings Papers on Economic Activity: Microeconomics* 1992: 341.

16. B. Malkiel and A. Saha, "Hedge Funds: Risk and Return," *Financial Analysts Journal*, November/December 2005; Nolke Posthuma and Pieter Jelle van der Sluis, "A Reality Check on Hedge Funds Returns," July 8, 2003, http://ssrn.com/abstract=438840.

17. Malkiel and Saha, "Hedge Funds," 81.

18. Ibid., 84–85.

Chapter 8. The Market Can Turn on a Dime

1. M. F. M. Osborne, "Brownian Motion in the Stock Market," *Operations Research* 7, no. 2 (March–April 1959): 145–73; Holbrook Working, "Note on the Correlation of First Differences of Averages in a Random Chain," *Econometrica 28*, no. 4 (October 1960): 916–18; both reprinted in *The Random Character of Stock Market Prices*, 123–61. See also Mark Rubinstein, *A History of the Theory of Investments* (New York: Wiley, 2006), 134–37.

2. The mathematician Benoit Mandelbrot (see *The Misbehavior of Markets*, by Benoit Mandelbrot and Richard L. Hudson [New York: Basic Books, 2004]) has argued cogently that a close relative of Brownian motion, the stable Paretian or Lévy process, fits the returns data better than strict Brownian motion. I shall (with only minor imprecision, from a strict mathematical viewpoint) use the terms random walk and Brownian motion interchangeably to encompass not only random walk and Brownian motion (the continuous random walk) but also the Lévy process.

Chapter 9. The Claims of Money Managers:
Smoking Our Brand Prevents Cancer

1. Malkiel and Saha, "Hedge Funds"; Posthuma and van der Sluis, "A Reality Check on Hedge Funds Returns."

Chapter 11. The Simple Rules of Nobel Prize Winners

1. Harry Markowitz autobiography, http://nobelprize.org/economics/laureates/1990/markowitz-autobio.html.
2. James Tobin, "Liquidity Preference as Behavior Towards Risk," *Review of Economic Studies* 25, no. 2 (February 1958): 65–86; William F. Sharpe, "Capital Asset Prices: A Theory of Market Equilibrium under Conditions of Risk," *Journal of Finance* 19, no. 3 (September 1964): 425–42.
3. Morningstar Inc. database study of 306 domestic equity funds with twenty years of data, December 2002; Charles D. Ellis, "The Loser's Game," *Financial Analysts Journal*, July/August 1975.

Chapter 12. There's No Such Thing as a Free Lunch

1. An exchange traded fund, or ETF, is just a different way of packaging a mutual fund.

Chapter 13. Investment Genius or the Thousandth Coin

1. Roger Lowenstein, *Buffett: The Making of an American Capitalist* (New York: Random House, 1995); see also http://www.berkshirehathaway.com/.
2. Some erroneous statements frequently heard about Buffett's results stem from the way Berkshire Hathaway reports its performance data. In its annual report, Berkshire displays annual percentage changes in book value. Next to that, it lists the annual percentage change in the S&P 500 index. The usual measure of the performance of a company's stock is the percentage change in its market value, not its book value. The percentage change in book value will fluctuate much less widely than the percentage change in market value.

   Berkshire Hathaway states the performance in terms of book value for a good reason. Buffett believes investors should keep their eyes on the long run, not short-term market fluctuations. To avoid becoming overly occupied with the short term, Buffett uses a measure that smooths over short-term market fluctuations, making them less noticeable.

   But to compare that measure with the percentage change in the S&P 500—a measure of the change in market value, not in book value—is to compare apples and oranges. It makes the performance of the company look much better when the stock market as a whole turns down.

   Berkshire Hathaway's book-value measure of annual performance was less than the S&P 500's annual percentage change in only four of the thirty-seven years from 1965 to 2001. The chance that could have occurred at random is only one in 577,125. But it's a meaningless measure. Stock market performance is measured by how much the price of a stock went up or down, not by how much the book value of the company went up or down.

The right way to compare a stock's performance with a market index is by using market values. On this measure, the number of years Berkshire Hathaway beat the market was not all that unusual. It certainly cannot disprove the hypothesis that the performance was the result of accident, or chance.

3. Data from Meir Statman and Jonathan Scheid, "Buffett in Foresight and Hindsight," *Financial Analysts Journal*, July/August 2002.

4. The standard deviation of Berkshire Hathaway stock over the period, calculated from Statman and Scheid's annual returns, was 33.2 percent. The standard deviation of the S&P 500 was 14.2 percent. The implied unsystematic standard deviation of Berkshire Hathaway stock was therefore $\sqrt{33.2^2 - (14.2\beta)^2}$ = 27.3 percent, or 4.7 percent on an annualized basis $(27.3 / \sqrt{34})$. Berkshire Hathaway's return was 26.2 percent, while the S&P's, adjusted for Berkshire Hathaway's systematic risk, was 13.7 percent. The probability that a normal random variable will take on a value of 26.2 or greater when the expectation is 13.7 and the standard deviation is 4.7 (i.e., the probability that the null hypothesis that Berkshire Hathaway's return was drawn from a normal distribution with expectation 13.7 percent and standard deviation 4.7 percent) is about 0.004, or 1 in 250.

Chapter 15. How Investors Delude Themselves

1. Sandra D. Atchison, "A 'Sure Bet' That Crushed Colorado Investors," *Business Week*, November 19, 1990.
2. Mitchell Zuckoff, *Ponzi's Scheme: The True Story of a Financial Legend* (New York: Random House, 2005).

Chapter 16. How Hedge Funds Operate and Are Sold

1. Malkiel and Saha, "Hedge Funds."
2. Roger Lowenstein, *When Genius Failed: The Rise and Fall of Long-Term Capital Management* (New York: Random House, 2000).

Chapter 17. How Consultants and Money Managers Sell to Institutional Investors

1. See http://www2.chass.ncsu.edu/garson/pa765/agent.htm.
2. F. Goltz, *Hedge Fund Indices as Asset Allocation Tools*, Working Paper, Edhec Risk and Asset Management Research Centre, May 12, 2005.

Chapter 18. Derivatives: The Good, the Bad, and the Ugly

1. Edward Winslow, *Blind Faith* (San Francisco: Berrett-Koehler, 2003).

Glossary

12b-1 fee   An annual charge to customers as part of some mutual funds' expenses, supposedly to cover the marketing of the fund. Much of this fee is often remitted back to the advisor who recommended the fund, causing a conflict of interest—advisors have an incentive to recommend the funds that remit back to them. For more information, see http://www.sec.gov/answers.shtml. and click "12b-1 Fees."

401(k) plan   A "defined contribution" employee pension plan in which participants contribute a pretax amount (possibly matched, up to a percentage, by the employer) and choose among investment choices offered by the plan.

403(b) plan   See *401(k) plan*. Similar to a 401(k) plan but offered to employees of educational and nonprofit organizations.

Accredited investor   An individual or an institution with a net worth of at least $1 million or income of at least $200,000 for each of the last two years (or joint income with a spouse of $300,000). See http://www.sec.gov/answers/accred.htm for details.

Active management   Investment managers who pick stocks (or bonds in the case of bond funds) to try to beat market averages.

Alpha   The percentage by which an investment manager beats a stock market average after adjustment for risk.

Anomalies   Patterns of investment that would have succeeded in beating the stock market in the past.

Arbitrage   Taking advantage of price differentials to make a profit—for example, buying a car in one state and then driving it to another state where it can be sold for a higher price.

Asset allocation   The percentages, adding to 100 percent, by which an investment portfolio is divided among major asset classes such as domestic stocks, foreign stocks, bonds, and real estate.

Asset–liability models   Pertains principally to pension funds; probabilistic modeling of the future liabilities of the fund—that is, the value of the obligation to pay future pensions—as compared with the future assets of the fund.

Assets (investment assets) The assets of an individual or an entity are the total net value of the individual's or entity's properties. Investment assets are the portion of total assets that are available to invest in liquid assets such as stocks and bonds.

Backfill bias The database bias introduced in prior years into a database of the performance of investment funds when a new fund volunteers to be added, along with its past data, after the fund has decided that its past performance figures are good enough to publicize.

Backtest Running a simulation of an investment strategy using stock (or bond) market data for a historical time period to see how it would have performed over that period.

Basis point Hundredth of a percent

Behavioral economics The theory that people do not act rationally in their economic behavior.

Behavioral finance The theory that investors do not act rationally.

Beta The extent to which a portfolio of risky securities of a certain type (e.g., domestic stocks) is effectively "leveraged"—that is, the extent to which the portfolio carries risk greater than (or less than) the capitalization-weighted average of all securities in the category. (Beta is equal to one if the risk is the same as that of the weighted average.)

Bias The tendency for a statistical sample from a population to be unrepresentative of the population as a whole. For example, databases of hedge funds are unrepresentative of the population of all hedge funds, because the databases include only those that voluntarily report (see *Self-selection bias*).

Binomial simulation Simulating a random process by means of tosses of a coin. Binomial simulation becomes equivalent to Monte Carlo simulation as the number of tosses becomes very large and the interval of time between them very small.

Black-Scholes formula A formula for the theoretical price of a put or call option, given the standard deviation of the underlying security.

Bond A form of security in which the capital provided by the investor is repaid with interest in fixed amounts on a fixed schedule over a fixed time period (usually interest is paid semiannually, and the principal is repaid at the end of the time period).

Brokerage A firm that is licensed to buy or sell securities, though large brokerages perform many other functions as well.

Brownian motion A randomly fluctuating process over time, such as the pattern often exhibited by the movement of securities prices. (See also

Random walk; the technical difference is that a Brownian motion occurs in continuous time, while a random walk occurs in discrete steps.)

Buy-and-hold A strategy of buying a portfolio of securities and holding them for a long time, without contemplating buying or selling them, regardless of their up and down movements.

Call option An option to buy a specified security (the *underlying*) at a specified future time (the *expiration date*) at a specified price (the *strike price* or *exercise price*). See Option.

Capital asset pricing model A theoretical model introduced by Nobelist William F. Sharpe and others, saying that the expected rate of return on a security (or portfolio of securities), in excess of the risk-free rate (e.g., that of a U.S. Treasury note), is proportional to the portion of the volatility of the security (or portfolio) that is correlated with the market as a whole.

Capital gains The increase in price over time of a security (or portfolio of securities). Capital gains are "realized" if the security (or securities) is sold, thereby incurring a tax liability in a taxable portfolio. Gains are "unrealized" if the security (or securities) is not yet sold.

Capitalization The number of shares outstanding of a public corporation multiplied by its price per share; a measure of the size or total value of a public corporation (that is, a corporation with publicly traded stock).

Capitalization weighting Refers to the weighting of the securities in a portfolio or market index (i.e., a hypothetical portfolio). The portfolio or index is capitalization weighted if the weight of each security in the portfolio is proportional to the total value of its shares outstanding in the market. (See also *Equal weighting*.)

CAPM See *Capital asset pricing model*.

Commissions Payments to brokers to execute trades.

Commodities Trading in bulk goods, such as grains, metals, and foods, and U.S. and foreign currencies, regulated and overseen by the Commodity Futures Trading Commission (CFTC).

Correlation (coefficient) A statistical measure of the extent to which two variables vary in the same direction or in opposite directions. The correlation coefficient ranges from an extreme of plus one (for moving together in the same direction in lock step) to the opposite extreme of minus one (for moving together in opposite directions in lock step). A value of zero means no correlation between the two movements.

Covariance Covariance is proportional to the correlation coefficient but is not scaled to be between minus one and plus one.

CPA Certified public accountant.

Credit life insurance   Insurance that pays off a mortgage or installment-plan loan when the borrower dies; usually extremely overpriced.

Currency risk   The possibility that the relative value of two currencies will change. It becomes a risk when, for example, a contract has been entered into to execute a trade or make or receive a payment in a foreign currency at a future date.

Data mining   The practice of performing undisciplined, repeated data studies in an attempt to find patterns in historical data. The danger is that it will uncover patterns that are merely random results, indicative of no inherent cause or design and of no value in predicting future patterns.

Day trading   The practice of frequent intraday trading of individual stocks. Day trading is in general a losing strategy because it generates substantial commission costs even at low commission rates.

Debt   For the investor, the amount loaned or invested in bonds or other fixed income. For the borrower (e.g., a company), the portion of corporate capital that has been financed by issuing bonds or other fixed income, as opposed to the equity portion obtained by selling shares of stock.

Debt/equity ratio   For a corporation, the ratio of the value of the portion of corporate capital obtained by issuing debt obligations such as bonds and other fixed income, to the value of the portion obtained by issuing shares of stock.

Defined-benefit pension plan   A corporate pension plan for the benefit of retirees in which the amount of retirees' future benefits is fixed, and the corporation is obligated to contribute to the pension plan sufficient amounts to ensure that those fixed benefits will be realized.

Defined-contribution pension plan   A corporate pension plan in which contributions by employer and employees are fixed, while the amounts of future retiree benefits are not predetermined but are whatever results from the growth of the contributions through investment.

Derivative   Any security or financial contractual obligation whose definition depends on the value of another security. Options and futures and combinations thereof are the chief examples of derivatives.

Directed brokerage   A method of payment for incidental services provided by a brokerage firm, such as research studies, in which payment is in the form of an agreement to use a certain amount of that firm's brokerage services. Also called *soft dollars*.

Discount broker   As opposed to a full-service broker, a broker who provides no advice or research but merely executes securities trades as directed by the customer, for a lower commission than a full-service broker.

Discount rate   The annual percentage by which future dollars must be discounted to arrive at their equivalent in present-day dollars. For example, if the discount rate is 5 percent, then $1.05 in one year is worth $1 now.

Diversification   Reduction in the risk of fluctuation in the value of a portfolio, or "volatility," by investing in a large number of securities. Maximum diversification is achieved with a capitalization-weighted portfolio of all market securities.

Dividends   Discretionary cash distributions paid out of earnings by a corporation to holders of shares of its stock.

Dollar-cost averaging   The practice of making regular periodic investments in stocks over a period of time. If, on the one hand, it is intended to provide a discipline to savers to invest regularly rather than spend all their income on consumption, it is a boon to wealth accumulation. If, on the other hand, it is intended as a method to earn more in the stock market by holding back a portion of investment assets and dribbling it into the market piecemeal, as opposed to investing it all at once, it is bad advice that will tend to impair wealth growth.

Dow (Dow Jones Industrial Average)   A composite index of the prices of thirty large company stocks chosen by the Dow Jones Company, weighted by its share prices.

Earnings   The profits earned by a corporation; corporate revenues after the deduction of costs and expenses.

Efficient frontier   A theoretical curved line on the graph of portfolio return versus risk (as measured by standard deviation) representing the portfolio with the highest expected return at each level of risk (as computed using Markowitz's mean-variance optimization methodology).

Efficient market theory   The theory that the market prices securities efficiently—that is, that market prices reflect all available information.

Endowment funds   Institutional investment funds owned by nonprofit organizations such as universities and foundations.

Equal weighting   Refers to the weighting of the securities in a portfolio or market index (i.e., a hypothetical portfolio). The portfolio or index is equal weighted if the weight of every security in the portfolio is the same—that is, if an equal dollar amount of every security is owned by the portfolio. (See also *Capitalization weighting*.)

Equity   A form of security (also called a *share*, or *shares*, of *stock*) in which the investor takes a percentage ownership of a company in return for his or her investment. Therefore, the capital provided by the investor to the company is repaid by the dividends that are paid out as a portion of the earnings of the company, or by the sale of the investor's ownership at some future time. In comparison with the stream of payouts to the investor from a conventional bond, which are fixed, the payouts to the equity investor are varying and uncertain.

Equity-linked contracts   A form of investment contract in which a security and an option are combined in such a way as to give the investor a combination of an equity-linked return (i.e., the value of the investor's investment goes up if the value of the underlying equity security goes up), while the investor is also guaranteed a specified minimum return over a given time period.

ETF   See *Exchange-traded fund.*

Exchange-traded fund   A mutual fund (usually an index fund) structured in such a way as to mimic a security. It can be bought or sold at any time of day, unlike a mutual fund, which can usually be bought or sold only once a day. ETF index funds may, under certain circumstances, be lower in cost than ordinary mutual funds.

Expense ratio   The ratio of the annual expenses of a mutual fund (exclusive of trading costs and front-end or back-end loads) to the value of the fund.

Fat tails   The tendency of securities price movements to exhibit a larger number of extreme events than might be expected from the law of large numbers, or from the hypothesis that price changes follow a mathematical "normal" distribution (i.e., a bell curve).

Financial planner   An advisor to individuals on investments and usually on other aspects of an individual's finances, such as taxes, insurance, and estate planning. See also http://www.sec.gov/answers/ finplan.htm.

Fixed income   Securities that offer a fixed or steady stream of payouts over time in return for an initial investment. See also *Bond.*

Full-service broker   A broker who offers investment research and advice as well as the service of buying and selling securities.

Fund of funds   A fund that an investor can select that allocates its assets among other funds, adding an additional fee for the service of selecting and packaging the funds into one.

Futures   A contract to purchase a commodity at a future time at a pre fixed price. For example, a euro future might be a contract to purchase 1,000 euros in six months for $1,300, without regard to the actual exchange rate at that time. Futures are often used as a hedge against risk, to protect against the possibility of a future loss due to fluctuating exchange rates.

Gains   See *Capital gains.*

GNMAs ("Ginnie Maes")   Fixed income securities offered by the Government National Mortgage Association, a quasi-governmental

(U.S.) entity that bundles mortgages on low-cost housing and reissues them to buyers as so-called GNMAs.

Growth stocks   Stocks in companies that are expected to have high future earnings growth rates and therefore have high price-to-earnings and price-to-book value ratios.

Hedge funds   Any mutual fund-like pooled funds that are unregulated or relatively unregulated because their investors are limited in number and kind (see *Accredited investor*) and are therefore presumably "sophisticated" and not needing government oversight. See also http://www.sec.gov/answers/hedge.htm.

Hedging   Any method of using securities or (more commonly) derivative securities to provide insurance against the risk of loss in a portfolio of securities (see, e.g., *Futures*). Some hedge funds use hedging, some do not.

High-water mark   The highest price of a portfolio prior to a drop in price; often used in the calculation of hedge fund performance fees to deny the manager current performance fees as long as the portfolio has not risen above the previous high-water mark.

Incentive fee   See *Performance incentive fee.*

Index fund   A fund that includes securities only according to a predetermined formula dictating the proportion of the securities in the portfolio, without regard to the current or past characteristics of the companies whose shares are owned. True index funds have very low expense ratios because they do not pay anyone to analyze and choose securities for inclusion.

Institutional investors   Investors that are entities like corporate pension funds or nonprofit organization endowment funds.

Institutions   See *Institutional investors.*

Investment advisors   "An investment adviser is someone who receives compensation for giving individually tailored advice to a specific person on investing in stocks, bonds, or mutual funds" (see http://www.sec.gov/answers/invadv.htm).

Investment assets   See *Assets.*

Investment managers   Companies that select and invest portfolios of securities for clients (also called *money managers*). Can be mutual fund managers or managers of separately managed accounts, such as for institutional investors or high-net-worth individual investors. Investment advisors and consultants often (for a fee, of course) select and recommend investment managers to investors. Investment management firms are among the most profitable, and most consistently profitable, firms in all of industry—in spite of the fact that on average they do not beat a naive, ultralow-cost buy-and-hold portfolio. Similarly, investment advisors and consultants exhibit no ability to select investment managers who will outperform a naïve buy-and-hold strategy.

Investment performance   Generally means the risk-adjusted rate of return on an investment.

Itô's lemma   A mathematical formula that describes the rate of change in one random process with a change in another random process on which it depends. Thus, it can describe the rate of change in the price of a financial derivative given the change in the underlying security on which it depends.

Kurtosis   A statistical measure that describes the extent to which a probability distribution has "fat tails"—that is, the extent to which extreme outliers occur.

Leverage   The extent to which an investment is financed by borrowing.

Life cycle funds   Mutual funds that change their asset allocation as the investor ages, generally investing a higher proportion in stocks when the investor is young and a lower proportion in stocks as the investor ages.

Liquidity   The ease and timeliness with which a security can be sold.

Load   A onetime fee for purchase or sale of a mutual fund, either a front-end load or a back-end load.

Market average   The investment performance of a hypothetical portfolio containing all marketable stocks, or a specific subset of all marketable stocks (e.g., U.S. domestic stocks), usually capitalization weighted but sometimes equal weighted or weighted by the price per share (as in the Dow).

Mean-variance analysis   An optimization algorithm proposed by Harry Markowitz in which security (or asset class) weightings within a portfolio of securities are derived in such a way as to maximize the expected return of the portfolio for a given level of variance (or standard deviation) of periodic returns. The method stumbles on the fact that accurate prospective values for the inputs cannot be obtained.

Modern portfolio theory   The body of mathematical theories of investment, generally including Markowitz's mean-variance analysis, the Sharpe et al. capital asset pricing model, and often the Black-Scholes option pricing model. Abbreviated MPT.

Money managers   See *Investment managers*.

Monte Carlo simulation   A method of simulating a random walk on a computer by generating (pseudo)random numbers to simulate security or market price movements. Monte Carlo simulation is frequently used to explore the probabilities of future results of investment, as in asset–liability studies.

MPT   See *Modern portfolio theory*.

Mutual fund "A mutual fund is a company that pools money from many investors and invests the money in stocks, bonds, short-term money-market instruments, or other securities" (see http://www.sec.gov/answers/mutfund.htm).

Opportunity cost Revenue foregone by choosing not to take advantage of an earning opportunity and doing something else instead.

Option A transaction reserving to the buyer of the option the right, for a price, to make a specified future purchase, or a specified future sale, at a specified future price, and within a specified future time period or at a specified future time.

Out-of-sample test A backtest performed using data for a historical time period or sample group, intended to attempt to confirm the prior results of another backtest performed using data for a different historical time period or sample group.

Passive management The practice of investing a portfolio of securities according to a formula that dictates the makeup of the portfolio, without regard to the characteristics of the companies underlying the securities; as opposed to active management, which attempts to pick securities based on the characteristics of the companies that issued them.

Pension funds Funds sponsored by corporations dedicated to the provision of retirement and other benefits to employees.

Performance fee See *Performance incentive fee.*

Performance incentive fee A fee paid to an investment manager that depends on the rate of return earned over a time period (usually a year) by the manager. A common performance incentive fee is 20 percent of gains. "Asymmetric" performance incentive fees (fees charged on gains but not rebated on losses) are not allowed for mutual funds, but are allowed for hedge funds.

Persistence The tendency for above- or below-average historical performance to continue into the future. No clear evidence has been found of persistence in investment performance.

Ponzi scheme An investment vehicle in which promised gains to investors are paid out of the deposits of new investors, but the vehicle itself generates no inherent returns (or insufficient returns to warrant the payouts). Also called a *pyramid scheme*, it requires an exponentially growing pool of new investors in order not to collapse into bankruptcy.

Portfolio insurance One of various means of ensuring or attempting to ensure that a portfolio of securities cannot lose more than a specified amount over a specified time period. The simplest example would be an S&P 500 index fund insured by the purchase of a put option on the S&P 500.

Portfolio optimization   See *Mean-variance analysis*.

Present value formula   A formula that expresses a future cash flow stream as a lump cash amount today by applying the discount rate for the appropriate time period to each future cash flow.

Price/earnings ratio   The ratio of the price per share of a stock to the earnings per share; can be different depending on the time period over which the earnings are calculated (or projected) and the definition of earnings.

Principal–agent theory   The theory of behaviors resulting when a principal, or owner, of a business or pool of capital entrusts its management to an agent who has self-interests different from those of the principal.

Put option   An option to sell a specified security (the *underlying*) at a specified future time (the *expiration date*) at a specified price (the *strike price* or *exercise price*). See *Option*.

Random walk   A randomly fluctuating process over time, such as the pattern often exhibited by the movement of securities prices. (See also *Brownian motion*: the technical difference is that Brownian motion occurs in continuous time while a random walk occurs in discrete steps.)

Rate of return on investment   The percentage increase in investment assets due solely to internal growth of the value of the assets, not counting any additional funds externally contributed.

Rationality   A vague term applying to assumed investor characteristics, usually interpreted to mean, minimally, that investors prefer a higher return on investment to a lower return, and a lower risk to a higher risk.

Real estate investment trusts (REITs)   "Entities that invest in different kinds of real estate or real estate related assets, including shopping centers, office buildings, hotels, and mortgages secured by real estate" (see http://www.sec.gov/answers/reits.htm).

Regression analysis   The simplest statistical method of choice for pummeling data to see if there are any patterns in it. Also known in elementary mathematics classes (in its two-parameter form) as *least-squares fit*. Regression analysis hypothesizes that several variables $V_0, V_1, \ldots, V_n$ fit a linear equation of the form "V_0 equals constant a_1 times V_1 plus constant a_2 times V_2 plus . . . constant a_n times V_n." It then estimates the constants a_1 through a_n and investigates whether the linear relationship is robust.

Regression toward the mean   A tendency for a wandering random variable to eventually move back toward its average value.

REITs   See *Real estate investment trusts*.

Return   See *Rate of return on investment*.

Risk assessment   A routine procedure applied by investment advisors usually involving a brief questionnaire to categorize an investor-client according to how much investment risk the client is able or willing to assume.

Risk-adjusted performance   The rate of return on an investment, adjusted for the risk of the investment. For example, if the risk of an investment of $100 is leveraged two-to-one by borrowing $100, thus making an investment of $200, and returns 10 percent on the original $100, its risk-adjusted return is reduced by a factor of two resulting in a risk-adjusted performance of 5 percent. Several methods have been proposed for expressing risk-adjusted performance.

Risk premium   The increase in expected annual percentage return on a risky investment in excess of the return on a (virtually) riskless investment such as U.S. Treasury bills.

S&P 500   See *Standard and Poor's 500.*

Scientism   The inappropriate imitation in the social sciences of the methods of the physical sciences, or "the erroneous transfer to social phenomena of the habits of thought we have developed in dealing with the phenomena of nature" (Friedrich Hayek).

Security   In investment, a contract or document showing ownership of a future contingent cash flow stream received in exchange for the investment of capital; usually a stock or a bond.

Self-selection bias   A bias introduced into a database by the fact that the data included in the database are selectively chosen by those who report the data. All hedge fund databases suffer from this bias.

Separately managed account   An investment account that is not a part of a larger pooled account such as a mutual fund or a hedge fund.

Socially responsible investments   Equity investments that are selected in part by screening the issuing companies for certain corporate practices that are deemed socially responsible by the selector.

Soft dollars   See *Directed brokerage.*

Standard and Poor's 500   A capitalization-weighted index of five hundred of the largest U.S. companies' stock prices; currently comprises over 70 percent of the total capitalization of all U.S. companies.

Standard deviation   A statistical measure of the variation or dispersion of a set of numbers; in investments, a measure of the variation or dispersion of periodic rates of return, such as daily or monthly (i.e., the volatility or variation of returns).

Stock   See *Equity.*

Stock market   Any marketplace in which shares of stock are bought and sold.

Style allocation   Usually, the percentages—adding to 100 percent—by which the equity component of an investment portfolio is divided among major equity asset classes such as large growth stocks, large value stocks, small growth stocks, small value stocks, international stocks, and emerging market stocks; can also apply to the categories of bonds and real estate.

Survivorship bias   Bias in a database of investment funds over a historical time period due to the fact that data for funds that did not exist at the end of the time period are not included in earlier periods.

TIPS (Treasury Inflation Protected Securities)   Securities issued by the U.S. Treasury similar to ordinary government bonds except that their principal values and interest payments rise or fall with inflation. See also http://www.treasurydirect.gov/indiv/products/tips_glance.htm.

Trading volume   The number of shares traded per day.

Transaction cost   The cost of buying or selling a stock or a bond, including brokerage commissions but also including (especially for large trades) losses due to the fact that the trade itself tends to move the market in a direction unfavorable to the buyer or seller.

Turnover   The percentage of the investments in a portfolio that is bought or sold annually. "Buy-and-hold" and passively managed portfolios generally have low turnover, while actively managed portfolios generally have higher turnover.

Value stocks   Stocks in companies that have low price-to-earnings and price-to-book value ratios.

Variance   Statistically, the square of the standard deviation; a measure of the variability of periodic rates of return.

Volatility   The variability, or degree of fluctuation, of periodic rates of return, usually measured statistically by standard deviation or variance, and considered a proxy for risk.

Wealth management   See *investment advisors.*

Wirehouse or wire house   By historical definition, a firm whose branch offices are linked by a communications system enabling the sharing of financial information, research, and prices; generally applied to mean large brokerage firms.

Wrap fee   A single percentage fee on total invested assets levied by an investment advisor or wealth management firm, claimed to cover all costs and expenses (though sometimes some costs are not covered, such as commission costs within a recommended mutual fund).

Bibliography

Altruist Financial Advisors. "Reading Room—Articles/Papers." http://altruistfa.com/readingroomarticles.htm, 2006 (accessed August 8, 2006). (Excellent list of books and articles on investing issues.)

Bernstein, William J. *The Four Pillars of Investing: Lessons for Building a Winning Portfolio*. New York: McGraw-Hill, 2002.

Bogle, John C. *Common Sense on Mutual Funds: New Imperatives for the Intelligent Investor*. New York: Wiley, 1999.

———. *The Battle for the Soul of Capitalism*. New Haven, CT: Yale University Press, 2005.

———. "The Mutual Fund Industry 60 Years Later: For Better or Worse?" *Financial Analysts Journal* 61, no. 1 (2005): 15–24.

Brown, S. J., W. N. Goetzmann, R. G. Ibbotson, and S. A. Ross. "Survivorship Bias in Performance Studies." *Review of Financial Studies* 5, no. 4 (1992): 553–80.

Carhart, Mark M. "On Persistence in Mutual Fund Performance." *Journal of Finance* 52 (1997): 57–82.

Conference Board. *The 2005 Institutional Investment Report: U.S. and International Trends*. New York: Author, 2005.

Cootner, Paul H., ed. *The Random Character of Stock Market Prices*. London: Risk Publication, 2000.

Eichenwald, Kurt. *Conspiracy of Fools: A True Story*. New York: Broadway Books, 2005.

Ellis, Charles D. "The Loser's Game." *Financial Analysts Journal* 31, no. 4 (1975): 19–26.

Fama, Eugene F. "The Behavior of Stock-Market Prices." *Journal of Business* 38, no. 1 (1965): 34–105.

———. "Market Efficiency, Long-Term Returns, and Behavioral Finance." *Journal of Financial Economics* 49 (1998): 283–306.

Friend, Irwin, F. E. Brown, Edward S. Herman, and Douglas Vickers. "A Study of Mutual Funds: Investment Policy and Investment Company

Performance." Report of the Committee on Interstate and Foreign Commerce, House Report No. 2274, 87th Congress, Second Session. Washington, DC: U.S. Government Printing Office, 1962.

Gardner, Tom. "Cash-King Portfolio Report." http://www.fool.com/CashKing/1998/CashKingPort980305.htm, March 5, 1998 (accessed August 8, 2006).

Goltz, F. "Hedge Fund Indices as Asset Allocation Tools." Working paper, May 12, 2005. Nice, France: Edhec Risk and Asset Management Research Centre.

Hayek, Friedrich A. *The Road to Serfdom*. London: Routledge, 1944.

Hitler, Adolf. *Mein Kampf*. Boston: Houghton Mifflin/Mariner Books, 1998.

Jenkins, Iain. "Determining the Fees: Hedge Fund Intelligence." http://www.hedgefundintelligence.com/ar/reports/2004_09/determining_the_fees.htm, 2004 (accessed July 10, 2006).

Jensen, Michael C. "The Performance of Mutual Funds in the Period 1945–1964." *Journal of Finance* 23 (1968): 389–416.

Kador, John. *Charles Schwab: How One Company Beat Wall Street and Reinvented the Brokerage Industry*. Hoboken, NJ: Wiley, 2002.

Lakonishok, Josef, Andrei Schleifer, Robert W. Vishny, Oliver Hart, and George L. Perry. "The Structure and Performance of the Money Management Industry." *Brookings Papers on Economic Activity. Microeconomics* 1992: 339–91.

Levitt, Arthur. *Take on the Street*. New York: Pantheon, 2002.

Lowenstein, Roger. *Buffett: The Making of an American Capitalist*. New York: Random House, 1995.

———. *When Genius Failed: The Rise and Fall of Long-Term Capital Management*. New York: Random House, 2000.

Malkiel, Burton G. *A Random Walk Down Wall Street*. New York: Norton, 2003.

———. "Returns from Investing in Equity Mutual Funds 1971 to 1991." *Journal of Finance* 50 (1995): 549–72.

Malkiel, B., and A. Saha. "Hedge Funds: Risk and Return." *Financial Analysts Journal* 61, no. 6 (2005): 80–88.

Mandelbrot, Benoit, and Richard L. Hudson. *The (Mis)Behavior of Markets*. New York: Basic Books, 2004.

Packard, Vance. *The Hidden Persuaders*. New York: McKay, 1957.

———. *The Waste Makers*. New York: McKay, 1960.

Posthuma, Nolke, and Pieter Jelle van der Sluis. "A Reality Check on Hedge Funds Returns." http://ssrn.com/abstract=438840, 2003 (accessed August 8, 2006).

Rauch-Neilson, Amy. "The Beardstown Phenomenon." http://www.betterinvesting.org/articles/bi/16/371, 2001 (accessed August 8, 2006).

Roll, Richard, and Robert J. Shiller. "Comments: Symposium on Volatility in U.S. and Japanese Stock Markets." *Journal of Applied Corporate Finance* 5, no. 1 (1992): 25–29.

Rubinstein, Mark. *A History of the Theory of Investments*. Hoboken, NJ: Wiley, 2006.

Schwert, G. William. "Anomalies and Market Efficiency." In *Handbook of the Economics of Finance*, ed. George M. Constantinides, Milton Harris, and René M. Stulz, vol. 1: 939–74. Amsterdam: Elsevier/ North Holland, 2003.

Sharpe, William F. "Capital Asset Prices: A Theory of Market Equilibrium under Conditions of Risk." *Journal of Finance* 19, no. 3 (1964): 425–42.

———. "Mutual Fund Performance." *Journal of Business* 39, no. 1, pt. 2, suppl. (1966): 119–38.

Statman, Meir, and Jonathan Scheid. "Buffett in Foresight and Hindsight." *Financial Analysts Journal* 58, no. 4 (2002): 11–18.

Surowiecki, James. *The Wisdom of Crowds*. New York: Doubleday, 2004.

Swensen, David F. *Unconventional Success: A Fundamental Approach to Personal Investment*. New York: Free Press, 2005.

Taleb, Nassim Nicholas. *Fooled by Randomness*. 2nd ed. New York: Random House, 2005.

Tobin, James. "Liquidity Preference as Behavior towards Risk." *Review of Economic Studies* 25, no. 2 (1958): 65–86.

Treynor, Jack L., and K. K. Mazuy. "Can Mutual Funds Outguess the Market?" *Harvard Business Review* 44, no. 4 (1966): 131–36.

Winslow, Edward. *Blind Faith*. San Francisco: Berrett-Koehler, 2003.

Zuckoff, Mitchell. *Ponzi's Scheme: The True Story of a Financial Legend*. New York: Random House, 2005.

Index

About the Author

MICHAEL EDESESS is an accomplished mathematician and economist with experience in the investment, energy, environment, and sustainable development fields. He was a founding partner in 1994 and chief economist of the Lockwood Financial Group until its sale to the Bank of New York in September 2002. Previously an independent consultant to institutional investors, his clients included several of the largest investment banking and consulting firms. His areas of expertise cover the range of applications of mathematics to investments, including performance and risk measurement; Monte Carlo methods for asset-liability, asset allocation, and pension planning models; dynamic hedging using futures and options; effective style mix determination; backtesting; and quadratic portfolio mean-variance optimization. Dr. Edesess has spoken at conferences on investment research and taught courses in international finance, economics, mathematics, statistics, systems analysis, and environmental policy at four universities. He has been published in the *Wall Street Journal* and the *Journal of Portfolio Management* and has been interviewed on CNBC.

In addition to his work in investments, Dr. Edesess is active in the fields of environmental and resource economics and international development. He currently chairs the board of International Development Enterprises USA, a nonprofit focusing on poor rural smallholders in developing countries, and has chaired the board of the Rocky Mountain Institute, a prominent energy efficiency think tank in Snowmass, Colorado, and the Rocky Mountain Advisory Board of Environmental Defense. He has written for numerous publications and spoken at conferences on energy, sustainable development, economics, and investment, with articles appearing in *Technology Review*, *Rising Tide*, the *Christian Science Monitor*, *Rocky Mountain News*, and *Pensions and Investments*. He holds a bachelor's degree from the Massachusetts Institute of Technology and M.A. and Ph.D. degrees in pure mathematics from Northwestern University.

About Berrett-Koehler Publishers

....

Berrett-Koehler is an independent publisher dedicated to an ambitious mission: Creating a World that Works for All.

We believe that to truly create a better world, action is needed at all levels—individual, organizational, and societal. At the individual level, our publications help people align their lives with their values and with their aspirations for a better world. At the organizational level, our publications promote progressive leadership and management practices, socially responsible approaches to business, and humane and effective organizations. At the societal level, our publications advance social and economic justice, shared prosperity, sustainability, and new solutions to national and global issues.

A major theme of our publications is "Opening Up New Space." They challenge conventional thinking, introduce new ideas, and foster positive change. Their common quest is changing the underlying beliefs, mindsets, and structures that keep generating the same cycles of problems, no matter who our leaders are or what improvement programs we adopt.

We strive to practice what we preach—to operate our publishing company in line with the ideas in our books. At the core of our approach is stewardship, which we define as a deep sense of responsibility to administer the company for the benefit of all of our "stakeholder" groups: authors, customers, employees, investors, service providers, and the communities and environment around us.

We are grateful to the thousands of readers, authors, and other friends of the company who consider themselves to be part of the "BK Community." We hope that you, too, will join us in our mission.

A BK Life Book

This book is part of our BK Life series. BK Life books change people's lives. They help individuals improve their lives in ways that are beneficial for the families, organizations, communities, nations, and world in which they live and work. To find out more, visit www.bk-life.com.

BE CONNECTED

Visit Our Website
Go to www.bkconnection.com to read exclusive previews and excerpts of new books, find detailed information on all Berrett-Koehler titles and authors, browse subject-area libraries of books, and get special discounts.

Subscribe to Our Free E-Newsletter
Be the first to hear about new publications, special discount offers, exclusive articles, news about bestsellers, and more! Get on the list for our free e-newsletter by going to www.bkconnection.com.

Participate in the Discussion
To see what others are saying about our books and post your own thoughts, check out our blogs at www.bkblogs.com.

Get Quantity Discounts
Berrett-Koehler books are available at quantity discounts for orders of ten or more copies. Please call us toll-free at (800) 929-2929 or email us at bkp.orders@aidcvt.com.

Host a Reading Group
For tips on how to form and carry on a book reading group in your workplace or community, see our website at www.bkconnection.com.

Join the BK Community
Thousands of readers of our books have become part of the "BK Community" by participating in events featuring our authors, reviewing draft manuscripts of forthcoming books, spreading the word about their favorite books, and supporting our publishing program in other ways. If you would like to join the BK Community, please contact us at bkcommunity@bkpub.com.